VIRGINIA WOOLF MISCELLANIES

VIRGINIA WOOLF MISCELLANIES

Proceedings of the First Annual Conference on Virginia Woolf

Pace University, New York
June 7–9, 1991

Edited by
Mark Hussey
and
Vara Neverow-Turk

Pace University Press
1992

Copyright © 1992 by
Pace University Press®
New York, NY 10038

All rights reserved
Printed in the United States of America

4720 Boston Way
Lanham, Maryland 20706

3 Henrietta Street
London WC2E 8LU England

Library of Congress Cataloging-in-Publication Data

Conference on Virginia Woolf (1st : 1991 : Pace University)
Virginia Woolf miscellanies : proceedings of the First Annual
Conference on Virginia Woolf, Pace University, New York, June 7-9,
1991 / edited by Mark Hussey and Vara Neverow-Turk.
    p.   cm.
1. Woolf, Virginia, 1882–1941—Criticism and interpretation—
Congresses. I. Hussey, Mark, 1956– . II. Neverow-Turk,
Vara. III. Title.
PR6045.072Z5787   1991   823'.912—dc20   92–4383 CIP

ISBN 0–944473–08–3 (cloth : alk. paper)
ISBN 0–944473–09–1 (pbk. : alk. paper)

 The paper used in this publication meets the minimum requirements of American National Standard for Information Sciences—Permanence of Paper for Printed Library Materials, ANSI Z39.48–1984.

Contents

Introduction
Recollections of the Proceedings

Woolf, Reading and Readers
Beth C. Rosenberg
Virginia Woolf: Conversation and the Common Reader   1

Alex Zwerdling
The Common Reader, the Coterie and the Audience of One   8

A Modernist Aberration: Reading Woolf in the Context of Postmodernism
Ann Marie Hebert
"What Does it Mean? How Do You Explain it All?"
Virginia Woolf: A Postmodern Modernist   10

Teresa Heffernan
Fascism and Madness: Woolf Writing Against Modernism   19

Roseanne Hoefel
Preserving a Discourse of Difference and a Difference of Discourse   28

Woolf, Class and Empire
Kathy J. Phillips
Woolf's Criticism of the British Empire in *The Years*   30

Beth Rigel Daugherty
Taking a Leaf from Virginia Woolf's Book: Empowering the Student   31

Jeanette McVicker
Vast Nests of Chinese Boxes, or Getting from Q to R: Critiquing Empire in "Kew Gardens" and *To the Lighthouse*   40

Woolf and Contemporary Writers
Antonia García-Rodríguez
Virginia Woolf from a Latin American Perspective   43

Deborah Straw
Tea with Virginia: Woolf as an Early Mentor to May Sarton   45

Contents

Carol Ascher
Reading to Write: *The Waves* as Muse — 47

Jane Lazarre
Structures of Common Experience: Learning from Virginia Woolf — 57

Elegies: Death and Mourning
Christopher Ames
Death and Woolf's Festive Vision — 62

Louise Poresky
Eternal Renewal: Life and Death in Virginia Woolf's *The Waves* — 64

A Video Project
Leslie K. Hankins
Virginia Woolf, Literary Tourism and Cultural Site-Seeing — 71

Virginia Woolf and Her Experimentalist Contemporaries: Mansfield, Richardson and Stein
G. Johnston
After the Invention of the Gramophone: Hearing the Woman in Stein's *Autobiography* and Woolf's *Three Guineas* — 88

Evelyn Haller
Virginia Woolf and Katherine Mansfield, or
The Case of the Déclassé Wild Child — 96

"A Rope to Throw the Reader": The Reading of Rhythm in Virginia Woolf
A Discussion moderated by Patricia Laurence with
John Briggs; Marilyn Zucker; Elizabeth Cabot;
Beth C. Schwartz; Leslie K. Hankins. — 105

John Briggs
Nuance, Metaphor and the Rhythm of the Mood Wave
in Virginia Woolf — 107

Woolf and War
Andy Delohery and Gail Fay — 119

Contents

Intertextualities: Woolf, Dostoevsky, Yourcenar, Weldon

Penny Colburn-McGuire
Interiors: Woolf and Dostoevsky   121

Denise Marshall
Dear Reader: Intercepting Romance and Transforming
Acculturation in Woolf and Weldon   123

Judith L. Johnston
"A Neccessary Bore" or Brilliant Novelist?: What Yourcenar
Understood About Woolf's *The Waves*   125

Reading at Random

Catherine Nelson-McDermott
Virginia Woolf and Murasaki Shikibu: A Question of Perception   133

Lisa Low
Two Figures Standing in Dense Violet Light: John Milton,
Virginia Woolf, and the Epic Vision of Marriage   144

Penny Painter
The Overlooked Influence of John Waller "Jack" Hills
on Virginia Woolf   146

Life/Studies: Psychobiography and Virginia Woolf

Judith Lutzer
Woolf and Freud: An Analysis of Invisible Presences   148

Jane Lilienfeld
"Like a Lion Seeking Whom He Could Devour":
Domestic Violence in *To the Lighthouse*   154

Louise DeSalvo
Virginia Woolf, Incest Survivor   164

Roger Poole
A Phenomenological Reading of Certain Photographs   172

Virginia Woolf Seeking Other Worlds With New Language, Vision and Ritual

Contents

Patricia Cramer
Notes from Underground: Lesbian Ritual
in the Writings of Virginia Woolf — 177

Merry Pawlowski
Virginia Woolf's *Between the Acts*:
Fascism in the Heart of England — 188

Penelope Cordish
Virginia Woolf's Mountain Top—That Persistent Vision — 191

Time, Embodiment and the Problem Of Separation in the Novels of Virginia Woolf
Amanda Grant
Life Without Boundaries — 199

Kathy Brady
Time, Space and Silence — 201

Hungry To Talk: A Roundtable Discussion of Teaching *To The Lighthouse*
Beth Rigel Daugherty and Mary Beth Pringle,
with Marcia McClintock Folsom; Nancy Topping Bazin;
Sally Jacobsen; Katherine Hill-Miller; Susan Yunis. — 203

"Mrs. Dalloway and The Aeroplane"
By Lisa Peterson with music by David Bucknam — 208

Leonard and Virginia Woolf Working Together
Wayne Chapman
Leonard and Virginia Woolf Working Together — 209

Janet M. Manson
Leonard Woolf, the League of Nations Society
and the Journal *War and Peace* — 211

Jean Moorcroft Wilson
Leonard Woolf: The Pivot or Outsider of Bloomsbury? — 213

The Rhetoric of Virginia Woolf's Feminism

Contents

Pamela L. Caughie with Anne Callahan
Virginia Woolf and Postmodern Feminism — 215

Catherine Sandbach-Dahlström
Tradition, Resistance and Rewriting in Virginia Woolf's Essays — 223

From *Melymbrosia* To *Between the Acts*
Laura Davis-Clapper
Why Did Rachel Vinrace Die? Tracing the Clues
from *Melymbrosia* to *The Voyage Out* — 225

Elizabeth Heine
New Light on *Melymbrosia* — 227

G. Patton Wright
Virginia Woolf's Uncommon Reader: Allusions in *Between the Acts* — 230

Appendix
Program for Virginia Woolf Miscellanies, June 7 - 9, 1991 — 234

Notes on Contributors — 238

Introduction: Recollections of the Proceedings

Virginia Woolf Miscellanies Conference
Pace University, 1991
The First Annual Conference on Virginia Woolf

The first *annual* conference devoted to Virginia Woolf studies took place at Pace University in the financial district of Manhattan over three perfect summer days—Friday, June 7 through Sunday, June 9, 1991. The conference was held in a great city on a river, a cosmopolitan city of bridges and jostling crowds, whose energy and variety Woolf would undoubtedly have applauded much as she did her own London. Almost 250 people gathered for the event which was not, it must be stressed, the first *conference* on Woolf studies. Calling the conference the "first annual" expressed the hope that it would become a habit for Woolf scholars, readers, and devotees to meet regularly and celebrate Woolf not only through scholarly exchange but through the antiphonal scraps, orts and fragments, first one thing, then another, of continuing conversations, new connections and lasting camaraderie.

Thus, as the *Proceedings* of the first annual conference go into print, the plans for the second annual conference are already well under way. The second annual conference, Virginia Woolf: Themes and Variations, will be celebrated Thursday, June 11 through Sunday, June 14, 1992 in New Haven, another city of bridges and harbors. The conference will be hosted by Southern Connecticut State University, a place Woolf would have valued because it began as a normal school for women aspiring to enter the profession of teaching, a school that, like Girton and Newnham, or the college Woolf imagines in *Three Guineas*, is decorated afresh by each generation.

The planning for what was to be the Virginia Woolf Miscellanies conference began in Washington, D.C. at the Modern Language Association Convention during the Virginia Woolf Society party. It was on the night of Thursday, December 28 that what at the time seemed just a casual conversation became the idea of starting a tradition of Woolf studies conferences. Soon, the call for papers was posted in the *Virginia Woolf Miscellany*. The submissions and suggestions and proposals and papers and inquiries and letters and phone calls began to come in and answers, responses, decisions, choices, problems and ideas began to evolve.

Then we began to meet rather more regularly. We talked on the phone. We sat over cappuccino and feasted on focaccia with eggplant in a restaurant in Greenwich Village as we sorted through stacks of materials and discussed publicity and registration forms, decided on registration fees and determined what hotels to suggest, imagined the dinner and the reception and commented that we now knew how Clarissa Dalloway felt when she was planning her party, but we didn't have Lucy to assist us and we knew the Prime Minister would not be coming.

After much work and anticipation, anxiety and effort, the day of the conference arrived. Like the dinner Woolf describes so vividly in *To the Lighthouse*, things began hesitantly. People were brought together in a room, they seemed cautious, a little stiff, then they began to converse. The first sessions were successful but quite formal. But then there was a meal at the Hunan Garden that first night and no one seemed to be moving the salt cellar uneasily—instead, everyone was suddenly talking and laughing and at ease.

The social trepidation that Clarissa Dalloway and Mrs. Ramsay exemplify gave way to the aesthetic tension of Miss La Trobe when Lisa Peterson's and David Bucknam's moving oratorio, "Mrs. Dalloway & the Aeroplane," was performed, reminding the audience of Woolf's love of harmony and the use of

Introduction

rhythm in her work, a topic that was explored in a roundtable discussion organized by Patricia Laurence. By sheer serendipity, Eileen Atkins was giving the two final performances of *A Room of One's Own* on June 7 and 8, a limited engagement that had miraculously been extended just until the last evening of the conference. Although the theater was sold out, even those few who did not have tickets were able somehow to get seats. The conference goers made the final performance a particularly lively event because they knew every line by heart and would begin laughing uproariously before the words were out of Atkins' mouth.

By the end of the conference, the more than seventy presentations, along with discussions, questions, comments, responses, and conversations, had created a very satisfyingly Woolfian polyphony. There were scholarly presentations on a range of topics from Woolf's postmodernist impulses to the challenges of editing her manuscripts. Alex Zwerdling spoke on Woolf's sense of her audiences. Kathy Phillips documented Woolf's complex critique of empire in *The Years*. Beth Daugherty and Mary Beth Pringle organized a roundtable discussion of ways to teach *To the Lighthouse*, a preview of their forthcoming MLA Teaching Approaches collection. Leslie Hankins narrated her remarkable videotape project on Woolf's St. Ives. Louise DeSalvo spoke on the implications of incest. Denise Marshall linked Woolf to Fay Weldon. Pat Cramer traced the lesbian coming-out narrative in *Mrs. Dalloway*. There was also a display of extremely rare Hogarth Press books and of books owned by Virginia Woolf, brought from the personal collection of Dr. Jean Moorcroft Wilson, who is married to Leonard Woolf's nephew Cecil and who, with him, runs Cecil Woolf Publishers. Linda J. Langham also generously brought examples of Hogarth Press first editions from her collection. The Scholar's Bookshelf did a brisk business in orders for Woolf-related works. And over 80 people stayed for the final reception, to finish conversations and say farewell.

From the start our intention had been to abide by Woolf's politics. There were to be no tufts of horsehair, nor highly ornamental silver pots. Although this decision could have resulted in some consternation and even dismay among those who like to be assured they are hearing from the "experts," it seems from all we've heard that the democratic and egalitarian atmosphere of a conference at which the famous, the potentially famous, the newcomer, the undergraduate, the common reader, and the lover of literature could all join together was greatly appreciated. More than anything else, though, this conference was marked by a collegiality, a real friendliness and tolerance, that is apparently rare. It is not, perhaps, so suprising that this should be the case, given that what the people who came had in common was a love of the work of Virginia Woolf.

Thus, when a casual conversation about the *Proceedings* began to seem like a plausible rather than a daunting project, we applied the same political standard: we invited submissions from all those who had participated, requesting the full text of papers from those panelists whose work had been particularly noted by the respondents to the conference evaluations, and abstracts from those who were publishing their work elsewhere. We requested summary statements from the organizers of roundtable discussions and decided that the only way we could represent the oratorio was to reproduce the program for the performance. And though we would have liked to use the conference program as the table of contents for the *Proceedings*, preserving the hours and dates as an allusion to Woolf's concern with the passing of time, we were not able to do so but we include it as an appendix. Those presenters whose work does not appear here are those who elected not to submit any materials for publication. The contents of the *Proceedings*, therefore, are as egalitarian as we could hope.

Most of these papers and abstracts are slightly revised versions of the actual presentations (some contributors even decided to modify their titles). Because these materials were originally intended to be read, the scholarly documentation of sources is not as rigorous as would be the case in a collection of articles. Also, because we wanted the *Proceedings* to be available in time for the second annual Virginia Woolf conference in June 1992, we decided not to undertake the laborious task of reconciling the authors' citation formats to a uniform style sheet. Thus, there are some variations in documentation throughout. Indeed, our insistence that the deadline was in fact the deadline did not allow contributors to revise at their leisure. These *Proceedings* are meant to represent what was *heard* at the conference as closely as possible (we would have liked to include what was *over*heard as

Introduction

well, and the questions and discussions that followed presentations, but transcription and recollection proved too arduous).

So many participants indicated their interest in the *Proceedings* that we believe the collection will both sustain dialogues begun in June 1991 and initiate further conversations and connections. We also are confident that the second annual Virginia Woolf: Themes and Variations conference will be succeeded by the third annual gathering of Woolf scholars, friends, fans, and fellow-travellers, and that these moments will live on, part even of people who never attended, laid out like a mist, spread ever so far.

In closing, we would like to thank those who made this conference and these *Proceedings* possible. At Pace University, the conference was wholeheartedly supported from the outset by Sherman Raskin, chair of the English Department. Patricia Ewers, President of Pace University, graciously opened the conference. Faculty at Pace were glad to serve as moderators for some panels, even putting up with very last minute changes of schedule. We would also like to thank Jillian Panfel, director of the Schimmel Theater and her staff, and Rebecca Martin who made conversations about the budget a pleasure. Stacey Schrader and Patrick Norton stalwartly monitored the registration tables, and, with Beth Rosenberg, heroically affixed eight thousand labels to conference announcements.

Evelyn Leong continued to prove herself an honorary lupine and appeared on the last day of the conference with wine, orange juice, cheese, fruit, flowers, and bread for the closing reception. Those who could not be with us at the conference were nevertheless invisible and felt presences from the very beginning.

We would particularly like to thank Caroline Tzelios, graduate assistant in the M. S. in Publishing program at Pace, who went well beyond the call of duty in helping to prepare this manuscript for publication, and of course we both wish to thank John Briggs and Kristina Masten for preparing the camera-ready copy.

... if only they could be brought together; so [we] did it. And it was an offering; to combine; to create ...

Vara Neverow-Turk & Mark Hussey
New York City, December 16, 1991

Woolf, Reading and Readers

Beth C. Rosenberg
Virginia Woolf: Conversation
and the Common Reader

Virginia Woolf's common reader has come to be understood as an ideal, almost real, person whose behavior is described in Woolf's criticism. Constructions of the common reader have attached the concept to Woolf's political and social beliefs, and to her preoccupation with her role as a critic and writer. The common reader, according to some critics, has become a persona adopted by Woolf to avoid the many authoritarian stances she argues against.

For example, Barbara Currier Bell and Carol Ohmann do not even acknowledge that the common reader is a concept borrowed from Samuel Johnson, wrought with eighteenth century connotations. For them, the common reader is an invention used to address her readers "amiably and unpretentiously," for Woolf is not "traditionally authoritarian, not an eminence" and therefore she needs a persona to communicate with her audience. Jean Guiguet takes the title "common reader" literally, and reveals his own will to class distinction by associating the epithet "common" with that of "average," a category broad enough to ensure Woolf's criticism a universality, and through which Guiguet sees Woolf as "opposed to learned, academic criticism." Still others see the common reader as a mask that allows a democratic relationship with a specific class of readers.[1]

However, the common reader is more than an ideal reader or a persona that Woolf uses to address her audience: *the common reader is also a metaphor for how texts operate and how knowledge is constructed.* With an understanding of the common reader as a rhetorical function, rather than a persona used to address political and social agendas, Woolf's title for her two collections of essays, *The Common Reader,* points to both its own textuality and the unifying themes of the books as a whole: not only does she describe how her reader reads, but her rhetoric mimics the very process she describes. The parallel between her common reader and her rhetoric is found in her concept of conversation and dialogue. The non-hierarchical quality of the common reader is merged with the concept of dialogue, while at the same time allowing the common reader to take on the other functions that dialogue implies.

Dialogue, as a model for constructing knowledge, is not fixed or static, but fluid, decentered, and process-oriented. Like the common reader, dialogue is anti-authoritarian and non-didactic, unsystematic and constantly changing with each interaction. Dialogue becomes part of Woolf's rhetoric, allowing opposing ideas to exist simultaneously and creating unity through contrariety in her "conversations" with herself.

Writing as conversation implies an interaction between the writer and her reader, between the speaker and her audience. In the essays Woolf makes much use of this relationship and we may then understand that for Woolf it is the conversational aspect of prose that gives prose its open-ended invitational quality. It is this aspect that Woolf investigates and develops throughout her growth as a writer, and it is this aspect that takes on a variety of forms: the conversational frame she gives many of the essays, the use of dialogue in her essays and novels, the conversational interaction between her prose and fiction, and the dialogical style found in the major novels. Conversation for Woolf means not merely an oral exchange between two or more people but ultimately the communication between different points of view, where one point of view is the function of every other point of view it comes into contact with. Conversation, or dialogue, is interactional and relational; Woolf's theory of language is based on this belief and it informs her notions of reading and writing.

Woolf's experimentation with dialogue and conversation took place early in her career. But before we can understand the relationship between the common reader (the rhetorical figure rather than the person) and conversation (as a rhetorical strategy), we can see how these ideas have their origin in essays such as "Byron and Mr. Briggs" and "Mr. Conrad: A Conversation."

Woolf tried to articulate the method of the common reader in the essay "Byron and Mr. Briggs," an essay that was intended as the introduction to the proposed book, *Reading*, but was never completed in the form suggested by the essay. However, as Andrew McNeillie points out, "the ideas behind it were subsequently developed and recast until they evolved and emerged as *The Common Reader: First Series* (1925)."

In "Byron and Mr. Briggs," the Mr. Briggs Woolf creates lived in the early nineteenth century, read Shakespeare, and resisted Coleridge's influence on his reading (480). The prototype of the common reader, Mr. Briggs has a certain kind of sense, a sense that Johnson defined and Woolf borrows. She tells us:

> When Johnson talked of the common sense of readers, no doubt he meant that the faculty of knowing what to use, what to neglect, is well developed among us, and can be trusted in the long run to whittle away even the enormous deposits which have heaped themselves over a man like Byron . . . . (485)

How is it that the common reader develops this faculty of knowing, and what is the easiest way for the reader to exercise his knowledge? The answer seems to be through conversation. What follows Woolf's analysis of the common sense of readers is a scenario of a conversation. The scene she describes verges on fiction and her characters' voices and points of view become Woolf's: "<Here is a little party of ordinary people, sitting round the dinner table, & talking, about Byron><gossiping; who will

marry who; what the Prime Minister said, have you read Byron's letters>" (494). The conversants are Terence Hewett, Rose Shaw, Clarissa Dalloway, and Mr. Pepper, and through their conversation Woolf enacts the way in which the common reader comes to construct the meaning and knowledge of what he reads.

Rose Shaw and Terence Hewet enter the library. In describing the exchange between them, Woolf also includes what appears to be irrelevant and domestic information. Rose and Terence discuss *Tristram Shandy* and, as Woolf tells us, "they were using literature partly in order to make them understand each other" (495). It is through conversation that they get to know literature, and by knowing literature they get to know each other. This is how the common reader operates—making literature and reading part of his life, making life part of his literature and reading. Conversation therefore functions as a means of understanding and constructing interpretations of literature, while it is through literature that they negotiate their way through social conversation.

This insight is pursued and developed by Woolf in "Mr. Conrad: A Conversation," written in 1923, the same year *The Common Reader* was being revised for publication. The essay is a conversation between Penelope Otway, the ideal common reader, and her friend, David Lowe. Penelope is "content to read and to talk, reading at intervals of household business, and talking when she could find company . . ." (76). On the particular day Woolf describes, Penelope Otway is visited by David Lowe, who finds her on the lawn surrounded by volumes of Joseph Conrad. Otway sees Conrad as a classic writer, whereas Lowe does not—the conversation concentrates on this disagreement.

Otway says that Conrad is "not one and simple; no, he is many and complex" (78). Conrad is like many modern writers, including Woolf, who have multiple selves and whose texts function to realign themselves with each other. In the following passage Penelope expands on her theory of what constitutes a "classic." We can also see this passage as the essay's commentary on itself, the description of how and why conversation and dialogue function in a text, and, finally, how this passage notes what Woolf attempts to achieve in her own fiction. Penelope explains:

> And it is when they bring these selves into relation—when they simplify, when they reconcile their opposites—that they bring off . . . those complete books which for that reason we call their masterpieces. And Mr. Conrad's selves are particularly opposite. He is composed of two people who have nothing whatever in common. (79)

To create a great novel, an author must find some way to unify his conflicting selves. This essay demonstrates a method with which Woolf is experimenting: it is the use of conversation to allow "particularly opposite" points of view to come into relation with one another and to interact.

Conversation for the common reader is both the process of obtaining knowledge and the very goal of that process. Just as we know Conrad through the interaction of his opposing selves, so too do we know Woolf through opposing views in the essay—she is both Otway and Lowe. Woolf refuses to tell her reader what to think about Conrad because she herself thinks many—often opposing—things. What Otway tells Lowe, Woolf tells us: we must read Conrad for ourselves. Then, after we have read him, we must, again like Otway, converse when we can—not to impose our views on others, but to clarify our thoughts, through contrast and opposition, for ourselves.

Woolf begins to merge her preoccupation with conversation and the common reader in the structure of the collection entitled *The Common Reader*. Before she settled on the final structure of her first *Common Reader*, she had another idea for its organization. On August 17, 1923 she writes in her diary:

> The question I want to debate here is the question of my essays, & how to make them into a book. The brilliant idea has just come to me of embedding them in Otway conversation. The main advantage would be that I could then comment, & add what I had had to leave out, or failed to get in . . . . Also to have a setting for each would 'make a book'; & the collection of articles is in my view an inartistic method. But then

> this might be too artistic . . . . There could be an introductory chapter. A family which reads the papers. The thing to do wd. be to envelope each essay into its own atmosphere. To get them into a current of life, & so to shape the book . . . .

Woolf was now considering framing *The Common Reader* in what she called "Otway conversation," the same method of experimentation in "Mr. Conrad." This frame, she felt, could allow her to say things that the structure of the traditional and "inartistic" book of articles could not. By constructing each of the essays in the form of a conversation between family members (much in the same way as she did in "Byron and Mr. Briggs"), she could place the essays into the "current of life". The family would read the papers and then talk with each other about them. It would allow Woolf to debate herself, to avoid committing herself to a fixed opinion or judgment, to allow opposing points of view to exist simultaneously, and to become both the reader and the writer in a single act. She decided, however, not to pursue this idea out of fear it would take too much out of her: "it might run away with me," she says, "it will take time." Here we find Woolf's awareness of the dangers of conversation. Her active mind and constant rethinking and reworking of ideas in her writing make her acutely aware of the nature of conversation in written discourse. Her ability to converse with herself, while it gave her one of her greatest critical insights, was her most troublesome and devastating skill because of her knowledge that the conversational mode does not have closure and resolution. Instead, she decided to begin with an essay entitled "The Common Reader."

The essay, her preface to the first collection, defines the common reader as one who "differs from the critic and scholar" (1). He is "guided by an instinct to create for himself, out of whatever odds and ends he can come by, some kind of whole . . ." (1). By beginning with this essay, Woolf establishes the organization of the collection. But are we to believe that what is to follow are just "a few ideas and opinions" that are "insignificant in themselves"? (2) It is not the humbleness of her endeavor that Woolf wishes to emphasize, but the process of construction and the lack of a fixed position. What the common reader does—

his purpose, motivation, and strategies—are the same as the writer; they both share an "instinct to create . . . some kind of whole." Reading is writing, and writing is reading: both are acts of interpretation and a construction of knowledge. And it is the acts of interpretation and construction that are the unifying themes of the collection.

By beginning the collection with her essay on the common reader, Woolf achieves a similar end to that of "Otway conversation." The essays are the expressions of a common reader, the creations and constructions of a mind in dialogue with a text. The essays do not contain the authority of the scholar or critic but rather the opinion and perception of a reader at a certain moment who, with his next reading experience or conversation, will create new meaning. The reader's mind is fluid, not static, and the essays in *The Common Reader* represent this constant flux and interaction, for they suggest the mind in conversation.

Note

[1] For M. Manuel the issue is whether Woolf is "referring to herself in the title or to the class of readers for whom she is writing" (28). The "figure of the Common Reader as it emerges from the two series of essays is, like the Tiresias of Eliot's *Wasteland*, an indefinite and all inclusive figure. . . . The Common Reader is nothing but a mask that Virginia Woolf wore in her role as a critic" (29). Vijay L. Sharma sees Woolf's reliance on the common reader as "a measure of critical sanity which derives its force from a democratic bias, which may well have been grounded in her father's political faith" (19). To ignore the centrality of the common reader's point of view would, according to Sharma, be to miss the uniqueness of Woolf's critical position: "While most of her contemporaries were shoring up academic criticism . . . she was trying to bring the high-brow activity in line with the needs of the average reader" (89).

Works Cited

Bell, Barbara Currier, and Carol Ohmann. "Virginia Woolf's Criticism: A Polemical Preface." *Feminist Literary Criticism: Explorations in Theory.* Ed. Josephine Donovan. Lexington: Univ. Press of Kentucky, 1975.
Guiguet, Jean. *Virginia Woolf and Her Works.* Trans. Jean Stewart. London: Hogarth, 1965.
Manuel, M. "Virginia Woolf as the Common Reader." *Literary Criterion* 7.2 (1966): 28-32.
McNeillie, Andrew. Introduction to *The Common Reader.* London: Hogarth; New York: Harcourt, 1925.
Sharma, Vijay L. *Virginia Woolf as Literary Critic: A Revaluation.* New Delhi: Arnold-Heineman, 1977.

Woolf, Virginia. "Byron & Mr. Briggs." *The Essays of Virginia Woolf.* Vol. I. Ed. Andrew McNeillie. New York: Harcourt, 1986.
———. "The Common Reader." *The Common Reader.* London: Hogarth; New York: Harcourt, 1925.
———. "Mr. Conrad: A Conversation." *The Captain's Death Bed and Other Essays.* Ed. LeonardWoolf. London: Hogarth, 1947. New York: Harcourt, 1925.
———. *A Writer's Diary.* Ed. Leonard Woolf. New York: Harcourt, 1953.

Alex Zwerdling
The Common Reader, the Coterie and the Audience of One

Although Woolf appropriated Dr. Johnston's phrase "the common reader" for her criticism, her attitude toward the audience of literature diverged significantly from his. It is true that all of her journalism and some of her more ambitious books (for instance *Night and Day, Orlando,* and *Flush*) were written for a general audience. In trying to appeal to a wide readership, she used the methods required for such an undertaking. These works do not rely on the reader's quick wit and reinforce traditional attitudes or disguise heterodox values under the veneer of charm.

Increasingly, during the course of her career, Woolf came to see such methods as a form of pandering and self-censorship. A writer interested in free expression must be willing to offend conventional readers, even at the risk of losing them. In the most fertile decade of her career—the one that produced *Jacob's Room, Mrs. Dalloway, To The Lighthouse,* and *The Waves*—she taught herself to address a much smaller audience, the "fit audience . . . though few" idealized in Milton's *Paradise Lost.* Like many of her fellow modernists, she thought of herself as writing for a coterie, a small circle of intimates she considered her ideal readers. In Woolf's case this coterie consisted primarily of her

Bloomsbury associates, who could be relied upon to read her work with care, to be sympathetic yet not uncritical, to be interested in both artistic and moral experimentation, and to be quickwitted enough to dispense with laborious explanations. The result was the highly compressed, allusive, and distinctly challenging art of these four novels, which helped to revolutionize fictional form by abandoning the more ponderous explanatory techniques of the earlier dispensation and by contesting traditional ideals. The reliable sponsorship of the coterie gave her freedom to experiment, to risk failure, to write as she pleased even if her thoughts were likely to offend and her methods to bewilder the common reader.

In the last years of her life, however, even this compromise between absolute freedom of self-expression and the need always to worry about the responses of an audience began to unravel. In writing *Three Guineas*, she came to feel that not even the coterie could be relied upon to sympathize with her most radical experiments, and that she would have to write initially at least for an audience of one. The appropriate genres for this kind of expression were the diary, the memoir not intended for publication, the letter to an intimate friend. Woolf was working toward something we might call the literature of solitude. She predicts its increasing importance in the late essay "The Humane Art," in which she imagines the writer talking "in the dark to himself about himself for a generation yet to be born" (*CE*, I, 104). Woolf saw such private works as antidotes to the pervasive hypocrisy of social discourse. But her appeal to posterity meant that she foresaw a day when the works that baffled the common reader of her own time and made her rely on a coterie, as well as the works that offended even her intimates might gradually be understood by a much wider circle of readers who were destined to be her true literary heirs.

A Modernist Aberration: Reading Woolf in the Context of Postmodernism

Ann Marie Hebert
"What Does it Mean? How Do You Explain It All?"
Virginia Woolf: A Postmodern Modernist

In Woolf's revolutionary novel *The Waves*, Bernard, after a lifetime spent constructing his own identity, concludes, "I am not one person; I am many people" (276). *The Waves*, like many of the novels, explores what Bernard calls "queer territory," territory in which reality is multiple and subjectivity is fragmented. Although Woolf is traditionally—and legitimately—accorded a place in the canon of high modernism, I will argue that, in her ontological and epistemological concerns, in her contesting of what Lyotard calls the totalizing master narratives, and—especially—in her refusal to reconcile contradictions, Woolf was a postmodern modernist. I am using the term postmodernism not as a chronological period, as that which follows modernism, and certainly not as the negative or the opposite of modernism, but rather as an ideological, philosophic and aesthetic stance, one that I see as an extension of the preoccupations of modernism and a lens that can help bring into focus the self-conscious contradictions and discontinuities of Woolf's fiction.[1]

Brian McHale distinguishes modernism and postmodernism

A Modernist Aberration

as having different primary concerns. He claims that the "dominant" of modernist fiction is epistemological, that of postmodernist fiction is ontological (9-10). While McHale makes some interesting arguments, I think this division is, ultimately, arbitrary and simplistic. Linda Hutcheon's definition of postmodernism as rendering visible the paradoxes of our ideologies is more persuasive. She argues that postmodernism "is a contradictory phenomenon, one that uses and abuses, installs and then subverts, the very concepts it challenges" (3). Woolf understood that which Hutcheon says postmodernism teaches—that one is implicated in the very structures that one contests.[2] In her fiction and her discursive texts Woolf foregrounds the contradiction of being inside and outside (the library, for example). Antitotalization, including the fragmentation of the subject, perhaps the most fundamental identifying mark of postmodernism, is the characteristic mode of Woolf's fiction.[3] Pamela Caughie argues, however, in her brilliant book, *Virginia Woolf and Postmodernism: Literature in Quest and Question of Itself,* not that postmodernism is an appropriate category for Woolf, but "only that her works are susceptible to analysis by means of this category" (21). While I agree that the analytical category, "postmodernism," says as much about the reader/critic as about the "nature" of Woolf's work, once the investment of the critic and the constructedness of the category are acknowledged, I would argue that classifying Woolf as a postmodernist is both useful and appropriate.

Postmodernism spawns multiplicity and, for Woolf, multiplicity was at the heart of her ontological and epistemological explorations, her experiments with form, and her representations of subjectivity. In her specific concerns with the nature of reality and how we know it, with the relationship between representation and reality, and with the problem of the subject, Woolf was a postmodern. Caughie sees this multiplicity or antitotalization, what she calls "equivocation," Woolf's "stance against certainty," as that which most distinguishes Woolf from Eliot and Joyce. Woolf shared the aesthetic concerns of the male modernists, but, as a woman who repeatedly used gender as a category of analysis, she perceived political and artistic implications that were of little concern to them. Excentric to the dominant male discourse she was both inside and outside the power-knowledge configuration. This feminine position gave a

11

different slant to her modernism which, I would argue, anticipated postmodernism.

From her diaries and letters of the thirties we know that Woolf read and discussed with her friends scientific theories, including those of modern quantum physics; thus, I think, she might enjoy the connection I am about to propose. One variation of quantum theory, the many-universes theory of Hugh Everett, developed at Princeton in the 1950s, can serve as a metaphor for Woolf's provisional working out of the ontological and epistemological questions that haunt her fiction: what is the nature of reality? how do we know? And, most threatening, but most important to Woolf, *who* knows?

The many-worlds, or multiple-universes, theory posits the existence of many other worlds, perhaps an infinite number of them, existing parallel to our own universe but forever cut off from it. Everett's interpretation is that the alternative realities at the quantum level do not collapse when we make a measurement (the dominant view of the wave-particle theory). Rather the act of observation forces the observer to choose one alternative which becomes part of what he or she sees as the "real" world; each of the alternative realities then goes on its separate way (Gribbon, 235-37). In *God and the New Physics*, Paul Davies claims, "every time an electron faces two choices, *both* alternatives occur, and the entire universe divides in two. Each universe is complete with inhabitants . . . each set of which believes that the electron has abruptly opted for one of the alternatives" (Davies, 173). Of course, the parallel universes theory can never, even in principle, be tested, because travel between quantum worlds is impossible.[4]

In all of Woolf's fiction, from *The Voyage Out* to *Between the Acts*, she, like the multiple-universes theorists of quantum physics, foregrounds contradiction. Believing that no essential "reality" can be known and that what is known is full of contradiction, Woolf inscribes the contradictions, hoping to get closer to a kind of truth. Her genius resides, in part at least, in the way in which she constructs multiple universes, replete with contradiction, and allows these parallel universes, these contradictory realities, to rest in juxtaposition, unresolved. If, as Bernard suspects in *The Waves*, writing is always, in a sense, lying, unresolved contradiction, she felt, was the truest lie that she could tell.

A Modernist Aberration

Woolf contests the metaphysical construction of reality as categorical, linear, defined, logical—the metaphysics which finds expression in *To the Lighthouse* in Mr. Ramsay's preoccupation with "subject and object and the nature of reality" (23). Woolf also contests all of the specifically masculine proliferations of knowledges, what Lily Briscoe calls the "inscriptions on tablets," all that "could be written in any language known to men" (51). If Lyotard is right, and I think he is, that postmodernism is, above all, incredulity toward metanarratives, then Woolf's aesthetics, philosophy, and politics are postmodern. Lyotard concludes *The Postmodern Condition* with a manifesto of sorts—"let us wage a war on totality; let us be witnesses to the unpresentable..."(82). This is Woolf's project.

As a supremely self-conscious writer, Woolf is forced to confront the question that Hutcheon argues is basic to postmodernism: from what position can one theorize a contradictory, disparate cultural phenomenon? (13) How does one stand outside the culture to critique the culture, outside metaphysics to critique metaphysics? Hutcheon quotes Stanley Fish's witty statement on what he calls the "anti-foundationalist" paradox that I think is important to keep in mind when discussing the "truth" of Woolf's fictions of multiplicity: "Ye shall know that truth is not what it seems and *that* truth shall set you free" (13). Woolf, intensely self-reflexive, is aware of this danger of creating her own metanarrative as she contests the traditional masculine ones. Thus, like Samuel Beckett, what she gives with one hand she takes away with the other. The contradictory universes contained in the everyday world are represented by Bernard in *The Waves* as:

> Must, must, must. Must go, must sleep, must wake, must get up—sober, merciful word . . . (234). We must find our coats. We must go. Must, must, must—detestable word... (293)

"Must...sober, merciful word." "Must...detestable word." For Woolf, both statements are true. She will never allow herself to rest in an unequivocal statement of truth. Neither praise nor blame of the quotidian is true in itself; only in the fullness of the contradiction does Woolf approach a fullness of meaning.

Her foregrounding of contradiction notwithstanding, part of Woolf's aesthetics was a longing for meaning. "What does it mean? How do you explain it all?" Lily wonders in *To the Lighthouse* (179). Critics have observed her obsession with unity, with an attempt to find (or construct) a "real" unity which underlies the multiplicity of appearances. "How do you explain it all?" During her father's illness in 1903, Woolf wrote to Violet Dickinson: "Please ask Hester L. to supply me with a god quick—not the Christian god."[5] Her representation of multiple universes always contains, just beneath the surface, a nostalgia for some kind of god who would give meaning to a seemingly meaningless universe and who would unify the disparate strands of life; however, she distrusted this impulse toward unity, suspecting that all unifying narratives are illusory. There is a revealing entry in the holograph manuscript of *To the Lighthouse* in which we see Woolf working with a series of motifs:

<u>To the Lighthouse</u>
Now the question of the ten years
The Seasons
The Skull
The gradual dissolution of everything
This is to be contrasted with the permanence of _____?
(Novak 57)

This blank space is quintessentially Woolf. "The permanence of _____?" To fill in this blank is the object of all her fiction—yet nothing solid, no ultimate permanence ever succeeds. She seeks a unifying reality which underlies appearance, but is deeply skeptical of its possibility. Minow-Pinkney says that there is a moment, in Woolf, when surfaces yield up an inner depth. "Truth is an *unveiling*," Minow-Pinkney says (109). Percival's name means to "pierce the veil," which seems to support her claim. I would argue, however, that, almost against her will, Woolf finds emptiness at the core of the conventional systems of truth. When Lily asks her question, "What does it mean? How do you explain it all?" she gazes at the scene around her and finds "curves and arabesques flourishing round a centre of complete emptiness" (179). In *The Waves* Percival is the unifying force which gives meaning to the characters' lives, he is "a God" (136). But, for the six characters and for Woolf, God is dead. Twice Bernard looks for him at the center of his life, only to find his place empty. He says, upon hearing of Percival's death: "Now then is my chance to find out what is of great importance, and I must be careful, and tell no lies. About him my feeling was: he sat there in the centre. Now I go to that spot no longer. The place is empty" (153). In Bernard's closing summary he is still longing for Percival: "Now to laugh with him . . . —that was what I wanted, to walk off arm-in-arm together laughing. But he was not there. The place was empty" (274). God is dead and the great systems of meaning which the eighteenth, nineteenth and twentieth centuries proffered for his replacement—reason, progress, science, history, psychoanalysis, even art—are, at best, partial.

Modernism's elevation of art and, ultimately, its trust in the efficacy of language, were seductive to Woolf. Repeatedly, however, she expresses a longing to capture what today, à la Kristeva, we call the semiotic—that which is inexpressible in language. Bernard is looking for: "a little language such as lovers use, words of one syllable such as children speak . . . . I need a howl; a cry" (295). Anticipating the postmodern feminist critique of phallogocentrism, Woolf argues that the symbolic fails to express the rawness of experience. When Percival dies Bernard goes to Jinny to confess his sorrow. They begin to reminisce: "we compared Percival to a lily—Percival who I wanted to lose his hair, to shock the authorities, to grow old with me; he was already covered over with the lilies." Bernard laments that their pain at Percival's death, as soon as it is encoded in the symbolic, loses its edge: "So the sincerity of the moment passed; so it became symbolical; and that I could not stand" (265). At another moment Bernard longs to replace words with music, "a painful, guttural, visceral, also soaring, lark-like, pealing song to replace these flagging, foolish transcripts." In despair he reflects on the inadequacy of language to represent the infinite variety of experience from complete indifference to tempestuous emotion to "horror, horror, horror—but what is the use of painfully elaborating these consecutive sentences when what one needs is nothing consecutive but a bark, a groan?" (250-51). This might almost serve as a definition of Kristeva's semiotic.

Bernard begins his summing up by saying, "I must tell you a story—and there are so many . . . ; and none of them are true" (238). None of them are true, Bernard senses, because of the nature of language and the nature of subjectivity. Many critics have suggested that the discovery of the self is the central theme in Woolf's novels. I agree, but would problematize the concept of the "self" as a coherent, knowable unit that can be "discovered." In the same years that Freud was splitting the psyche Woolf was exploring the discontinuities of the self in her fiction. In her narrative strategies she was a prophet of the self-in-progress, the subject-in-process of postmodernism. The multiple universes metaphor is nowhere more compelling than in Woolf's representation of subjectivity as multiple and discontinuous. Traditional, i.e. realist, representations of the individual are of a unitary, coherent, unambiguous character who acts in a unified way. Self-consistency within the text is an important measure of its success. Woolf's characters, on the other hand, have inconsistent feelings, actions, and words; this inconsistency is consistent with reality, she believed.

In her representation of subjectivity as split and as never fully present to itself, Woolf anticipates Lacanian theory. *The Waves* is, above all, a study of the construction of multiple subjectivities. The six characters are constituted as the extreme of Woolf's usual existential paradox of both solitary and blurred identities: "I am alone," Bernard says (11). And yet, although there is no dialogue, no character interaction, and no dramatic line, there is a tenuous, fragile communion among the six individuals. Early in the text Bernard says, "when we sit together close, we melt into each other with phrases. We are edged with mist. We make an insubstantial territory" (16). And that is an exact description of the relationship of the six voices.

Each self in *The Waves*, provisional, located in and constructed by language, is not an essence, independent of time and history. Louis says, ". . . these attempts to say, 'I am this, I am that,' which we make, coming together, like separated parts of one body and soul, are false'" (137). The voices constantly struggle to know themselves, to differentiate themselves, to achieve recognition of their identities by the others, to tell their

A Modernist Aberration

stories ("The time approaches when these soliloquies shall be shared" [39]) and to somehow overcome their existential aloneness. Differentiation and identification, however, are unresolved among the six. Neville muses:

> How useful an office one's friends perform when they recall us. Yet how painful to be recalled, to be mitigated, to have one's self adulterated, mixed up, become part of another. As he approaches I become not myself but Neville mixed with somebody—with whom?—Bernard? Yes, it is Bernard, and it is to Bernard that I shall put the question, Who am I? (83)

The advent of the other jeopardizes hard-won singularity. And yet—a contradiction—the plural self is made a single being by the other's glance: "To be contracted by another person into a single being—how strange," Bernard thinks (89). A process of becoming both single and plural, construction of a subjectivity, requires an audience: "I need eyes on me to draw out these frills and furbelows," says Bernard. "To be myself (I note) I need the illumination of other people's eyes..." (116). The other threatens the subject's coherence and unity and yet recognition by the other is essential for the construction of identity.

The search for a coherent self, one which resolves all the contradictions is, ultimately, futile. There is no core identity to be discovered *under* all of the apparent contradictions. Bernard, the teller of stories and, perhaps, the closest to an authorial voice, speaks the contradictions: "I am one person—myself" (87). "I am more selves than Neville thinks" (89). "I am not one person; I am many people; I do not altogether know who I am—Jinny, Susan, Neville, Rhoda, or Louis: or how to distinguish my life from theirs" (276). Bernard's fragmented subjectivity—"For this is not one life; nor do I always know if I am man or woman, Bernard or Neville, Louis, Susan, Jinny or Rhoda" (281)—leads, in the most terrifying passage of the book, to an experience of nihilism—no, annihilation. This experience of Bernard's, I suspect, represents Woolf's deepest fear:

> A man without a self.... A dead man. With dispassionate despair, with entire disillusionment I surveyed the dust dance; ... mutable, vain. I, carrying a notebook, making phrases, had recorded merely changes; ... How can I proceed now, I said, without a self, weightless and visionless, through a world weightless, without illusion? (285).

This chilling glimpse of "dispassionate despair" and "entire disillusionment" is one of unalleviated horror. The world and the self, usually overlaid with habit, drop away, and Bernard—and the reader who is, as a result of Bernard's explicit address to "you," complicitous in the narrative at this point—experience a moment of non-being as *we* gaze into an abyss.

In the final words of the text Bernard regains a sense of his own subjectivity; desire replaces despair. But Woolf, anticipating postmodernism, has disrupted the modernist master narrative, especially the conventions of representation. Suspecting that fragmentation, not unity, underlies appearance, she foregrounds contradiction and discontinuity and constructs reality and subjectivity as divided and plural. In her decentered many-universe theory of fiction, Woolf is, clearly, a postmodern modernist.

Notes

[1] Although this paper will argue Virginia Woolf's affinity with postmodernism, I do not discount her classification as a modernist. Her distrust of tradition, her persistent experimentalism, her love of the poetic image and, above all, her elevation of art mark her as a modernist. Her hope for art as a unifying force and as the replacement for the lost values of the past, particularly science and religion, continually gave way, however, to a skepticism about the efficacy of art. Woolf anticipates, I believe, the suspicion of Beckett and of the late-twentieth-century postmodernists that language is, ultimately, unreliable.

[2] One of Hutcheon's startling claims about postmodernism is that it is self-consciously didactic, an unusual claim for a position that problematizes truth. Woolf, too, in her concern with subverting conventional assumptions about the nature of truth, language, time, gender and subjectivity, is didactic, in the postmodern sense—certainly a different sense than that of Dickens or George Eliot, however.

[3] Woolf's postmodern modernism includes a nostalgia for Romanticism with its vivid emotion and its hope that Nature might provide a unifying force

A Modernist Aberration

in the place God had vacated. In *The Waves* Bernard becomes Byron for a period and, in an allusion to Keats' "Ode to a Nightingale," Louis says, "I am half in love with the typewriter and the telephone" (167). Bernard's last soliloquy, in which he addresses the reader as a stranger to whom he is compelled to tell his life's story has textual echoes of Coleridge's "The Rime of the Ancient Mariner" (238).

⁴The many-worlds or parallel-universes theory is not a majority view, but is a rather respectable one among physicists. For an introduction to the theory see John Gribbon or Paul Davies; for an elaboration, see Bryce DeWitt and Neill Graham's *The Many-Worlds Interpretation of Quantum Mechanics*.

⁵Dickinson correspondence, Berg Collection, quoted in Jane Novak's *The Razor Edge of Balance*.

Works Cited

Caughie, Pamela L. *Virginia Woolf & Postmodernism*. Urbana and Chicago: U. of Illinois P., 1991.
Davies, Paul. *God and the New Physics*. New York: Simon and Schuster, 1983.
DeWitt, Bryce and Neill Graham, eds. *The Many-Worlds Interpretation of Quantum Mechanics*. Princeton: Princeton U.P., 1973.
Gribbon, John. *In Search of Schrodinger's Cat: Quantum Physics and Reality*. Toronto and New York: Bantam Books, 1984.
Hutcheon, Linda. *A Poetics of Postmodernism*. New York and London: Routledge, 1988.
Lyotard, Jean François. *The Postmodern Condition: A Report on Knowledge*. 1979. Trans. Geoff Bennington and Brian Massumi. Minneapolis: U. of Minnesota P., 1984.
McHale, Brian. *Postmodernist Fiction*. London and New York: Metheun, 1987.
Minow-Pinkney. *Virginia Woolf and the Problem of the Subject*. New Brunswick, N.J., Rutgers U.P., 1987.
Novak, Jane. *The Razor Edge of Balance: A Study of Virginia Woolf*. Oxford, OH: U. of Miami P., 1975.

Teresa Heffernan
Fascism and Madness: Woolf Writing Against Modernism

In a year long course entitled "The Origins of Modernism" given at the University of Toronto, one woman appeared on the reading list, Virginia Woolf. What is more problematic is that in that one hour of that year long course that was devoted to Woolf we were also asked to deal with feminism. Feminism in this context is thus read as continuous with canonized modernism. What I would like to suggest in this paper is that Virginia Woolf's writing in fact challenges the parameters of canonized modernism and that if we continue to read and gender the canon of modernism as male, Woolf's feminist texts cannot be slotted unproblematically into this list.[1]

As Woolf reflects on the nature of a post-war modernist aesthetic in *A Room of One's Own*, she poses the question:

> What was the truth about these houses, for example, dim and festive now with their red windows in the dusk, but raw and red and squalid, with their sweets and bootlaces, at nine o'clock in the morning? And the willows and the river and the gardens that run down to the river, vague now with the mist stealing over them, but gold and red in the sunlight—which was the truth, which was the illusion about them? (16)

Woolf's inquiries are, in many ways, indicative of the concerns of the modernist movement: she questions the status of truth, she implicitly challenges the tyranny of classical or realist art, and she is interested in the process of representation.

Yet, for the modernist (and here I would like to clarify that I mean canonized modernism) this new aesthetic is both liberating and disquieting—advocates of modernism at once encourage radical experimentation, a demystification of the traditions of the past, the dissolution of borders,[2] and an interest in alternate perspectives, while simultaneously the members of the avant garde are concerned with legitimizing this new aesthetic. Hence, there is a tension evidenced in much of the work of this period between a privileging of the marginal, an interest in anarchism, and an embrace of the other (the child, the primitive, the insane) and the concern with unity, structure, and the authority of the artist. The radical impulse of modern art, literature, and criticism is at the same time accompanied by what Roger Fry refers to as a sense of nostalgia for the "well-ordered system" of the past and

A Modernist Aberration

at the extreme becomes, to borrow a phrase from Gianni Vattimo, "a neurotic reaction to the opening of new horizons."

The longer version of this paper locates this tension in an analysis of the modernist agenda; to summarize this section very briefly—it considers the valorization of the "purity" of the aesthetic and the elevated status of the "prophetic" artist in Kandinsky's and Klee's work; it also considers the writing of master narratives, such as Freud's discourse on psychiatry which Foucault has named "a monologue of reason about madness"; and finally it considers the privileging of "progress" and the discourse of science in Eliot and Pound's work which encouraged a search for "universal" laws that existed outside and beyond the interests of the individual subject. These various modernist positions invite divisions between the "ignorant masses" and the "enlightened artist" and hence necessarily produced new marginalized groups who were behind or on the periphery of the "true" path, a drama that plays itself out in the modernist's fear of contamination by the masses and the feminine. Andreas Huyssen has looked at the fear of the feminine and a fear of the masses as a "fear of nature out of control, a fear of the unconscious, of sexuality, of the loss of identity and stable ego boundaries" (52). Huyssen argues that although the modern artist professes contempt for the bourgeoisie, this fear of seduction and this fear of play supports both the bourgeois work ethic and the bourgeois desire for a stable society. I think it is also possible to read some points of convergence between this high art/mass culture discourse of modernism, which is also always inscribed as a masculine/feminine discourse, and fascist ideology. Despite attempts to read the modernists as occupying a neutral political stance, I would like to challenge the assumed boundary between the private and public and between the personal and the political on which this reading of neutrality depends. The rigid borders constructed around the autonomous artist parallel to some extent the defence of national boundaries and the program of nationalism; the prophetic artist is played out in the political sphere by the charismatic leader; the explicit misogyny, the fear of contamination, and the obsessiveness about the purity and unity of the aesthetic in modernism finds a parallel in the general resistance to plurality evident in the racist and sexist policies in the fascist agenda. Finally, the radical need to defend both the self and the state works itself out in both a metaphorical and literal exaltation of war.

Virginia Woolf's commitment to feminism in many ways sets her apart from the more conservative aspects of the modernist movement—if we return for a moment to the quote from *A Room of One's Own* with which this paper opens, we find Woolf is unwilling to respond to the question she poses regarding the division between truth and illusion (she ends or rather doesn't end the speculative moment with the non-conclusion "for no conclusion was found"). In contrast with many of the modernist artists who are concerned with locating the foundations of truth, Woolf's comments are at times indicative of her impatience with this search. At the opening of *A Room of One's Own*, it is not without some irony that she admits to her failure as a lecturer to provide her audience with "a nugget of pure truth... to keep on the mantlepiece forever" (1).

A Room of One's Own helps to illuminate some of the points of contention between Woolf and her fellow artists. As a female, masculine histories and fictions have written Woolf and her gender into the role of "other." Women have been/are silenced in a patriarchal structure which locates power in the masculine "self" and which is supported by a discourse of truth. Patricia Waugh writes:

> Subjectivity, historically constructed and expressed through the phenomenological equation self/other, necessarily rests masculine 'selfhood' upon feminine otherness. The subjective centre of socially dominant discourses (from Descartes's philosophical, rational 'I' to Lacan's psychoanalytic phallic/symbol) in terms of power, agency, autonomy has been a 'universal' subject which has established its identity through the invisible marginalization or exclusion of what it has also defined as 'femininity' (whether this is the non-rational, the body, the emotions, or the pre-symbolic).(6)

Ironically, even as Woolf is attempting to recover a history of women, her role as "other" is affirmed when she is forced by the

Beadle from the turf of the fellows and scholars and onto the peripheral gravel surrounding the university grounds.

Thus, unlike many of her male counterparts who have been immersed in and have benefited from the rhetoric of truth, Woolf, who has been excluded from this discourse, is not nostalgic about abandoning it. It is precisely such claims to "truth" which have allowed for the oppression of women and which have driven men to defend at any cost their privileged position. She writes in *A Room of One's Own:*

> Possibly when the professor insisted a little too emphatically upon the inferiority of women, he was concerned not with their inferiority, but with his own superiority. That was what he was protecting rather hot-headedly and with too much emphasis, because it was a jewel to him of the rarest price... By feeling that one has some innate superiority—it may be wealth, or rank, a straight nose, or the portrait of a grandfather by Romney—for there is no end to the pathetic devices of the human imagination—over other people (34).

The longer version of this paper includes a more detailed analysis of *To the Lighthouse* which focuses specifically on the construction of gender in a patriarchal society and posits that because Mr. Ramsay plays the authoritative, rational, powerful male who is truth, Mrs. Ramsay must play the subservient, intuitive, self sacrificing female who is non-truth. In *A Room of One's Own*, Woolf's privileging of the concept of androgyny suggests that she perceives this division of gender as problematic.

Mary Daly argues that the notion of androgyny was a pitfall for early feminist theorists: "Experience proved that this word [androgyny], which we now recognize as expressing pseudowholeness in its combination of distorted gender descriptions, failed and betrayed our thought... When we heard the word echoed back by those who misinterpreted our thought we realized that combining the `halves' offered to consciousness by patriarchal langauge usually results in portraying something more like a hole than a whole" (387). However, Woolf's notion of androgyny does not concern a combining of halves. Woolf does not propose that the sexes be considered identical, nor does she imply that the traditionally "feminine" traits replace the traditionally "masculine" traits; allowances for difference are critical in her writing and politics: "It would be a thousand pities if women wrote like men, or lived like men, or looked like men, for if the two sexes are quite inadequate, considering the vastness and variety of the world, how should we manage with one only?" (*A Room of One's Own*, 84). Woolf's interest in the possibilities of androgyny originate in her recognition of the limitations of reading gender in dichotomous terms. Her texts suggest that in a patriarchal structure the social construction of masculine and feminine (structure and structurelessness, reason and intuition, object and subject) are, to borrow a Derridian term, false opposites. In *To the Lighthouse* the destructive potential of this dichotomy is realized in the offspring of Mrs. and Mr. Ramsay who are the literal and logical product of binary gender constructions: Prue dies in childbirth—the loss of the female self; and Andrew dies in war—the fight to defend the self.

In *A Room of One's Own*, and *To The Lighthouse* the political and social ramifications of setting up the sexes as oppositional are considered. Mr. Ramsay is locked into a way of perceiving the world that demands a defense of what is "true"; his faith in the ability to access a universal "right" depends upon an insistence on the inadequacy of different perspectives. In *A Room of One's Own*, Woolf links this "unmitigated masculinity" to fascism: "And in a restless mood in which one takes books out and puts them back without looking at them I began to envisage an age to come of pure, self-assertive virility, such as the letters of professors (take Sir Walter Raleigh's letters for instance) seem to forbode, and the rulers of Italy have already brought into being" (98).

But if the masculine—the unified autonomous ego—taken to an extreme, concludes in fascism, the "unmitigated" feminine is associated in Woolf's writing with madness and death. In *To The Lighthouse* while the male is absorbed in shoring up his identity, the female must concern herself with supporting that identity: "it behooves the woman, whatever her own occupation may be, to go to the help of the young man opposite her so that he may expose and relieve the thigh bones, the ribs, of his vanity, of his urgent desire to assert himself" (105).

The female in a patriarchal structure can only exist in relation to the male—her "non-truth," her fundamental "absence" is through the inscription of the masculine world allowed some limited degree of legitimacy; in *To the Lighthouse* Mrs. Ramsay inhabits this world: "she let it uphold her and sustain her, this admirable fabric of the masculine intelligence, which ran up and down, crossed this way and that, like iron girders spanning the swaying fabric, upholding the world, so that she could trust herself to it utterly . . ."(122). Hence, the escape from patriarchy becomes problematic in Woolf's texts—when Mrs. Ramsay begins to fall through the gaps in the "iron girders" constructed by the masculine world, she loses a sense of self. On her trip to the lighthouse, she strays from the supportive structure of masculine society and finds herself stranded in a structureless, selfless world which provides no defense against death. Similarly, in *A Room of One's Own*, the fate of the female who attempts to transgress the designated gender boundaries is inevitably tragic; society does not validate a female subject that is independent of a male. By abandoning the iron girders she falls through the gaps, descends into the abyss, and like "Shakespeare's sister" ends in suicide or, like the "lost novelist," wanders "the highways crazed" (48). Because of the repression of what Dale Spender in *Man Made Language* refers to as "female talk," the attempt to escape patriarchy to some extent can only be an illusion—an escape into a silence which itself is encoded by patriarchy.

Lily Briscoe resists the limited role assigned to females in the patriarchal drama but is also excluded from the masculine role which allows for the assertion of self through the creation of meaning; hence she too confronts the possibility of falling into a non-space, an absence, a death. But her resolution at the end of *To the Lighthouse* to draw the line on the blank page announces her rethinking of the restrictive masculine-feminine constructions; Lily Briscoe is at once conscious of the absence and the need for structure. As long as the artist can create, put marks on the blank page, she prevents the descent into madness and death; she can still script in the face of unreason and disorder. Foucault writes in *Madness and Civilization*:

> Madness is the absolute break with a work of art; it forms the constitutive moment of abolition, which dissolves in time the truth of the work of art; it draws the exterior edge, the line of dissolution, the contour against the void. Artaud's oeuvre experiences its own absence in madness, but that experience, the fresh courage of that ordeal, all those words hurled against a fundamental absence of language, all that space of physical suffering and terror which surrounds or rather coincides with the void—that is the work of art itself; the sheer cliff over the abyss of the work's absence. (287)

Lily Briscoe's line is in Foucauldian terms that "sheer cliff over the abyss."

Virginia Woolf, in her diaries, articulates a similar tension between the pull of madness, the void, selflessness and the desire to resist that pull through writing, the assertion of self, the creation of a structure. Art for Woolf, like Lily, becomes a defense against madness and death: She writes in a diary entry: "Yet I've been absorbed all the morning in the autobiography part of *Three Guineas*. And the absorption is genuine: and my great defense against the cold madness that overcame me last night . . . Meanwhile suffer me now and again to write out my horror, this sudden cold madness, here" (199).

The ability to conceive of something other than a feminine/masculine dichotomy allows Lily Briscoe to draw the line. In a *Room of One's Own* Woolf locates that possibility in the utterance and representation of female experience which necessarily disrupts gender roles as the subsequent supply of signifiers play at the edge of the abyss. The positing of texture and variety against a void resists binary constructions.

Woolf's interest in androgyny should be read in the context of the dangerous implications of phallogocentric gender divisions; an "unmitigated" masculine courts fascism while the "unchecked" feminine slips into madness and death. In *A Room of One's Own*, *To The Lighthouse*, and *Three Guineas* construction and creation are necessary to introduce programs for change, to improve the status of women, to review art by and about women, and to address the problems of a war-torn Europe. The coherent assertive subject allows for creation and production and is the agent of change; however, the "girders" that support this self are always already flexible—not "iron" but elastic and contingent.

Woolf's deconstruction of the socially constructed divisions between masculine and feminine in a patriarchal structure (and the implied dichotomies that accompany this division) encourage her to search for alternative forms of expression. Her dismissal of the concept of "femininity" as existing only in relation to "masculinity" encourages her to disrupt the notion of a fixed center, an autonomous subject, a universal truth that works itself out against margins, absence, non-truths. In other words, Woolf's writing is not easily accommodated by a modernist agenda—as long as modernism continues to be read as and gendered male, Woolf's texts will continue to render problematic this inscription. Her texts will speak from the margins—not from the position of the sanctified "other," not as a testament to the gaps or spaces in the monolithic male canon—but, to quote Gayatri Chakravorty Spivak, from the margin as the "place for the argument, the place for the critical moment."

Notes

[1] Reading the canon as "male" leads to the gendering of the canon as male and not vice versa; by "male" I am referring to the construction of gender in phallogocentric terms or under patriarchy.

[2] The transgression of borders is evidenced, for example, in the modernists' preoccupation with interdisciplinary studies that gave rise to such groups as the famous school of design, the Bauhaus.

Works Cited

Bell, Quentin. *Virginia Woolf*. Vol. 2. London: The Hogarth Press, 1973.
Daly, Mary. *Gyn/ecology*. Boston: Beacon Press, 1978.
Foucault, Michael. *Madness and Civilization*. New York: Vintage Books, 1973.
Huyssen, Andreas. *After the Great Divide*. Bloomington and Indianapolis: Indiana University Press 1986.
Waugh, Patricia. *Feminine Fictions: Revisiting the Postmodern*. New York: Routledge, 1989.
Woolf, *A Room of One's Own*. London: Grafton Books, London, 1989.
———. *To the Lighthouse* . Middlesex, England: Penguin Books, 1969.

Roseanne Hoefel
Preserving A Discourse of Difference and
A Difference of Discourse

In two of her major critical works, Virginia Woolf explores women's position of contra/diction within patriarchal discourse. She postulates this situatedness on a literary critical level in *A Room of One's Own* as a difference of discourse and theorizes it on a cultural basis in *Three Guineas* as a discourse of difference. Among her strategies in this project are *mimetisme* and literary creation in *A Room of One's Own*. Self-effacing *mimesis* allows Woolf to demonstrate that, as a woman, she has been socioculturally, economically, intellectually deprived, which in turn enables her to establish an empathy motif. In this way, Woolf diffuses antagonism and resentment toward her topic. Further, Woolf deliberately formulates the argument as story, "making use of all the liberties and licenses of a novelist" (*Room* 4). Such techniques lead toward two very significant ends: storytelling puts theory (of women's writing of fiction) into practice; and deliberating the thought processes privileges process over product in the function of language, thus making it less contained than patriarchal language.

The apologetic tone accompanying her mimetic tact(ic) in *A Room of One's Own* is a luxury neither Woolf nor the world-at-large can afford ten years later, when Woolf theorizes a discourse of difference for women in *Three Guineas* (1938). With an urgency which is informed by her less-censored engagement with her anger, Woolf presents (to a male audience, this time) a utopian alternative (feminist education), which she then has to withdraw (31-35), since such would set women up for failure without patriarchy. Here, Woolf attempts to change the terms of the discourse by: a) prioritizing the establishment of institutions which preserve female difference and b) giving women access to subjectivity, knowledge, and power.

Using a consciousness- rather than action-centered materialistic logic, Woolf offers coalition as an alternative to either merging or separation among men and women. She prefers to suspend the contradiction between the sexes and genders, and

A Modernist Aberration

live either in the contradiction between the two worlds, or at the margins, for she feels that 1) being locked into patriarchal constructions and dualities is worse than being locked out (99-100) and that 2) union is too total an effusion since it obliterates both. Rather than integration (which breeds likeness), difference, for Woolf, is a construction we can better use as a base for *transforming* the entire structure. Wanting to be a pacifist without being passive, Woolf is left with the dilemma that non-participation in the male economy of sameness—an economy which breeds itself, repeats the same mistakes with increasingly disastrous effects—is the only way to help.

Woolf, Class and Empire

Kathy J. Phillips
Woolf's Criticism of the
British Empire in *The Years*

Virginia Woolf's *The Years* (1937) depicts a society both deadened and deadly. The novel counterpoints emptiness in England against constant references to the British Empire. Many of the Pargiters have been to the colonies, spreading their civilization. Yet the family's hypocrisy, loneliness, and dullness, typical of a whole society, represent nothing worth exporting. Repressed sexuality and emotion become distorted into money lust and militarism, turning the eminently "nice" Pargiters into the perpetrators of an unjust Empire. As Leonard Woolf says in *Empire and Commerce in Africa* (1920), the "evil" of imperialism is carried out not by monsters, but by ordinary people under the sway of an evil system (353). Virginia and Leonard Woolf essentially agree about the folly of Empire. As a Socialist, Leonard traces the root of the problem to economic imperialism and eventually to capitalism. Woolf concurs and adds other causes, such as gender relations. From *The Voyage Out* to the end of her career, Woolf consistently links dominance of "inferior" races with dominance of "inferior" women. No one has yet studied the extent of Woolf's criticism of Empire. She draws on specific details from Leonard's book and from other books published at their Hogarth Press about the Empire in Africa and India. Whereas her source materials judge the Empire through discursive commentary, she condemns it through powerful visual imagery and juxtaposition.

Work Cited

Woolf, Leonard. *Empire and Commerce in Africa: A Study in Economic Imperialism.* New York: Macmillan, n.d.

Beth Rigel Daugherty
Taking a Leaf from Virginia Woolf's Book: Empowering the Student

Anybody who studies Virginia Woolf's relationship with her reader knows there is something special about it. In fact, most critics use the language of empowerment when they discuss the writer/reader relationship in Woolf's essays. For example, Lyndall Gordon says Woolf's essays invite the reader "to become a co-worker" and their tone "infuses the reader with agency" (182). Marcia McClintock Folsom mentions the "profoundly encouraging effect of Woolf's peroration" in *A Room of One's Own*, which continues to tell young women, more than 60 years later, that "they must write" (254). Edward Bishop points out how Woolf's metaphors "enlist the reader as an active partner in this delicate and difficult business of communication" (584). Jane Marcus notes how Woolf erases the difference between lecturer and lectured in *A Room of One's Own* so that we all become readers, and "the original meaning of the word *lecture* is restored, 'the action of reading'" (176). Steve Ferebee says Woolf "pointed toward a future generation of critics" (361), reader response critics who "find meaning not only in the text but also in the reader" (343). Debbie Olhoeft, in an Otterbein College Distinction Project on Woolf's voice, says, "She puts herself in the audience with us, making herself one of us" (8). In other words, Woolf identifies with readers and in doing so, empowers them.

Many reasons for this cooperative writer/reader relationship have been posited, and I have no quarrel with any of them. However, I would like to suggest an additional influence. The traits often mentioned as part of Woolf's writer/reader relationship also happen to be the traits associated with good teaching: speaking in a personal, conversational tone; giving information about process; using narrative; making information vivid, real; providing context; and giving students a voice. And although we do not usually think of Virginia Woolf as a teacher, at a crucial time in her life, she *was*. For two and a half years, the young Virginia Stephen taught working class adults at Morley College; furthermore, evidence in her early diaries, letters, and Morley College teaching reports juxtaposed with the empowering techniques she uses in the essays most like teaching, those that began as "lectures," suggest that the Morley College students helped shape the writer/reader relationship we see permeating Virginia Woolf's work.

To provide a little background, when Virgina Stephen begins teaching at Morley College in January 1905, she is not quite 23. The Stephen children have just moved to Bloomsbury, she has met Leonard Woolf for the first time, Leslie Stephen had died the year before, and she is recovering from an illness. She has to get Dr. Savage's advice about "my capabilities of work at present" (*PA* 220) before she can say "yes" to Miss Mary Sheepshanks, the acting Principal at Morley, who approaches her about teaching a class. She writes every morning, working on reviews, which she has just begun to publish. In 1905, then, Virginia Stephen is becoming more independent, adjusting to living without her parents in a new place, and developing the lifelong routines that would make her such a productive writer. When the shy, upper-middle class Virginia Stephen arrives at Morley for her first class on January 18, 1905, she walks into the Old Vic, the Victoria Theatre. What had once been a theatre famous for low melodrama, public drinking, and prostitutes and thieves had been turned into the Royal Victoria Coffee Hall in 1880, when various kinds of better entertainment could then be enjoyed for a few coppers. Some classes were added to Miss Emma Cons' reform efforts in 1885, and in 1889, the educational work was separated from the entertainment and named Morley Memorial College for Samuel Morley, the wealthy hosiery manufacturer who put the place on a sound financial basis before he died. Founded by a woman and consistently run by women for many years (even when they were not allowed to speak up at board meetings!), Morley was co-ed from the start. Classes were held behind, above, and at the sides of the stage while the entertainment continued. Courses in science, literature, history, languages, music, etc. were not meant to improve wages but to enrich lives.

Morley College was in Lambeth, near the border of Southwark, two of London's worst districts. (The college still exists, by the way, but unfortunately, all its records were destroyed by a bomb in 1940.) Southwark provided Dickens with much of his material for *Oliver Twist*, and in 1890, one of its parishes was *the* poorest district in London. Most students at Morley were working class and would have ended their education at 14 or younger. According to Denis Richards, author of a history of Morley College, nearly one-half of the population of Southwark and North Lambeth was below the poverty line in 1890, which meant being in one of the following four groups: the lowest (no family life, no work, alcoholism, crime, etc.); the very poor, with small and irregular earnings; the poor with well-paid but irregular work; and the poor with low regular wages. Above the poverty line were the working class in regular employment, who ate well and regularly, then the foremen and highly paid artisans who could actually save money, and then the middle classes, with servants, who were only 10% of the population (Richards 22-24; citing Charles Booth's survey, *Life and Labour of the People in London*).

So Virginia Stephen travels to Lambeth after dinner on Wednesday nights to teach "anaemic shop girls who say they would write more but they only get an hour for their dinner, and there doesn't seem much time for writing" (*Letters*, I:210). Unlike Vanessa and Adrian, who try teaching there but quit almost immediately, Virginia keeps at it for two and a half years, perhaps because the experience of writing every morning and confronting a real audience every week was teaching her so much about how to reach readers.

In fact, I want to suggest that Woolf makes a crucial discovery at Morley. She sees a similarity between herself and the struggling outsiders attending classes there, an identification she then duplicates over and over again: in whom she talks to, in what she says, and in how she says it. Thus, a cooperative writer/reader relationship begins to take shape in Woolf's mind during those years at Morley. The lectures that became essays—"Mr. Bennett and Mrs. Brown," "How Should One Read a Book?," "The Narrow Bridge of Art," *A Room of One's Own*, "Professions for Women," and "The Leaning Tower"—all have a pedagogical sub-text, one that can be traced back to Morley.

For example, Woolf's development of a conversational tone, such as in the opening line of *A Room of One's Own*, "But, you may say, we asked you to speak about women and fiction—what has that got to do with a room of one's own?" (3) may have grown out of a lesson she learned from her Morley students. Naturally enough, with no training as a teacher and little experience as a student, Virginia Stephen worries about whether her first lecture on prose will interest her students. She works two mornings on it, and on January 17th writes in her diary, "Finished my Prose lecture which must still be written out, as I cant trust my self to speak from memory — & with writing before me I cant go far wrong" (*PA* 223). Only two women show up to hear her thoughts on Sir Thomas Browne, and although they are "[n]ice and intelligent," they are also "readier to talk than listen" (*PA* 224). Three days after this discouraging start, she's at it again, writing an "odd kind of lecture" about the Stephen trip to Italy (*PA* 225). Four students come, and when she describes *this* class to Violet Dickinson, she writes, "*we discussed* Venice" (*Letters*, I:177); my emphasis). By February 8th, her enrollment has gone up to seven, and on March 8th, she tries the experiment of "only writing short notes, which I shall put into words on the spur of the moment." Why? Because she notices that "Directly I begin to read, their attention wanders." This adjustment to her audience must have worked, because she writes later that night, "To my women, & managed the speaking all right — it is certainly better than reading" (*PA* 234, 249). When she shifts from Sir Thomas Browne to a description of the Stephen journey to Italy, her students' reactions probably also influenced Woolf's later willingness to include herself and her own experiences in her lectures: "we discussed Venice, and I showed them pictures, and they were nice and friendly and full of interest, and told me about their Aunts who said that there was water in all the streets in Venice, and was it true..." (*Letters*, I:177). In a letter to Madge Vaughan, Virginia Stephen admits she "would rather get to know them [her students] than instruct them" (*Letters*, I:173), and she may have later realized that listeners/readers have a similar desire. Thus, in "Mr. Bennett and Mrs. Brown," Woolf begins her discussion of character in fiction by telling about her train journey from Richmond to Waterloo, and in "Professions for Women," she describes her entry into the writing profession by asking her audience to picture "a girl in a bedroom with a pen in her hand. She had only to move that pen from left to right—from ten o'clock to one. Then it occurred to her to do what is simple and cheap enough after all—to slip a few of those pages into an envelope, fix a penny stamp in the corner, and drop the envelope into the red box at the corner. It was thus that I became a journalist" (284).

Several other techniques for including readers seem to have grown out of strategies she used at Morley. For example, at the same time Woolf includes herself in the story I just quoted, she also emphasizes process, sharing with her audience *how* she did something. In "How Should One Read a Book?" she takes seriously and tries to answer a question others might dismiss as obvious, covering the sequence of reading from the point of confusion at the library door to the act of literary criticism. As Debbie Olhoeft writes in "Virginia Woolf's Voice: Reverberating Presences," "the very question posed in the title is a question Woolf voices to herself and answers in her essay, for herself and us. And the answer to this question is the basic framework for dialogue within Woolf's community" (14). Woolf's openness to questions and her practice of voicing them in her lectures may have grown out of that early decision to let her students become part of the class, letting them talk, discuss, and ask questions.

She also often uses narrative, vivid images, and the familiar to explain abstractions: an arm-waving beadle becomes the male establishment shutting women out; food reveals the power structure; a leisurely walk from house to house and garden to garden defines English literary history; the novel genre is a cannibal; a sign saying "Trespassers will be prosecuted" represents class barriers; peeking in windows becomes biography; the internal barrier holding women back is a seductive, whispering Angel who must be stabbed with a pen. Compare how she tries at Morley to "make the real interest of history—as it appears to me—*visible* to them" (Bell 203; my emphasis). She generally includes one good scene for her students to focus on or writes a "pot boiler" (*PA* 227): "I have been making out a vivid account of the battle of Hastings. I hope to make their flesh creep!" (*Letters*, I:191). She tries to put "flesh & blood" into the shadowy past (Bell 203) by using humor, making them write about themselves, bringing in pictures, and lending them books. She and Vanessa even meet six women at the National Gallery one Saturday to walk through the early Italian paintings (*PA* 246). Woolf's self-deprecating tone as a lecturer—"Even if I could answer the question for myself, the answer would apply only to me and not to you" ("How" 1); "Lies will flow from my lips, but there may perhaps be some truth mixed up with them; it is for you to seek out this truth and to decide whether any part of it is worth keeping. If not, you will of course throw the whole of it into the wastepaper basket and forget all about it" (*Room* 4)—can already be seen in her 1905 Report on Teaching at Morley College. She is sure her methods are superficial and fast; she writes, "Of course it was not possible in the way I took to make them know anything accurately; my task, as I conceived it, was rather to prepare the soil for future sowers" (Bell 203). Hear *A Room of One's Own*? In a letter to Violet Dickinson, she mentions that Miss Sheepshanks thinks her gift is "rather influence than direct intellectual teaching" (*Letters*, I:264). Years later, she says in *A Room of One's Own* that she cannot fulfill the "first duty of a lecturer—to hand out after an hour's discourse a nugget of pure truth to wrap up between the pages of your notebooks and keep on the mantelpiece for ever. *All I could do was to offer you an opinion upon one minor point*—a woman must have money and a room of her own if she is to write fiction" (3-4; my emphasis).

Surely Virginia *Stephen's* anger at Morley College for providing no context for student learning has something to do with Virginia *Woolf's* attention to context and history. As Jane Marcus has pointed out, the audience at *A Room of One's Own* left her lecture with a reading list of women authors (78), a list that may seem obvious after two decades of Women's Studies but would *not* have been obvious to her audience. Those listeners also were given a history of how Girton and Newnham got started and a description of how to do research (Marcus 176).

Finally, Virginia Woolf identifies with her audience, aligning herself with outsiders: her lectures are delivered only to students, women, and working men (Marcus 165), the same audience she had at Morley. The one lecture that included a few educated men in the audience, "The Narrow Bridge of Art," is the least useful pedagogically. The young Virginia Stephen may not always speak glowingly about her students (she sounds like many tired composition teachers I know, for example, when she writes "I have been teaching a Milkman to write English for 2 hours; and the effect is so singular that I had better say no more. It is like floating your brains in cold mist" [*Letters*, I:281]), but she is clearly on their side. She understands that their attempts to "piece together what they 'hear'; to seek reasons; to connect ideas" are hampered by their previous lack of education; she, too, experienced such frustration. She is much more angry at the institution than at her students, wondering why it does not do more to show students how the "disconnected fragments" of lectures and classes are "part of a whole" (Bell 203-04). She finds her students enthusiastic, "refreshing after the educated" (*PA* 218) and admits that they possess "more intelligence than I expected; though that intelligence was almost wholly uncultivated" (Bell 203). In July 1905, she writes, "But of this I am convinced; [t]hat it would not be hard to educate them sufficiently to give them a new interest in life; They have tentacles languidly stretching forth from their minds, feeling vaguely for substance, & easily applied by a guiding hand to something that [they] could really grasp" (Bell 203). Furthermore, the seeds of *A Room of One's Own*, that 1929 feminist landmark that would point out the connection between what one *has* and what one *does*, are in that 1905 draft report. Miss Stephen reports that Miss Burke has written an account of her own life:

> It did not take up many pages, & only described certain memories of childhood; it was a curious little production, floundering among long words, & involved periods, with sudden ponderous moral sentiments thrown into the midst. But she could write grammatical sentences, which followed each other

logically enough; & she had evidently some facility of expression; in other circumstances, I suppose, she would have been a writer! (Bell 203)

In other circumstances, she would have been like Miss Stephen...

The other circumstances? 500 pounds a year and a room of one's own. The idea that money equals freedom of expression underlies both *A Room of One's Own* and "Professions for Women," but Woolf may have first seen this connection between money and integrity when she talked with Miss Williams at Morley in 1905. Miss Williams, "[t]he germ of a literary lady," works for a religious newspaper whose editor tells her whether a book review is to be favorable or unfavorable, thus eliminating the need for her to read the book before reviewing it! (Bell 202). By the time Woolf delivers her "Leaning Tower" lecture to working class men in 1940, her identification with outsiders has become so automatic and so strong that she uses and *publishes* the pronoun "we" to mean herself and the working men against the "they" of educated men in the tower; furthermore, she reassures those listeners that the great writers "do not mind if we get our accents wrong, or have to read with a crib in front of us" (181).

In "Mr. Bennett and Mrs. Brown," Woolf writes that "A writer is never alone. There is always the public with him" (332). She embodies this concept *within* her lectures by giving her audience a voice. Remember the first sentence of *A Room of One's Own* quoted earlier? Well, the end of that lecture also centers around objections the audience may have to her talk—she makes the audience's concerns legitimate, takes their possible questions seriously. She also frequently points out how difficult the audience's tasks are; she does not minimize what she asks them to do—write, read, think, furnish their metaphoric room differently, trespass. But she also points out the power they have. In "How Should One Read A Book?", for example, she reminds her listeners right up front that they should come to their own conclusions, take no advice about reading. Only if they agree that they can reject anything she says, thus maintaining the "independence that is the most important quality that a reader can possess," can she be truly free to "put forth a few ideas and suggestions" (1).

She also names the power they *will* have if they put forth massive effort. At the end of *A Room of One's Own*, they will bring to life a great female writer, Shakespeare's sister; at the end of "How Should One Read a Book?" their reactions will help make writers' books "stronger, richer, and more varied" (11). At the end of "Mr. Bennett and Mrs. Brown," their insistence that authors tell the truth about Mrs. Brown will help bring about a great age of English literature (336-37). At the end of "Professions for Women," women who finally have rooms of their own can remake social structures (289). At the end of "The Leaning Tower," working men have the power to create a classless society if they simply start trespassing on the young educated men's ground and read: "literature is no one's private ground; literature is common ground" (181). These endings are, I think, Woolf's tribute to her Morley students. When she names the power the reader potentially has at the end of these essays, she names the power her students *actually* had: they "[stole] into the air and [became] part of the atmosphere" she breathed as she worked ("How" 11).[1] They became part of the public that was always with her, part of her voice; they helped Woolf shape the writer/reader relationship that now shows *us* how to empower our students.

Notes

[1] Morley College and its students also became part of Woolf's novels. For example, at the beginning of *The Voyage Out*, Mrs. Ambrose is relieved to see a school built by the London County Council for Night Schools in this "city of innumerable poor people" (12). The "degenerate poet" Virginia Stephen teaches at Morley College on Waterloo Road, the young man "who rants and blushes, and almost seizes my hand when we happen to like the same lines" (*Letters*, I 313), becomes Septimus Smith who falls "in love with Miss Isabel Pole, lecturing in the Waterloo Road upon Shakespeare" (*MD* 128).

Works Cited

Bishop, Edward L. "Metaphor and the Subversive Process of Virginia Woolf's Essays." *Style* 21.4 (1987): 573-588.

Ferebee, Steve. "Bridging the Gulf: The Reader In and Out of Virginia Woolf's Literary Essays." *College Language Association Journal* 30.3 (1987): 343-361.

Folsom, Marcia McClintock. "Gallant Red Brick and Plain China: Teaching *A Room of One's Own*." *College English* 45.3 (1983): 254-262.

Gordon, Lyndall. *Virginia Woolf: A Writer's Life*. New York: Norton, 1984.
Marcus, Jane. *Virginia Woolf and the Languages of Patriarchy*. Bloomington: Indiana UP, 1987. 163-187.
Olhoeft, Debbie. "Virginia Woolf's Voice: Reverberating Presences." Distinction Project. Otterbein College. 1991.
Richards, Denis. *Offspring of the Vic: A History of Morley College*. Foreword by Harold Nicolson. London: Routledge and Kegan Paul, 1958.
Woolf, Virginia. "How Should One Read a Book?" *Collected Essays*. Vol. II. New York: Harcourt, 1953. 1-11.
———. "The Leaning Tower." *Collected Essays*. Vol. II. New York: Harcourt, 1953. 162-181.
———. *The Letters of Virginia Woolf: Volume One, 1888-1912*. Ed. Nigel Nicolson and Joanne Trautmann. New York: Harcourt/Harvest, 1977.
———. "Mr. Bennett and Mrs. Brown." *Collected Essays*. Vol. I. New York: Harcourt, 1953. 319-337.
———. *Mrs. Dalloway*. New York: Harcourt/Harvest, 1925.
———. "The Narrow Bridge of Art." *Collected Essays*. Vol. II. New York: Harcourt, 1953. 218-229.
———. *A Passionate Apprentice: The Early Journals, 1897-1909*. Ed. Mitchell A. Leaska. San Diego: Harcourt, 1990.
———. "Professions for Women." *Collected Essays*. Vol. II. New York: Harcourt, 1953. 284-289.
———. "Report on Teaching at Morley College." *Virginia Woolf: A Biography*. Quentin Bell. New York: Harcourt/Harvest, 1972. 202-204.
———. *A Room of One's Own*. New York: Harcourt/Harvest, 1929.
———. *The Voyage Out*. New York: Harcourt/Harvest, 1920.

Jeanette McVicker
Vast Nests of Chinese Boxes, or Getting to from Q to R: Critiquing Empire in "Kew Gardens" and *To the Lighthouse*

This paper explores what I call Woolf's critique of Empire, i.e., her critique of ideology and power and the social formations and discourses through which they are exercised. In these two particular works, the subtlety of Woolf's critique reveals her deep awareness of the complex network of power relations expressed through the academy, technology, and the mastery of nature and temporality. While I argue that this critique can be detected in the whole of Woolf's work, her commitment to the aesthetic principles of modernist practice prevented her from indicting literature and art along with other cultural institutions. Nevertheless, recognition of the depth of her critique is crucial for a contemporary reading of Woolf's work and life: first, it focuses the historical context of her situation so that her feminism has broader implications for other "subjected subjects," i.e., it reads her feminist critique of patriarchy against the larger frame of the Western tradition; second, it assigns to Woolf a pivotal role in the transformation of modernist literature, from one preoccupied with the aesthetic concern for newness, to one which would become with the existentialists a "literature of engagement."

"Kew Gardens" provides a capsulized version of Woolf's critique of Empire if one reads from an ideological position. The function of marriage in suppressing desire and youth, evidenced by the first couple's interchange, becomes a critique of patriarchal dominance in the last couple's scene, as the young man thrusts his companion's parasol in and out of the flower-bed and "bears her on" toward tea. Alternately, the second couple's dialogue makes several references to the devastation caused by war, while the third couple's fragmented conversation addresses issues of class and imperialism. These couples represent among other things, ideological binary oppositions: male/female, age/youth, wealth/poverty, sanity/madness. As a whole, the story frames the larger opposition between civilization and nature.

In the concluding paragraph of the story, one is presented with a final, overarching facet of the theme of Empire: the drive toward technological progress, bringing together its roots in a patriarchal, militaristic and class-oriented system. Everything is caught up in the exhausting mechanization of London life. The images of dehumanizing, sterile technology at the close of this story suggest Woolf's keen awareness that the repressiveness of Empire touches all aspects of life; that even a place of beauty such as Kew Gardens was caught up in that web, having been designated a state institution in 1841, as the home of the Royal Botanical Gardens.

Whereas "Kew Gardens" addresses the technological and social implications of the stamp of Empire, *To The Lighthouse* addresses this theme primarily at the sites of culture and education. Woolf establishes several important ideological connections through the character of Mr. Ramsay. The subtle rendering of the tyranny that can be exerted by an obsession with facts, reason, and the compulsion to order life and manipulate truth is a masterful critique of patriarchy and traditional enlightenment thinking. But Woolf presses her critique further, adding the controlling metaphor of Tennyson's poem, and the image of Mr. Ramsay as a tragic romantic hero firmly standing by his quest (to conquer other lands and nature), together achieving a devastating critique of the relay between patriarchy, philosophy, imperialism, and state art in the perpetuation of power by the proponents of Empire. Woolf's multilayered portrait of Mr. Ramsay and his desperate attempt to construct reality by means of linear thinking, depicted as his dogged pursuit of R—as something that can be mastered, letter by letter—suggests the will to power inhering in Cartesian-based rationality. That "cogito," as Woolf demonstrates here and elsewhere, is the "I" of the western tradition, the "shadow across the page" which has eclipsed a "multitude of others": women, the working classes, the victims of colonization, the insane, etc.

But time and again, Woolf ends up deflecting the theme of Empire (here, with the final brushstroke of Lily's painting). Thus, while this theme is consistent throughout her writings, her critique never fully acknowledges the overwhelming degree to which Empire subverts all ideology to its hegemonic purposes. Woolf's intense aesthetic commitment to the modern and to the redeeming function of art in society were in direct conflict with her impulse to expose and critique the ideology of Empire. Thus, for all the socio-political awareness in her work, the unified vision so prevalent in modernist art takes priority. But acknowledging that it is artistic resolution which wins out rather than the full implications of social critique does not and should not lessen the importance of that critique. It is this dimension that gives real impact to her feminism, read within the larger context of the Western tradition, one dominated not only by patriarchy, but also by racism, classism, militarism, etc. It is this same dimension which Woolf contributed to the transformative movements of modernism. Reading with these insights allows us to glimpse more fully the complexities in Woolf's writings, and to explore the historical and political implications of her insights.

Woolf and Contemporary Writers

Antonia García-Rodríquez
Virginia Woolf from a
Latin American Perspective

While there is no one "Latin American" perspective, certain factors do exist which might lead us to believe that there are very basic differences between, for example, an English woman and a Chilean woman. These factors might be elements as diverse as religion, family and the roles of male and female. But as women, there are certain factors that all women share in common. A concentrated study of comparisons and influences between Hispanic women writers and women writers from other cultures doesn't exist, but needs to be conducted. In much of the fiction and non-fiction written by women there are certain recurrent themes and patterns. There is a constant need to rid oneself of obstructions, of internalized patriarchal norms and expectations. An intertextuality exists among sometimes very different writers. This intertextuality at times can be found in dedications, epigraphs, quotations and in autobiographical writings. If we look at these sources, sometimes it is clear that many women writers explain their vocation, their politics and their sense of being a part of some sort of tradition of women writing through the works of other women authors.

In this century, it was Virginia Woolf who lit the fire of one of the most gifted Latin American women: Victoria Ocampo. Ocampo could trace her ancestry back to the original European founding families of Argentina. From infancy, she was surrounded by the advantages of wealth and privilege. Yet, in spite of her aristocratic environment, as she approached adolescence she became increasingly aware of how much she was circumscribed by the conventions of her class. In her lifetime Ocampo met and befriended some of the most important cultural figures of the 20th century, all men: Jose Ortega y Gasset, Borges, Garcia Lorca, Valery, Ravel, Miro, Malraux, Huxley, Gide and Waldo Frank, to name just a few. She later stated that her friendships opened her eyes to fundamental problems of the dialectic between the sexes. She, along with some of the most influential Latin American writers of our century, founded the literary review *Sur*, or *South*, in 1931. The very first issue of *Sur* established a precedent that future issues would continue: a mixture of American and European contributors and a combination of articles about both continents. Woolf's *A Room of One's Own* and *Orlando* were first published in Spanish by the Sur Publishing House, translated by none other than Borges.

It was in 1934 that Ocampo and Woolf met in London at the opening of a Man Ray exhibit. Both of them entered the date in their diaries. Ocampo would visit Woolf many times and always remained in awe of her. They found that they shared many of the same ideas about women and literature. They had grown up in circumstances that were similar, and they had had to overcome many of the same obstacles that had destroyed many women writers before them. Ocampo believed that no one had expressed as well as Woolf the concept of psychic wholeness, as symbolized by the androgynous mind described in *A Room of One's Own* and *Orlando*. Woolf was the first to express this concept from a woman's viewpoint.

After Woolf's death, Ocampo wrote about her in many essays and talked about her on many occasions. In 1954 she wrote "Virginia Woolf in Her Diary," which is a short work in which Ocampo articulates many of the thoughts and feelings that she was unable to share with Woolf. She later stated that in writing it she had an opportunity to understand Woolf's place in her own development.

This, I believe, is the importance of Woolf's influence on Ocampo. For Ocampo, the fact that Woolf wrote, that she existed, was an important role model and influence. It helped Ocampo come to a sort of self-discovery and gave her the impetus to write and the courage to publish her own work. However, we cannot forget that very few women have enjoyed the advantage of participating in writers' groups such as the Bloomsbury circle or have been at the center of highly regarded literary magazines, such as *Sur*. Latin American women writers have written mostly in isolation, with less contact and assurance of an audience than their male counterparts.

Deborah Straw
Tea With Virginia: Woolf as an Early Mentor to May Sarton

At various times in her 50-year career, poet, novelist and keeper of journals May Sarton has acknowledged Virginia Woolf as one of her very important influences. At the very least, the two writers had animated conversations over tea each time Sarton visited London and exchanged letters in the mid to late '30s, the last years of Woolf's life and the formative years for Sarton as a writer.

Although Sarton's opinion of the role of Woolf on her development as a writer seems to change as she ages, the relationship, in my opinion, has left its mark on her thought, work and life. Woolf seems to have been an important role model or informal mentor in three ways—in the way that Woolf exemplified the work of the woman writer; in Woolf's role in relationship to less experienced writers; and in Woolf's literary influence.

And, although the two women write in quite different styles, often about different subject matter, each has a very distinctive voice that can be discerned throughout the entire body of work. This consistency in voice and vision of life may be coincidental, but Woolf certainly provided a clear example of this kind of consistency and excellence for May Sarton.

May Sarton first met Virginia Woolf at a dinner party given by Elizabeth Bowen in 1936. Sarton was 24. Over the next several years, Sarton and Woolf had tea each time the younger writer was in London. Each time they met, they discussed literature and the writing of novels. Apparently, Woolf always plied the younger writer with questions—about herself, her work and her relationships. The two often discussed their writing methods, Sarton listening attentively to any advice she could glean from the famous writer.

They spoke of the role of literary criticism. Sarton gave her first novel, *The Single Hound*, to Woolf when it appeared, although it seems that Woolf never gave her any feedback on it. Woolf and Sarton also discussed the importance of keeping a writer's notebook. Woolf kept notebooks for essay ideas and also extensive journals. Sarton has published five journals to date. At least one idea for a novel, the basis for *The Education of Harriet Hatfield*, first appeared in her journal, *The House by the Sea*.

The ideas which Woolf expressed in *A Room of One's Own* may have had at least an unconscious impact on the younger writer's life and development of writerly habits. Sarton has led her life primarily alone and is probably best known for her portrait of the woman living and working in solitude.

Like Woolf, Sarton has often invited younger writers to tea, but, also like Woolf, she realizes the extreme demands on a recognized author. She offers carefully thought-out advice, but, like Woolf, does not read all unsolicited manuscripts she receives. As did Woolf, Sarton has often felt hounded by these requests from aspiring writers and her readers, but she has continued a tradition of nurturing which she inherited from her mother.

As far as literary influence, Sarton believes Woolf had little effect on her work. Certainly the former's fiction style is more accessible and transparent. Sarton can be read more easily on first sitting than Woolf. But Sarton has admitted that her first novel, *The Single Hound*, has a Woolfian streak (*Paris Review*, 89).

But, in the large theme of their novels, the two women share much. The study of relationships and their quality is at the center of both women's work. Friendship and love are paramount in both. They have created sensitive characters interested in growth and in helping others to grow and change.

Woolf, according to Sarton, "was always in every book exploring new territory" (personal letter, March 4, 1991). And so have Sarton's books followed this pattern, tackling themes which are challenging to both writer and reader—dying of cancer, confronting homophobia, coming to grips with aging, etc.

May Sarton has the kind of power and magic for many readers and aspiring writers that Woolf, I strongly suspect, had. And she too has developed a highly original vision of life, apparent in all the genres of her work.

In the spring of 1991, Sarton told me, "she (VW) did not change my life. But if I had not known her, my life would have been impoverished" (personal conversation, April 20, 1991). Her poem, "Letter from Chicago" (*Land of Silence* 153) testifies to the loss Sarton felt at hearing of the death of Virginia Woolf.

Works Cited

Sarton, May. Conversation with the author. 20 April 1991.
———. *Land of Silence*. New York: Rinehart & Co., Inc., 1953.
———. Letter to the author. 4 March 1991.
Saum, Karen. "The Art of Poetry XXXII." (an interview with May Sarton) *Paris Review*, 25, (1983):81 - 110.

Carol Ascher
Reading to Write: *The Waves* as Muse

"Put your foot on this brick [said Bernard to Susan]. Look over the wall. That is Elvedon. The lady sits between the two long windows, writing. The gardeners sweep the lawn with giant brooms. We are the first to come here. We are the discoverers of an unknown land." (186)

That the lady is writing gives proof of Bernard's childish adventure. Yet the lady who sits between the two windows may well be writing this very novel in which Bernard has crept over the wall to peer at Elvedon. And while, of the six childhood friends, even Bernard will only scribble notes in a notebook, it is this book, *The Waves*, that inevitably inspires me to write.

    I myself had to be reminded one day early this spring that the word inspiration comes from the Latin *in spirare*, to breathe in. That is, inspiration doesn't just spring isolated from one's talented innermost soul. One must first breathe deeply—take something in. Say the image of a woman at a desk between two long windows. Or the rhythm of beautifully chosen words. For many writers and poets, and I can't exclude myself, ambition, competition, imitation, even envy can disguise themselves as inspiration, quickening one's attention and one's creative energy. It was to such poor resemblances to inspiration that Harold Bloom must have been referring when he wrote of the "anxiety of influence." His subject was writers, understood as male, and he was saying that, as deeply important as the work of another man can become, the young writer (also of course male) must also fight it off, as he would fight off his father, in order to proceed with his own destiny. Put bluntly, as tradition passed it on long before Bloom, only women are muses. A man can be influenced—uneasily—by another man, but he certainly can't have a man for his muse.

> "I see the lady writing. I see the gardeners sweeping,
> said Susan. "If we died here, nobody would bury us."
> (186)

How dangerous is Woolf's world where a woman sits writing! I think it's less dangerous now, even a short 60 years later, when scores of Virginia Woolf's literary sisters and daughters have had the luxury of hearing our muses. Still, who is muse to the lady at the window? Who to the women writers here in this room? Can a woman have a man as her muse?

woman = muse for man
man = muse for woman

It's a tempting little bit of symmetry. But Woolf thought it wouldn't work: "we think back through our mothers if we are women," she said. "It is useless to go to the great men writers for help, however much one may go to them for pleasure" (*Room* 79). Why? Because, according to Woolf, if the writer is a woman, "the weight, the pace, the stride of a man's mind are too unlike her own to lift anything substantial" (*Room* 79). "Women alone stir my imagination," she once confessed, which might, partly, have been because of the fit of their phrases. Woolf's daughters in literary criticism have tried to come up with a more sociological answer. The Patriarchy distorts the symmetry in the equation, they've said, meaning that the trouble lies in power and the arrangements of family life. I suspect, however, that, insofar as it's hard for a distinctively male voice to be muse to either woman or man, the reason goes to something deeper, more primitive, that even equality-loving men taking on childcare would only partly shift. Experiencing the muse, as I see it, means simultaneously a heightened alertness to one's own thoughts and a removal of the guard who usually stands so vigilantly at the door to the secret rooms of one's mind. To be inspired by the muse, one has to let go as one did once at the breast, sucking and listening dreamily but attentively to the little stories or songs whispered by one's mother, who was still almost oneself.

Of course, the return to this early, unguarded state has to be somewhat different for men (writers or otherwise) than it is for women. For us women, however disconcerting it may be to discover that one's first love is for another woman, we don't lose our gender identity in the regression. However, while, for men, the eroticism is acceptably, romantically heterosexual, the gender crossing is marked with danger. Here is Robert Graves, our own twentieth century expert on the muse, describing the seductive horror for men of returning to this unguarded state, which, however, must be entered—and conveyed—in a "true poem":

The reason why the hairs stand on end, the eyes water,

> the throat is constricted, the skin crawls and a shiver runs down the spine when one writes or reads a true poem is that a true poem is necessarily an invocation of the White Goddess, or Muse, the Mother of All Living, the ancient power of fright and lust—the female spider or the queen-bee whose embrace is death. (12)

Seeking inspiration, our literary heroes once breathed in the intoxicating fumes from specially-prepared cauldrons, while in later centuries they have sought out the beauty of Mother Nature or a woman, imagined or real—the Virgin Mary, Milton's "heav'nly Muse," or Yeats's Maud.

Meanwhile, as Woolf's story of Judith, Shakespeare's sister, makes so clear, there are good reasons why the muse didn't breathe into the imaginations and pens of women for all those long centuries. Or, more accurately, why our foremothers were unable to act on their moments of inspiration. In addition to their lack of education, income, and "a room of one's own," there was the exhaustion, and often early death, of uncontrolled childbearing, and of course households that had to be maintained without electricity and running water. Besides, our great great grandmothers were themselves acting as muses to their husbands and brothers, even as they poured their frustrated ambitions into their gifted sons.

Luckily, towards the end of the eighteenth century a change came about to which Woolf would give "greater importance than the Crusades or the Wars of the Roses. The middle-class woman began to write" (*Room* 68). Why was this of such great importance? Certainly it was no small thing for the silent half of civilization to begin to add their different stories and peculiarly paced phrases to what we know about the world. While I must claim a special literary father, Henry James, a literary father is not a literary mother. James' gift of magnification—of dilating the moment to catch the nervous twitch of a finger or the tiniest wince between the eyes—is a more distant gift than that subcognitive treasure, sometimes eidetic sometimes rhythmic, that I receive from Woolf. No, a man is never exactly a muse. Though I don't think it's useless to go to the fine male writers for help, and some certainly offer me more than many women writers do, they can't "stir my imagination." There is something closer, more compelling, in a work by a woman for me, if only because behind each white page somewhere a lady sat writing at her desk between two windows.

Mother and Death—this is what Graves thought one had to breathe in as one opened oneself to the muse. In fact, Mother and Death enclose all Woolf's novels, for she saw the two standing like awesome bookends on each side of our years. Yet it is *The Waves*, that rhythmic ode to the ocean, the 24-hour round of the sun, and the much longer arc of a life, which constricts my throat, in gratefulness, not fear—and which, over and over, has made me yearn to pick up my own pen. *The Waves* isn't for surfers. No sentence yields itself without my sinking—down, down, and so, even as I give myself to its rich confessions, I am inspired about the possibilities of writing. Am suddenly alive to the subtle effusions of my own mind. Listen to Jinny:

> "I tremble, I quiver, like the leaf in the hedge, as I sit dangling my feet, on the edge of the bed, with a new day to break open. I have fifty years, I have sixty years to spend. I have not yet broken into my hoard. This is the beginning." (212-13)

And so flow the ecstatic early pages of this marvelous, largely present-tense novel, whose rolling succession of soliloquies reproduces the ceaseless roll of waves.

As the sun lifts itself over the horizon, the childhood chums begin to differentiate themselves, one from another. Fatherless Rhoda thinks of herself as a nobody, who must imitate her friends if she is to avoid feeling like "'the foam that races over the beach or the moonlight that falls arrowlike here on a tin can'" (265). Louis is an outsider, because he is from Brisbane and has an Australian accent. And Neville, who cannnot help yearning for the handsome Percival, wonders if he is "'doomed always to cause repulsion in those I love'" (235).

After Percival's accidental death in India, the sun no longer stands in the middle of the sky, and a new reflectiveness imperceptibly tones down the book's youthful energy. As the waves seem to lengthen, adulthood brings concession and reevaluation to each of the six in different ways. And in Bernard's final, evaluative soliloquy, *The Waves* sinks meditatively at last into past tense.

> "But we were all different. The wax—the virginal wax that coats the spine melted in different patches for each of us.... Louis was disgusted by the nature of human flesh; Rhoda by our cruelty; Susan could not share; Neville wanted order; Jinny love; and so on. We suffered terribly as we became separate bodies." (344)

But let me go back a step to Woolf's own inspiration, for *The Waves* wasn't breathed to her as surges of prose while she obediently held her pen—certainly not at the beginning of this difficult, extraordinarily inventive novel. I think it's important to understand this: that inspiration, intelligence, and stringent discipline are so often entwined. In late December, 1928, at the age of 47, Woolf wrote in her journal,

> Why admit anything to literature that is not poetry—by which I mean saturated? Is that not my grudge against novelists? that they select nothing? The poets succeeding by simplifying: practically everything is left out. I want to put practically everything in; yet to saturate. That is what I want to do in *The Moths* [she was at this point calling *The Waves* that]. It must include nonsense, fact, sordidity: but made transparent. (*A Writer's Diary* 138)

And, while she had rhetorically argued that it was "useless to go to the men writers for help" (*Room* 79), she now directed herself to read Ibsen and Shakespeare and Racine. Influence? Inspiration? I don't know. In any case, she was clearly trying to bolster herself for some great task.

Woolf and Contemporary Writers

And in March, 1929, Woolf spoke more clearly about her method of calling on the Muse. "... I am going to enter a nunnery these next months; and let myself down into my mind" (*WD* 140). And two months later, "Now about this book, *The Moths*. How am I to begin it? And what is it to be? I feel no great impulse; no fever; only a great pressure of difficulty. Why write it then? Why write at all?" (*WD* 141). Why? Because of the "great pressure of difficulty" she felt. Because of some amorphous urgency that demanded to be expressed. And another three months went by, and it was September, and she was still saying, "but it forms very slowly; and what I want is not to write it, but to think it for two or three weeks say—to get into the same current of thought and let that submerge everything" (*WD* 143-44).

And finally, in October, not through "reeling it off; but sticking it down" (*WD* 145), she began. And in December, she was still saying,

> I write two pages of arrant nonsense; compromises; bad shots; possibilities; till my writing book is like a lunatic's dream. Then I trust to some inspiration on re-reading; and pencil them into some sense. Still I am not satisfied. I think there is something lacking. I sacrifice nothing to seemliness. I press to my center. I don't care if it is all scratched out. And there is something there. (*WD* 149)

What is there, after the inspiration of the reread, after the crossout and the edit, and the press to her center, and still more scratching out, is a chorale of speech that isn't speech; the hushed music of waves, all so harmonious yet each unique; an opera of utterances from the silences between what is usually said. This is Louis, in charming defense of his own pedestrian need for order.

"I am half in love with the typewriter and the telephone. With letters and cables and brief but courteous commands on the telephone to Paris, Berlin, New York

> .... I love punctually at ten to come into my room; I love the purple glow of the dark mahogany; I love the table and its sharp edges; and the smooth-running drawers. I love . . . the date on the wall; and the engagement book. Mr. Prentice at four; Mr. Eyres sharp at four-thirty." (291-2)

At the bottom of this speech, which is never as guarded as speech, but always too intense, prosaic, lyrical, revealing, is the desire to be known, at best by another of the six friends, but, since even Bernard, the curious and compassionate storyteller, understands everything, "except [in Neville's words] of what we most feel" (223), then to be known by oneself; to be able to say, as Louis does, "I am this. I am that" (270).

How this novel is about the imagination itself! As flight, as joyful play, as a reach for order, and as relief from pain. In childhood, Bernard molds his bread into pellets and calls them people; later he keeps an alphabetized notebook of his "valuable observations upon the true nature of human life" (221). Rhoda sails white petals in a brown dish basin, keeping her ships at close range, for she never finds the world a good enough place to live in. Even Susan shapes her "natural happiness" with the romance that only language enables:

> "I shall go to bed tired. I shall lie like a field bearing crops in rotation; in the summer heat will dance over me; in the winter I shall be cracked with the cold. But heat and cold will follow each other naturally without my willing or unwilling. My children will carry me on; their teething, their crying, their going to school and coming back will be like the waves of the sea under me" (266).

The Waves is about drawing on life to make art, as Bernard unceasingly hopes to do; on giving weight and meaning to one's personal pain through art, as Neville does with his love of Catullus, or Louis with his "thousand lives" taken from history;

and even about inspiring others to art, as does Susan, who is the novel's only mother, and must, after the lady between the windows, be its second muse. "'She was born to be the adored of poets [says Bernard of Susan], since poets require safety; some one who sits sewing...'" (348). How much more inspiring is the needle than the pen in the hand of a woman, at least to men.

And finally, as the sun disappears behind the horizon, *The Waves* is about imagination's limits, because (in Bernard's words) there is too often distraction, pretence and vanity, because "this difference we make so much of, this identity we so feverishly cherish'" (377) both engenders and hinders art; and because even a night sky, "'clear like the inside of a blue stone,'" yields the understanding that, "'Heaven be praised... we need not whip this prose into poetry. The little language is enough'" (359).

Inexplicable death has by now again diminished the group: this time it was Rhoda, by her own hands. And for the pain of death, "'words are lacking [we are hearing Bernard]. There should be cries, cracks, fissures, whiteness passing over chintz covers, interference with the sense of time, of space'" (359). The life that remains for Bernard is too raw and ragged to domesticate in art. While Elvedon, "'where the lady sat writing'" (343), is still sharp in his memory, a disturbance, Bernard himself can no longer imagine transforming his or anyone else's life into a story:

> "My book, stuffed with phrases, has dropped to the floor. It lies under the table to be swept up by the charwoman when she comes wearily at dawn looking for scraps of paper, old tram tickets, and here and there a note screwed into a ball and left with the litter to be swept up. What is the phrase for the moon? And the phrase for love? By what name are we to call death? I do not know" (381)

Yet the loss of egotism and control which age brings, and even the conviction that life is too much for art, draws me in more deeply, and makes *The Waves* an even more powerful muse. For it is through Bernard's understanding that I too glimpse a different vision of true art. How, like fine friendship, art can depend on anonymity, as much as on a sturdy ego; on the ability to merge as much as to be separate; on the willingness to overcome "'this identity we so feverishly cherish'" (377) as the urge to be the subject of biography.

Whatever Woolf's private arrogance, jealousies, competitiveness and hoardings, *The Waves* offers me a meditation that is generous, wise, and maternal. "Masterpieces are not single and solitary births" (*Room* 68), she had said a few years earlier, meaning that we are all part of a creative flow, each point dependent on all others. Yet because we *are* all separate points, I know each work of art affects everyone differently. Some readers, men and women, will find *The Waves* abstract, precious, obtuse, narrow in its social scope. But to me, the music, lyrical beauty and deep intelligence of the novel makes it transcend all such limitations. In insisting on an active reader, *The Waves* asks me to drink more deeply of its waters, and so nourishes me for my own art. Because Woolf has mined treasure from usually well-guarded layers, I find courage to explore the very different agitations of my own hidden mind. As if cast ashore by one long pull of the moon on the sea, *The Waves* assures me that there will always be lives, from whose idiosyncratic pain and quiet patience can spring new imaginative flights and new art, including mine.

References:

Robert Graves. *The White Goddess.* 1948.
Virginia Woolf. *A Room of One's Own.* New York: Harcourt, Brace & World, Harbinger Books. 1929.
Virginia Woolf. *The Waves.* New York: Harcourt, Brace & World, Harvester Books. 1931.
Virginia Woolf. *A Writer's Diary.* London: Triad/Panther Books. 1978

Jane Lazarre
Structures of Common Experience:
Learning from Virginia Woolf

In the fall of 1985, I was teaching women's literature courses at both City College and Yale University. The students at City College were mostly African-American and Latina women returning to study after having raised children to school age. The students at Yale were . . . students at Yale—in that semester almost all white, children of relative or extreme privilege. Yet, in both these classes, at two colleges with extremely diverse populations, the highpoint of the course, a kind of epiphany of all the themes discussed during the semester, was the reading of *To The Lighthouse*.

With both groups it was necessary, at first, to read Woolf's language together, to become acquainted with the structures of her prose, the backs and forths and ins and outs of time and point of view. Both groups of students picked up the skill quickly—just about the moment they saw how Mrs. Ramsay walked to town with Charles Tansley while still remaining in the window with James. From then on, it was smooth sailing, as it were. We rode in and out of the mother's consciousness, the father's linear intellectuality, the adoptive daughter/artist, Lily—and discussed the themes which seemed to all of us to be intensely personal to our lives—a universality within which we could recognize ourselves. I don't mean by this now much debated and deconstructed word—universality—a falsely homogenized vision of dominating voices masking authentic and important difference, but rather a perception of felt, shared experience beneath equally authentic and profound diversity.

As far as diversity goes, in fact, I too came from a very different background than Woolf's. I am first generation, Russian Jewish, a child of the working class, radical left. Yet, like the students at Yale and City College, I read Virginia Woolf and feel I am reading about my own mind. As a writer of fiction, this deep spiritual and intellectual identification is invaluable to me, because I read fiction primarily to try to understand life—which most often feels dumbfounding, confusing, paradoxical, even despairing. I write and read fiction, I think, not only as a sometimes desperate hope of faith in connection between myself and the world, but as a search for faith in that connection: those commonalities between us, and between ourselves and the world, which are the source, I believe, of a sense of meaning.

As a young artist, I took faith and meaning from Woolf's writings about writing and consciousness. In her autobiographical essay, "A Sketch Of The Past," she tells the story of writing *To The Lighthouse*—how, in her forties, after a lifetime of being haunted by her mother, who died when Virginia was 13, she finally wrote the novel that would free her from this haunting. My mother too had died when I was a child, and that semester, when I took the train back and forth from the broken down rooms of City College to the elegant towers of Yale, I was nearing 40 and trying to begin my fourth book which was to be, one more time, about the impact of this loss on my life. By that time, I had read and taught *To The Lighthouse* many times, and had been really transformed in my own consciousness by the unlayering of a woman's mind while in the act of creation. Almost like a religious novice invited to the naming of mysteries, I witnessed Lily Briscoe thinking about her painting, planning her painting, stopped from painting. I marvelled at the depth and accuracy of Woolf's description of a woman steering the vessel of her consciousness through the stormy chaos of desire for union with the quintessential mother figure, Mrs. Ramsay; through fear and insecurity of a particular kind all women artists still know: "women can't write, women can't paint;" through the intrusions of Mr. Ramsay's demands and needs, but also of Lily's identifications with him, her "wanting him too." Like an orphan looking at a suddenly discovered photograph of a long lost relative, I followed the thread of Lily's fear that she would not be equal to the task of continuing her work, knowing that it would be "rolled up and stuffed under a sofa." But I also recognized her ecstasy, that moment of incomparable and indescribable wholeness, that passing but transforming moment of faith when we have had our own vision. All this framed, for me, what has come to seem, as I near 50, the heroic story of a woman trying over a lifetime to make art, a quest which, for me, involves bringing the most precise possible language through the chaos of emotion and idea to a moment of clarity; of meaning.

This part of my identity as a woman writer, laboring at the

craft—which is another way of saying discipline—was also greatly influenced by Woolf, and again, by Lily Briscoe. At the famous dinner scene, Mrs. Ramsay is silently pressuring Lily to take her place in the conventionally domestic, gendered scheme of things. Lily moves toward accommodation, back into resistance, flounders in the chaos and anxiety in between. And all the while, she is moving that salt cellar around. Placing it here, then there, she enables herself to think about her painting: its structure, its balance, the part of making art that is about form, and skill, and control. These capacities, so necessary to the attainment of the spiritual epiphanies of her vision, keep her steady at the dinner table too. In other words, she keeps a sense of self, the boundaries represented by her capacity to work, that combination of dedication and real knowledge we call "discipline."

Reading this scene over and over as I taught it for many years, I learned something crucial about the function of writing in my life; that apart from the quality of my work, the pursuit of its craft and discipline—from the discovery of a more precise word to the shape of a whole novel—this pursuit literally keeps me sane. And it is, I think, this notion of discipline and work that seems to possess a universal meaning for readers and students of all sorts. Like those students at Yale and City College, my current students at the Eugene Lang College identify with this statement of faith: that we are pushed and pulled by all manner of stormy feeling, desire, thought—some creative, some profoundly threatening to survival—but that discipline, agency, dedication to craft in many activities, many sorts of work, can keep us afloat. I have found that this awareness is especially important for many women students, as it has been very important for me.

During the fall of 1985, on the train between Grand Central Terminal and New Haven every Wednesday, when I began the novel which in a way was the least autobiographical work I'd ever begun, characters and situations came to me I'd never known in their particularity. Yet, my motivation was as intensely autobiographical as ever: to write a story of how it felt to me to have wanted to be an artist since early childhood. I took from Woolf the translation of the writer into a painter—a choice which was deepened and enriched by the fact that like Woolf's sister, Vanessa, my sister, Emily Lazarre, is a painter, and by the fact that I had been a painter before becoming a writer. This story, which became my novel *The Powers of Charlotte*, included many other stories about mothers, fathers, sex, marriage, motherhood, because for me being a writer always grows out of and along with, rather than standing separate from, all the stories of my life. Like Woolf's experience in writing *To The Lighthouse*, I feel I penetrated my own loss of a mother deeply enough in this novel to have stopped a certain haunting. But in the work of the novel, I was trying to use the important lessons I'd learned from Woolf about pattern and form. I used a three part structure, the middle piece a story of the destruction of a house, in a way, but also one of pregnancy and birth. I took as my risky theme a woman artist's consciousness as she tries to encompass the thrilling dangers of experience, mystery, defiance of convention, but also the everyday realities, even the apparent dullness at times, of the making and remaking of art, the making and remaking of family. Toward the end, in a personal tribute to Virginia, I placed several central women characters in a bay, now shallow and eminently navigable, in sight of an old, snail-encrusted lighthouse.

When I think back on my involvement with Virginia Woolf, and bring all these years of reading up to the present (I taught *Lighthouse* as recently as this past semester, and teach sections of "A Sketch Of The Past" every year when I try to convey to college freshmen the idea of pattern and structure in writing, how "making a scene come right" can give one the "rapture" of perceiving pattern: "a sense of what belongs to what"), I see that all along I have been learning about the condition for making art, an education in consciousness that literally began for me in my early twenties when I first read *A Room Of One's Own*. Once, when I had small children, this education involved learning how to give to them meaningfully and consistently without—to paraphrase—giving until I died. I had to be Mrs. Ramsay, in a way, and be Lily too. Now, with my children grown up, the idea of conditions includes (in addition, of course, to the struggle of navigating between making a living and writing fiction) reconstructing every day the confidence and energy to continue writing despite the knowledge that everything may end rolled up under the sofa; to keep taking my work seriously despite the failures and discouragements so endemic to the life of an artist, especially in this time of publishing on an industrial scale which, combined with the new marketplace of MFA programs, threatens a literary homogenization, a kind of "censorship" as Carol Ascher has called it, that has been previously unknown. Yet, to give language to the deepest, most particular stories of our lives, and to work hard to develop out of whatever talent we possess the capacity to tell our stories clearly, honestly and even beautifully—this does seem to be a fundamental human need that connects us. We do take life from each other's work and stories and become something more than we were before. I am different, for example, for reading and in a way becoming Sethe, in Toni Morrison's *Beloved*. Sethe is a woman in fiction who has affected me more deeply that anyone since Lily. In these women I have experienced that enhancing, imaginative ambiguity of self-discovery and self-creation. Obviously, I did not live Sethe's life—the life of an African-American escaped slave—any more than I lived Lily's. But my life has been structured, in a way, by the same themes as Toni Morrison uses to structure her novel about Sethe and her murdered daughter, Beloved. The stories of my life have been structured, shaped, given meaning by the themes of memory, its dangers and salvations; of the intricate interior reflections of the human need for liberty; of the endlessly overlapping identities of motherhood and daughterhood. Clearly, we cannot ever completely understand the talent, or the genius, that enables writers like Morrison and Woolf to create works which are both rooted in and defy the boundaries of cultural and historical particularity. But we can analyze the structures of their work and, in so doing, come to appreciate the learned, disciplined capacity that enables me, or any other reader—not only to see myself in Lily and Sethe—but, in reading and rereading their lives, to in some sense become them.

"Is it meaningful," another Wolf asks—this one the German writer Christa Wolf—"beyond the need for personal confession, for one individual to come face to face with herself in language?" Answering that question, for me, requires finding the ever-renewed courage to explore my particular story. The depth of this exploration will always depend on the steady development of my craft. But the courage cannot exist without a deepening faith that there is some common reflection of us all that is as real as our differences. That faith is gleaned, for me, in part, from all the students, including myself, who have found our lives described in the work of Virginia Woolf.

Elegies: Death and Mourning

Christopher Ames
      Death and Woolf's Festive Vision

"Oh! thought Clarissa, in the middle of my party, here's death." This suggestive juxtaposition in *Mrs. Dalloway* initiates Clarissa's meditation upon the presence of death at her "offering" to life, the passage that forms the climax to a novel which can be read as an extended meditation on mortality. Clarissa Dalloway moves in her thoughts from viewing the news of Septimus Warren-Smith's death as an outrageous intrusion to affirming its rightful place in the festive setting. Through Clarissa, Woolf explores the ritual encounter with mortality in a modern and secular context where the ancient carnival triumph over death is reenacted at an upper-class private party. Her exploration of the "party consciousness" in *Mrs. Dalloway* begins a career-long engagement with issues of contemporary celebration: how do individuals, so essentially separate, find the spirit to celebrate life together? Woolf sees any authentic affirmation of life as necessarily grounded in an imaginative encounter with the inevitability of death.

But the party or festivity is not the only cultural structure for affirming life in the presence of death: Woolf demonstrates that her fiction is engaged in precisely that festive enterprise. This conception of literary purpose is reflected in the artist figures in Woolf's fiction and their struggles with artistic expression in the face of mortality: Bernard hyperbolically battling a personified and capitalized Death in *The Waves*; Lily Briscoe viewing the completion of her painting and her vision in terms of Mrs. Ramsay's death; Miss La Trobe in *Between the Acts* interpreting the lapses in her pageant as "death, death, death." Clarissa Dalloway is explicitly not an artist, but bringing people together is her creative gift: like Woolf as novelist, Clarissa facilitates a commingling of many voices under one roof and resists imposing her personal authority too strongly on the other selves of her party.

Mrs. Dalloway, then, provides a crucial perspective on Woolf's fiction and on her ideas about death and celebration. The novel imagines individual extinction against the continuation of communal life and consciousness, a mystical sense that can best be understood in terms of the carnivalized consciousness Bakhtin discusses as intimately bound up with developments in the novel genre. The carnival spirit, which Woolf links with the party through her descriptions of Clarissa's offering as a ritual, celebrates "the very process of replaceability, and not the precise item that is replaced" (Bakhtin 125). Bakhtin's description of carnival as "the festival of all-annihilating and all-renewing time" (124) concentrates the engagement of festivity with mortality in a way that resonates with Woolf's treatment of death in *Mrs. Dalloway* and later works. For Clarissa Dalloway as creator of the party and Virginia Woolf as creator of fictions, the celebration of life is a daring act taken against the forces of inevitable extinction.

Works Cited

Bakhtin, Mikhail. *Problems of Dostoevsky's Poetics*, ed. and trans. Caryl Emerson. Minneapolis: U of Minnesota P, 1984.
Woolf, Virginia. *Mrs. Dalloway*. New York: Harcourt Brace, 1925.

Louise Poresky
Eternal Renewal: Life and Death in Virginia Woolf's *The Waves*

Virginia Woolf constructs *The Waves* on certain basic inversions. For instance, she calls the novel a "play-poem" but it is written in prose, and there is no dialogue, just soliloquies. The characters do not act; they reflect, and in the pure present tense of meditation. Besides these structural inversions, the central thematic one, upon which any understanding of the novel depends, is that between life and death.[1] The novel follows its six characters from nursery school to old age. As they move through college or into their business and family lives, we think we are witnessing their maturing into life. But, as I will show, they are actually dying, emotionally and spiritually.

A seventh character, Percival, physically dies in the middle of the novel. The other characters, as adults, repeatedly recall him and compare their lives to his. In the process they progressively see that what they have been calling life—identities and possessions—has been depriving them of life. The irony is that Percival, who saw no limits to his life, loses his life; and the other characters, who take him as a model and a projection of a life they were too frightened to live, mourn when he dies over what they lost or never had. The waves, heard throughout the novel, remind us, however, that death carries with it a promise of renewal. The waves form and rise into existence, then break and dissolve. But they also return to the sea, their source, where they reform into new waves. They thus participate in a life and death cycle that promises a return to the beginnings, and an eternal renewal.[2]

Bernard opens the first set of soliloquies by describing eternity. He sees it in a ring that "quivers and hangs in a loop of light" (9). His words recall the opening lines of Henry Vaughan's poem "The World": "I saw eternity the other night/ Like a great ring of pure and endless light." Other characters also hear and see things that participate in eternity: colors meeting, birds singing, a globe hanging. Now life seems to endure. Experience, sensation, and imagination have no limits. By the time of Percival's farewell dinner, the characters have transferred their

Elegies: Death and Mourning

childhood belief in endurance onto Percival. Then, with his death, they see their own lives as incomplete and flimsily built on delusion.

Woolf links the beginning of the characters' lives to the beginning of humanity through her biblical allusions. For instance, Bernard escorts Susan to the imaginary world of Elvedon, a ringed wood with a wall around it, like Eden. There the two children see a lady sitting between two long windows, writing; in the beginning was the word, this vision tells us, and the word was with woman. Meanwhile, Elvedon is cleaned and protected by the gardeners, who, like the guardians of Eden, scare away intruders. But into this new and magical world comes the threat of death: a gardener spots Bernard and Susan, and the world instantly becomes hostile. Bernard tells Susan to follow him "without looking back" (18), as if they were Lot and his wife fleeing Sodom, their once fertile estate. A haven becomes hostile, Eden becomes Sodom, and humankind is driven by fear into an alien and mortal world.

The Eden story connects Elvedon to Neville's early and recurring vision of "death among the apple trees" (24). The tree of knowledge that leads to the fall from grace and the imposition of mortality, dooms humankind to moments that do not endure, to fragile connections between people that often break, and to psyches that fragment.

The children separate: the boys go to one school, the girls to another. And then Bernard and Neville attend college, while Louis goes into business; Jinny and Rhoda enter the London social life, and Susan returns to the country. As the children separate from each other, they also begin psychically to fragment within themselves. They deny certain parts of life and cling to others for a spurious sense of wholeness. For instance, Bernard makes phrases and thus appears to have a grasp on his experience; yet he is afraid of life, and in fact uses phrasemaking and notetaking to maintain a distance between himself and others. Susan tells herself she is fully content with her life as a mother; yet the purposelessness of her life creeps into her consciousness at night, when the children are asleep. Jinny communicates with others through her body, and is motivated by her passions; yet she is afraid to look at her reflection in the short mirror for in it she sees only a part of herself. Rhoda, unable to look at herself in any mirror, fears she has no face and does not exist in the real world; so she often psychically splits off to a distant world of marble columns and pools. Louis, who feels connected to life only when he meditatively sinks into the earth's center, and sees order in life only when he conducts business, goes on hearing the chained beast stamping on the shore (67), for he knows that to live in the past or to acquiesce to the present is to die. And Neville yearns for intimacy, first with Percival, then with anyone who would come to him; yet he finds his identity not in the fulfillment of that intimacy, but in its denial.

The dissociation the characters feel from each other and within themselves leads them to ask "Who am I?" and "What am I?" Meanwhile, true identity appears in the figure of Percival. He is the only character who simply says, "I am," for he is the only one who chooses life over death. The legendary Percival was brought up in the forests of North Wales in total ignorance of chivalry, committing one gaucherie after another. He does receive instruction in the use of arms and manners, and he does get to the Grail castle, but he fails to ask the mysterious question: "Whom does one serve with the Grail?" Woolf's Percival also grows up in ignorance of refined and intellectual things, and though he reaches India in his heroic purpose to bring the west to the east and thus round out the vast world, soon after his arrival his horse stumbles; Percival falls and dies senselessly. Besides the legendary connections, Woolf's character suggests Christ in that both hold a last supper with their disciples; and as the characters in *The Waves* unite in love of Percival, so Christ's disciples take their first communion with him. Woolf builds her Percival out of symbolism, ritual, and tradition drawn from pagan fertility cults, Christian sacraments, and Medieval sentiments. She thus portrays the "I am" in a character whose associations transcend culture, century, and religion.

At Percival's farewell dinner, Bernard explains that they have come together out of love for Percival and through that love they can believe in their own endurance. He says, "We have proved, sitting eating, sitting talking, that . . . We are not slaves bound to suffer incessantly unrecorded petty blows on our bent backs. . . . We . . . stride not into chaos, but into a world that our own force can subjugate and make part of the illumined and everlasting road" (146). The characters then disperse, and,

Elegies: Death and Mourning

despite Bernard's speech, a wide margin of indifference spreads. Percival dies at the very center of the novel. Just as in *Mrs. Dalloway*, Clarissa is outraged at the Bradshaws—what business had they, Clarissa wanted to know, to talk of death in the midst of her party (280)—so Percival's death intrudes on life. But just as Septimus in *Mrs. Dalloway* preserved life through his suicide, so Percival's death preserves the idea of life and defies the human fear of death. And just as with Septimus's death, closeness drew apart, rapture faded, and one was alone, so with Percival's, the unity the characters experience at the dinner disappears, their rapturous connection with Percival fades, and each is left alone to either confront or avoid grief.

The chief mourners in *The Waves* are Neville, Bernard, and Rhoda. With Percival's death, Neville feels unknown, disconnected from any identity, unable to pass the immitigable tree. Beneath that tree, Neville feels the pain of death and for the moment welcomes it. At the time of Percival's death, Bernard's son is born and Bernard cannot distinguish joy from sorrow. He goes to the National Gallery to escape the rush of life and there confronts his own death: "Behold then, the blue madonna streaked with tears. This is my funeral service. We have no ceremonies, only private dirges and no conclusions, only violent sensations, each separate" (157). And with Percival's death, Rhoda feels alone in a hostile world. She goes to the river with a bunch of violets in hand and ceremoniously joins Percival in his death with the words, "Now I will relinquish; now I will let loose.... We will gallop together... where the swallow dips her wings in dark pools and the pillars stand entire."

Louis, Susan, and Jinny, unlike the mourners, try to avoid grief. Louis immerses himself in business activities; Susan croons to her infant to ward off the dangers of life; and Jinny follows her body's imagination.

Though some characters mourn, and others deny their grief, all six, in reaction to Percival's death, voice their doubts about how alive they have been. In the process they catalog their losses. At the end of a day's work Bernard asks himself, "What is lost? What is over?" He answers his own question: friends, some by death, and delusions about his own artistic and intellectual strengths. He acknowledges that he will never see savages in Tahiti spear fish or a lion spring in the jungle. But he goes as far as he can—to Rome—where, because he lets go of possessions—wife, children, house, dog—"Tahiti becomes possible" (189). He pleads with one moment to wait and then, as he leans over the parapet and peers out into the waste of water, he sees a fin turn. In this bare visual impression, Bernard receives a sign that life contains the unexpected, visions and miracles do occur, and a powerful, mystical life exists beneath the waste of water we call life.

Susan also examines her possessions—her family and garden—and begins to see that though she acquired them for security, familiarity, and protection, they have actually taken her life away. She sums up by saying, "I have had peaceful, productive years. I possess all I see" (190). Yet she feels fenced in, planted down and "sick of natural happiness" (191). As a child she went to Elvedon, a magical land of beauty and terror. Now she holds her scissors and snips off hollyhocks. She has lost her imagination, her passion, her courage to explore and meet the unexpected.

Louis, at the end of his day, leaves the office and retires to his attic where he reads "O western wind," a medieval lyric, by the identity-less poet, Anonymous. As the poem's speaker yearns for his love to be in his arms, and he to be in his bed again, so Louis yearns for "continuity and permanence" (203), lost long ago, and he is willing to die to regain them. Rhoda's soliloquy, the last in this sequence, is an apostrophe to life. It begins with "Life, how I have dreaded you" (203) and continues with what life has exacted: "What dissolution of the soul you demanded in order to get through one day, what lies, bowings, scrapings" ? (204).

The characters meet for the last time when they come together for a dinner at Hampton Court. Illusions collapse as the characters compare their pasts to their present lives. Neville asks himself and the others, "What have you made of life" (211)? He recalls when "all simmered and shook" and he and the others "could have been anything" (214). But now, they are bound within the limits set by their self-imposed identities.

In the last chapter, Bernard takes on the identities of all the characters, uniting them once again through his imagination, and sums up their lives. He tells their story to a stranger, and like the Ancient Mariner, tells it to do penance. The Ancient Mariner repents for killing the albatross; Bernard, for the death of authenticity and, with it, the loss of the "I am."

The biblical opening of his story—"In the beginning, there was the nursery" (239)—connects his story to that of the world. He then describes the characters' emerging consciousness and how they were then reduced and numbed by life. Meanwhile, Percival remained whole and removed from life, though loved, worshipped, and envied by the others. He had a magnificent equanimity, Bernard says, that preserved him from meanness and humiliation. Bernard describes how age made the fiery and furtive life of childhood into order, method, and no more than entries in an engagement calendar. As an adult, Bernard found himself thankful that he "need not whip this prose into poetry" (263).

Bernard leans over a gate and looks out, but this time "No fin breaks the waste of this immeasurable sea" (284). No sign of eternity, no remnant of human origins, no indication that the power of exaltation exists. He is left as a "man without a self... A dead man" (285). He walks shadowless and makes no impress upon the earth (287). Unladen by an identity, however, he becomes "immeasurably receptive" (291) and, like Lear, takes upon him "the mystery of things" and goes "like a spy without leaving this place" (291).

Bernard now can go beyond Rome, and on to "the remote verges of the desert lands where the savage sits by the campfire" (291). There, he becomes aware of a new desire, something rising beneath him like a proud horse. The enemy advances. It is Death against whom he rides with his spear couched and his hair flying back, like Percival. He strikes spurs into his horse and cries out, "Against you I will fling myself, unvanquished and unyielding, O Death!" (297). In this imagined ride against Death we are reminded of Don Quixote, for Bernard's act, the last of the novel, is illusory though heroic.

As Woolf records in her diary in September 1926, "it is not ourself but something in the universe that one's left with." So the novel ends with the words— *"The waves broke on the shore"* (297). Individual identities break and dissolve on the sand. But just as the fallen waves gather themselves on the sand and return to the sea, so do identities return to eternity. The sea, the origin of humankind, sweeps up the broken waves and receives them again into its vastness.

Notes

[1] James M. Haule lists over 40 entries for "death" or "deaths" in his *A Concordance to The Waves by Virginia Woolf*.

[2] Most critics agree that Percival symbolizes a heroic ideal for the other characters and that his death confronts them with the emptiness of their actual lives. As just one example, Lucio Ruotolo says that Percival's "death occasions a sense of solitude and emptiness" (158). However, these same critics see no renewal in the novel's ending, but rather a dissolution and collapse into nothingness. Even Maria DiBattista, who otherwise detects the mystical dimension of Woolf's novel, recognizes no victory over death, mutability, and silence, but a "comic enlargement of reality" that dismisses the life it creates (189).

Works Cited

DiBattista, Maria. *Virginia Woolf's Major Novels: The Fables of Anon*. New Haven: Yale University Press, 1980.

Haule, James M. *A Concordance to The Waves by Virginia Woolf*. Oxford: Oxford Microform Publications, 1981.

Malory, Sir Thomas. *Le Morte d'Arthur*. Ed. Keith Baines. New York: New American Library, 1962.

Ruotolo, Lucio P. *The Interrupted Moment: A View of Virginia Woolf's Novels*. Stanford: Stanford University Press, 1986.

Woolf, Virginia. *A Writer's Diary: Being Extracts from the Diary of Virginia Woolf*. Ed. Leonard Woolf. New York: Harcourt Brace Jovanovich, 1953.

———. *Mrs. Dalloway*. New York: Harcourt Brace & World, 1925.

———. *The Waves*. New York: Harcourt Brace Jovanovich, 1931.

A Video Project

Leslie K. Hankins
Virginia Woolf, Literary Tourism
and Cultural Site-Seeing

Writers' Sites and Critics' Labyrinths

It is proof of the snobbishness which, no doubt, veins us through that the mere thought of a literary pilgrim makes us imagine a man in an ulster looking up earnestly at a house front decorated with a tablet, and bidding his anaemic and docile brain conjure up the figure of Dr Johnson. But we must confess that we have done the same thing dozens of times, rather stealthily perhaps, and choosing a darkish day lest the ghosts of the dead should discover us, yet getting some true pleasure and profit nevertheless. We cannot get past a great writer's house without pausing to give an extra look into it and furnishing it as far as we are able with his cat and his dog, his books and his writing table. We may justify the instinct by the fact that the dominion which writers have over us is immensely personal; it is their actual voice that we hear in the rise and fall of the sentence; their shape and colour that we see in the page, so that even their old shoes have a way of being worn on this side rather than on that, which seems *not gossip but revelation.* (Woolf, a review of *A Literary Pilgrim in England* ... by Edward Thomas 161; my emphasis)

Writers' sites are immensely intriguing to other writers, scholars, and readers. The culture industry seizes the initiative, marketing tours of various writers' homes and landscapes; historical preservation societies embalm the remains of writers' homes and rooms and literary tourists troop through, sign the guest books and marvel at the orts and fragments of the writers' lives displayed as artifacts. The entrepreneurs of literary history are obviously on to something. But we might probe the complex desires behind our attraction to writers' sites and the ideological forces behind the culture industry's attempts to meet that desire. What are the sites of literary history and how they are marketed? What is left out of the embalmed sites, or what is left in? How does the embalming process fetishize the writer? What aspects of the writer are preserved, and what are eliminated? Whose interests are served by these sites? What about the writers' sites might be significant to our understanding of their work or their role in cultural history? What does this whole process tell us about literary studies? art and culture? the culture industry as a whole?

Newly back from my travels to Talland House, Asheham House, and Monk's House, recording my responses, I noted residual guilt feelings from touring Woolf's sites. Though there is a voyeuristic element in such projects as if we were attempting to insinuate ourselves unseen into the living space of another, that libidinous aspect did not wholly explain my feelings of discomfort. Part of the awkwardness came from the feeling that the overall project was illegitimate, that the fascination with writers' sites was misguided, that it was tracking the personal, which was inherently wrong. This sense that the personal was forbidden, suspect or extraneous to art and scholarship, is deeply embedded in the aesthetics of modernism and postmodernism (for different reasons perhaps) and in the academic institutions.

A Video Project

When that desire for the personal is forbidden, it comes out, like most repressed desires, in exaggerated form; the literary tour guides cater to that exaggerated desire. This bit of analysis helped to explain a little vignette from the tour of Monk's House. In an effort, I suppose, to give the site that lived-in look, an ashtray full of half smoked cigarette butts of the kind of shag tobacco Woolf smoked were placed on the table in the sitting room of Monk's House. It was an interesting touch, but on reflection, such fetishizing of personal details seemed to exemplify what is suspect in the whole scholar-pilgrim enterprise. The relationship between the personal and the cultural in such sites seems radically askew.

How can we re-place the personal in perspective, so that we neither make a fetish of the personal life of a writer nor deny it? Contemporary theories which attempt to place the personal in cultural and historical contexts offer possibilities; feminism, arguing that "the personal is political" looks in personal experiences for the common ground from which to launch a social critique. Materialist critics or critics of the everyday look at personal artifacts as cultural artifacts and construct analyses accordingly. Woolf placed the individual life in that sort of cultural milieu:

> Consider what immense forces society brings to play upon each of us, how that society changes from decade to decade; and also from class to class; well, if we cannot analyse these invisible presences, we know very little of the subject of the memoir; and again how futile life-writing becomes. I see myself as a fish in a stream; deflected; held in place; but cannot describe the stream. ("A Sketch of the Past" 80)

Well-preserved writers' sites seem to ignore the stream and give us the fishbowl without the fish (to continue Woolf's figure). Yet, our fascination remains. . . .

Efforts to analyze the desire to visit writers' sites do not quell it, however. By problematizing the desire we may bring sharper minds to the tour and look for, not only what is offered, but what is withheld. In my project to analyze the sites of Virginia Woolf, I embarked upon different stages of literary tourism. I went on the packaged tours, visiting Monk's House on one of the open Wednesdays, and I toured Charleston Farmhouse with the many others filing through the rooms. That provided one version of literary pilgrimage. But I also had the opportunity to tour behind the scenes; as a scholar (rather than simply one of the literary commoners), I received permission to videotape Monk's House (under the supervision of a gentleman from the National Trust) and to videotape Charleston House before the hours for regular tourists. Being backstage before the tours opened gave me the sense that such sites are selected and staged presentations as fully as any play about the figures. Perhaps most rewarding were the solitary treks I took myself, simply launching out in blind hikes across the South Downs pursued by ominous clouds—hiking for hours across the Downs in search of Asheham, for instance. Though Quentin Bell thought my hiking somewhat foolish, noting that one could reach Asheham by driving on a main road these days, to me that sense of descending upon Asheham from the Downs, as Woolf first found it, felt more "authentic"[1] than any of the carefully reconstructed site-experiences marketed about. Asheham House and Talland House, both probably ruined from the point of view of historical preservation, seemed to me to still contain traces of life in curious ways. The yard of Asheham is now a chemical waste dump, top-secret and off limits (how sublime) and Talland House has been broken up into tourist flats. The central staircase is gone and there have been various renovations and additions; the orchard Woolf described so lovingly has been paved and turned into a pay parking lot for tourists going down to sun at Porthminster Beach. But the balconies still offer that compelling view and the air is still gummy and dense with sounds of pumps, waves, gulls, rooks and voices.

When I slept in Talland House, looking across the bay through the ornate balconies of either the nursery or Woolf's parents' bedroom, I stayed up late rereading *To the Lighthouse* and Woolf's autobiographical writings. Watching the lighthouse beam (not so impressive now that it is an electric bleep rather than the searching sweeping light of yesteryear), I felt intimidated by ghostly presences before waking to videotape dawn at

A Video Project

Porthminster Beach. There was a backdrop of guilty indulgence in my time at Talland House.[2] I strolled the lawn (Lily's lawn) reciting phrases from *To the Lighthouse*, I confess. I felt rapture, ecstasy. And I was worried. "How," I asked again and again, "how can I market this for academia? How can I disguise this delight? How can I legitimize this quest and fulfillment?" A first hurdle of the scholarly rationalizing had been met by the application for the initial grant: the Pre-Dissertation Feasibility Fellowship which came up with the money to send me to England. Other hurdles awaited: the prospectus meeting, the dissertation defense, more grant-writing, and conference presentations. Interestingly enough, I witness in the audiences to whom I show my videotape of Talland House the same approach-avoidance that characterized my own—moved and intrigued, but hesitant and a bit shamefaced. We all feel more comfortable when I place the literary pilgrimage within the legitimizing frame of cultural critique.

But we did not invent these mixed feelings about the genre of literary tourism or literary pilgrimages. Once again, when we reach that lookout we find that Woolf was there before us. By writing about, and analyzing, my responses to the whole scholar tourist or scholar pilgrim enterprise on which I embarked, I am following in the footsteps of Woolf—not only tracking her actual footsteps by trekking over the Downs—but also partaking of one intellectual pilgrimage that may be traced in her writing. For she too probed her mixed feelings about her interest in writers' sites, and she wrote out her fascination, repudiation, apology, dismissal, and fulfillment of those desires in humor and in argument in her essays and reviews.

Virginia Woolf from "Literary Pilgrim" to Cultural Historian

Woolf was intrigued by writers' sites, though she found literary pilgrimages somewhat suspect and on occasion adopted an apologetic tone. Contemporary critics follow Woolf in this perhaps voyeuristic desire, as the caravans to Charleston Farmhouse and Monk's House and guided tours through Woolf's Bloomsbury indicate. We also seem to follow her in our apologetic demeanor. What is the lure of writers' sites? Do we seek "gossip" or "revelation"? And what is the source of our awkwardness or guilt about our interest in writers' sites? Similar questions fascinated Woolf; following the dialectical play of her mind as it pondered such questions throughout her career may lead us to a more profound perspective on writers' sites. Woolf's earliest published essays introduced the topic of *literary geography*, or the scholarly interest in the homes and landscapes of great writers. She was not always kind to the genre. In one of her first published pieces, "Haworth, November, 1904" in *The Guardian*, 21 December 1904, she theorized about the precarious scholar-pilgrim enterprise itself: "I do not know whether pilgrimages to the shrines of famous men ought not to be condemned as sentimental journeys" (5). With that rhetorically complex double negative, Woolf emphasized her vacillation between fascination with such pilgrimages and caution that such jaunts fetishize the writer and slight the works. Woolf frequently struck a cautionary note about such projects;[3] she acknowledged her mixed feelings in mock confession in the 1917 review cited as the epigraph to this essay.

Throughout her career Woolf wavered between condemnation of and eager participation in such critical ventures.

In "Literary Geography" (1905), her first publication for the *Times Literary Supplement*, a review of two such books, Woolf was particularly harsh in her judgment of the author of a book on Dickens: "Of all books therefore the books that try to impress upon the mind the fact that great men were once alive because they lived in this house or in that are those that seem to have least reason for their being, for Thackeray and Dickens, having done with earthly houses, live most certainly in our brains" (35). Woolf scornfully dismissed the work as trivial and misguided:

> He knows not only every house where Dickens lived, but every lodging that he took for a month or two in the summer; he tells us how Dickens seemed to prefer 'houses having semi-circular frontages' and describes the inns where Dickens lodged and the mugs from which he is said to have drunk and the 'stiff wooden chair' in which he sat. A pilgrimage, if one followed this guide, would be a very serious undertaking; and we doubt whether the pilgrim at the end would know very much more about Dickens and his writings than

he did at the beginning. (34).

Even after that indictment, however, Woolf found some value in the book:

> The most vivid and valuable part of the book is that which describes the various dwelling places of Dickens as a young man before he was famous and could afford a 'frightfully first-class family mansion', as he calls it. It was while he lived in these dreary and dingy back streets in Camden Town and the neighbourhood of the Debtors' Prison that Dickens absorbed the view of the life which he was afterwards to reproduce so brilliantly. (34).

According to Woolf, then, biographical spaces might be of interest as they shaped the spatial sensibilities of the author who wrote out such spatial formations in his or her fiction. She legitimized the critics' curiosity in some instances, "[w]hen the house of a great writer or the country in which it is set adds something to our understanding of her books" (5).[4] In the case of Dickens, Woolf acknowledged that the formative role of dwelling place for the youthful proto-artist was worth study. For Woolf studies, this might justify the study of the contrast between 22 Hyde Park Gate and Talland House, St. Ives as part of Woolf's developing sense of spatial aesthetics.

In her 1905 essay, Woolf warned about the dangers of equating the writer with the place written about and the pitfalls inherent in the quest of the scholar pilgrim. At the same time as she noted the perils, Woolf recognized the lure of spatial pilgrimages:

> We are either pilgrims from sentiment, who find something stimulating to the imagination in the fact that Thackeray rang this very door bell or that Dickens shaved behind that identical window, or we are scientific in our pilgrimage and visit the country where a

> great novelist lived in order to see to what extent he was influenced by his surroundings. Both motives are often combined and can be legitimately satisfied, as, for instance, in the case of Scott or the Brontës, George Meredith or Thomas Hardy. (*Essays* 1:32)

In her own time, Woolf begged the question of the legitimacy of literary pilgrimages when it came up in reference to the Brontës and Haworth Parsonage. After presenting arguments against the genre Woolf rebelled against her own strictures: "However, I am not taking away my only excuse for visiting Haworth" (6).[5] As late in her career as 1932 Woolf proved susceptible to the draw, as her essay "Great Men's Houses" testified.[6]

If aspects of literary tourism sometimes amused Woolf,[7] her orientation to the genre shifted to outrage and hostility when her own space became a mecca for unscrupulous journalists. Quentin Bell printed her vitriolic poem, "Fantasy Upon a Gentleman who Converted His Impressions of a Private House into Cash" in which she described such a trespasser, a journalist who insinuated himself into Monk's House uninvited, as a "bug:"[8]

> A bug; Always on the wall. The bug of the house
> that comes. But if you kill bugs they leave marks
> on the wall. Just as the bug's body bleeds in pale
> ink recording his impressions of a private house
> in the newspapers for cash. (494)

In anger Woolf described the figure as a housebreaker, violating her space:

> Sitting there, in the chair in the spring of the year;
> taking time, air, light, space; stopping the
> race of every thought; blocking out with his tweeds
> the branches; the pigeons; and half the sky. (493)

The indictment echoed her harsh judgment of Milton's bogey in *A Room of One's Own*: "Indeed my aunt's legacy unveiled the sky to me, and substituted for the large and imposing figure of a gentleman, which Milton recommended for my perpetual adoration, a view of the open sky" (39) and "if we look past Milton's bogey, for no human being should shut out the view" (118). Like Milton's bogey, the trespassing literary tourist occupied not only Woolf's room, but her mind.

For a scholar attempting a study of Woolf's spatial art and critique, including her biographical sites, such words are particularly sobering.[9] Certainly her argument makes superficial scholarly tourism out of the question. But the study of biographical and fictional spaces need not begin and end with the realtor's guide to literary Woolf. In *A Room of One's Own*, Woolf argued that the relationship between the writer and the site occupied the threshold of cultural history and biography:

> What were the conditions in which women lived, I asked myself; for fiction, imaginative work that is, is not dropped like a pebble upon the ground, as science may be; fiction is like a spider's web, attached ever so lightly perhaps, but still attached to life at all four corners. . . . these webs are not spun in midair by incorporeal creatures, but are the work of suffering human beings, and are attached to grossly material things, like health and money and *the houses we live in*. (*A Room of One's Own* 43-4; my emphasis)

Her move in this pivotal essay to shift the focus from sites of great writers to the hypothetical sites of women writers and to the actual sites of women in culture was a breakthrough in her art and critique. The shift from Shakespeare to the hypothetical spaces of his imaginary sister allowed Woolf to combine her fictional power with ideological argument. Using writers' sites to lead to cultural critique helped Woolf to bridge art and critique. In "Great Men's Houses," dated March 1932, one segment of a five-part series for *Good Housekeeping*, she explored again the genre of literary pilgrimage beginning with familiar ideas and moving to cultural critique. The essay opened with echoes of her earlier essays in the genre:

> London, happily, is becoming full of great men's houses, bought for the nation and preserved entire with the chairs they sat on and the cups they drank from, their umbrellas and their chests of drawers. And it is no frivolous curiosity that sends us to Dickens's house and Johnson's house and Carlyle's house and Keats's house. We know them from their houses — it would seem to be a fact that writers stamp themselves upon their possessions more indelibly than other people. Of artistic taste they have none; but they seem always to possess a much rarer and more interesting gift — a faculty for housing themselves appropriately, for making the table, the chair, the curtain, the carpet into their own image. (23)

But Woolf quickly moved into a cultural critique of the Victorian system and the domestic enslavement of women:

> All through the mid-Victorian age the house was necessarily a battlefield where daily, summer and winter, mistress and maid fought against dirt and cold for cleanliness and warmth. The stairs, carved as they are and wide and dignified, seem worn by the feet of harassed women carrying tin cans. The high panelled rooms seem to echo with the sound of pumping and the swish of scrubbing. The voice of the house — and all houses have voices — is the voice of pumping and scrubbing, of coughing and groaning. (24)

In a fascinating sleight of pen Woolf shifted from the traditional emphasis on the males who had inhabited the "houses of great men" to the women behind them, from the battlefields and masterpieces of great men to the daily battles of the women: "Thus number 5 Cheyne Row is not so much a dwelling-place as a battlefield — the scene of labour, effort and perpetual struggle"

A Video Project

(25).

Woolf's complex mapping of the relationship of writer to landscape, setting and place formed a key part of one narrative for her work—a narrative of her spatial art. Her manipulations of space as part of a cultural critique shaped *To the Lighthouse* and *The Waves*, appropriately, for these texts interrogated the site of her most intense personal visions, the childhood summer home of Talland House. That Talland House was an intense and magical site of ecstasy and insight for Virginia Woolf is an interesting bit of biographical information; that she in *To the Lighthouse* and *The Waves* re-created that site as a cultural critique warrants *our* attention. Because the home was drenched with magic and sentiment, it was the ultimate challenge for her ability to rework sentiment into what she could acknowledge as art. Talland House became the touchstone in Woolf's spatial theory which most clearly illustrated her shift from spatial aesthetics to cultural critique. For Woolf, Talland House was a *site of passage*.

Talland House full view.
  At times I can go back to St Ives more completely than I can this morning. . . I feel that strong emotion must leave its trace; and it is only a question of discovering how we can get ourselves again attached to it, so that we shall be able to live our lives through from the start.
        ("A Sketch of the Past" 67)

The Waves balcony: the waves and dawn over the lighthouse from the balcony of Talland House.
"*The sun had not yet risen . . . The birds sang their blank melody outside.*"
(First poetic interlude of *The Waves*)

A Video Project

As the echo of Woolf's words dies away and the visual images fade one is left with some resonance of *To the Lighthouse* and *The Waves*: "I see it—the past—as an avenue lying behind; a long ribbon of scenes, emotions. There at the end of the avenue still, are the garden and the nursery" ("A Sketch of the Past" 67). It is imperative to pause on that threshold, however, for Talland House was not just another pretty place! It was to Woolf a site in cultural history. When Woolf wrote against the patriarchal system, she founded her critique on the private home; in *Three Guineas* she argued "the public and private worlds are inseparably connected ... the tyrannies and servilities of the one are the tyrannies and servilities of the other" (142). The personal and cultural history were one. As the home in *To the Lighthouse* had its secrets—the Swiss maid sobbing in the attic and the daughters daydreaming of escape—the lovely compelling site of Talland House was also the site of the incestuous molestation of Virginia as a child, as she wrote in "A Sketch of the Past": "There was a small looking-glass in the hall at Talland House.... There was a slab outside the dining room door for standing dishes upon. Once when I was very small Gerald Duckworth lifted me onto this, and as I sat there he began to explore my body" (67-69). This horror took place in the same hall bathed in golden arched light which Woolf described as the "cathedral space of childhood." How can we hold both images of the family home in our minds? Which is "true"? Was Talland House the idyllic nostalgic haven or the prison house of the family? Writing of James looking at the lighthouse, Woolf gave us a clue:

> James looked at the Lighthouse. He could see the white-washed rocks; the tower stark and straight; ... So that was the Lighthouse was it?
> No, the other was also the Lighthouse. *For nothing was simply one thing.* The other Lighthouse was true too. (276-7; my emphasis)

In the same way, Talland House was "not simply one thing." It was both *Woolf's* childhood summer home, *and* an outpost of the brutal patriarchal bourgeois system. Class and gender forces crystallized in this site, as the patriarchal family home as a critical concept overlaps with the concept of the bourgeois home. For Woolf, as for Walter Benjamin, a house, a home, a street, crystallized the social, cultural, personal, and political forces into *dialectical images* or *insights in sites,* images which encode historical tensions. In "Time Passes" Woolf captured the fragility of the pointedly shabby patriarchal home ("the house was ramshackle after all" [190]) as an abandoned site on the fault line of culture. It was the triumphant vision of Woolf to capture *both* the nostalgia *and* the repudiation, the sob of longing and the curse in the throat—for nostalgic sites are the threshold of revolution.[10] That mix of attachment and loathing gives the dialectical push to a new consciousness. Like Benjamin, Woolf did not simply reject nostalgia but used it—to recognize and exorcise the ghosts who inhabit the past.

As Woolf's stark and uncompromising vision and exposé of the patriarchal myths of home and center, Woolf's spatial art and critique provided a passageway for the twentieth century. Abandoning the patriarchal home, moving in and finally out of a room of one's own, seeking a dwelling place for the twentieth century, she dismantled the past, remodelling with its orts and fragments. Her spatial pilgrimage toured Talland House from different perspectives, placing it within different contexts, but always, siting and reciting Talland House:

> Behind us lies the patriarchal system; the private house, with its nullity, its immorality, its hypocrisy, its servility...
> (*Three Guineas* 74)

> There at the end of the avenue still, are the garden and the nursery.
> ("A Sketch of the Past" 67)

> But for a moment I had sat on the turf somewhere high above the flow of the sea and the sounds of the woods, had seen the house, the garden, and the waves breaking. The old nurse who turns the pages of the picture-book had stopped and had said, 'Look. This is the truth.' (*The Waves* 287)

A Video Project

Notes

[1] Such a desire for authenticity, of course, may merely carry the error further.

[2] I am purposely here including (albeit in a footnote) that messy personal sentimental voice of my experience—the confessions of a scholar groupie—because they are so carefully censored out of our scholarly writings.

[3] This is a timely warning for the Woolf scholar tempted by tour caravans to Charleston Farmhouse, the opening of Monk's House, and the appearance of books such as *Charleston: Past and Present* and *Virginia Woolf: Life and London: A Biography of Place* by Jean Moorcroft Wilson, 1987. Such books, particularly the Wilson book, are useful introductions into Woolf's places and may lead readers into more in-depth analyses of those places in cultural history.

[4] Though she cited Gaskell's assertion that Haworth and the Brontës reflect each other, Woolf was more skeptical of the link between landscape and literary creation: "How far surroundings radically affect people's minds, it is not for me to ask; superficially, the influence is great, but it is worth asking if the famous parsonage had been placed in a London slum, the dens of Whitechapel would not have had the same result as the lonely Yorkshire moors" (5-6). In the essay Woolf stepped back from the common literary critical fascination with homes of great writers to consider broader issues of the influence of landscape and degrees of legitimacy of the quest. Her tongue-in-cheek tone sought to dampen the ardor of the scholar groupie: "This marked the shrine at which we were to do homage"(6) and she undercuts the project with her flat statement "There is nothing remarkable in a mid-Victorian parsonage, though tenanted by genius . . ." (8).

[5] Here and in her comment about transplanting the Brontës to the London slums, the essay contains traces of Romantic genius theory—the belief that the genius will transcend environment, that geniuses are born, not created by environment. Later she becomes much more profoundly aware of the shaping structures of home, especially the very ones in which there is "nothing remarkable," the typical Victorian home with the "angel in the house" for instance. Here the home structure is but a cardboard backdrop for the drama of genius; later its active role will be more fully explored.

[6] This essay was part of Woolf's series of articles for *Good Housekeeping*, May 2, 1932, 21:3, 18-19, 102.

[7] Woolf's multi-faceted response to the relationship between writer and physical setting enjoyed a fantastic moment of play in "Dostoevsky in Cranford," a review in the *TLS* on 23 October 1919 of Dostoevsky's *An Honest Thief and Other Stories . . . from the Russian* translated by Constance Garnett:

> It is amusing sometimes to freshen one's notion of a great, and thus semi-mythical, character by transplanting him in imagination to one's own age, shore, or country village. How, one asks, would Dostoevsky have behaved himself upon the vicarage lawn? (113)
> Yet we are perpetually conscious that, if Dostoevsky fails to keep within the proper limits, it is because the fervour of his genius goads him across the boundary (114).

By transplanting the figure to another landscape, Woolf was able to suggest the importance of spatial and cultural setting.

[8]In Appendix B of *Virginia Woolf, A Biography.* 1972.

[9]Imagine what she would have said to the "bug" had he been carrying a video camera. A subtitle for this video pilgrimage to Talland House might be: "Guilt Tripping Down Memory Lane" . . . for how can we justify peeking through the escalonia hedge to seek some glimpse of Talland House and Virginia Woolf? Should we feel like guilty trespassers? or in seeking the writer's site are we seeking (to quote Woolf) "not gossip but revelation"?

[10]Woolf merged *her* mother with the homes she dominated; Talland House and Hyde Park Gate defined Julia Stephen, as Woolf wrote in her autobiographical works: "She was the whole thing; Talland House was full of her; Hyde Park Gate was full of her" ("A Sketch of the Past" 83). In lectures and essays, Woolf expands this merging of person and place in her formulation in 1931 of "The Angel in the House" as a cultural icon who literally haunts the house and cripples the woman artist. Woolf's indictment of the Victorian woman as the "Angel in the House" is in "Professions for Women" a paper read to the Women's Service League and collected in *The Death of the Moth and Other Essays*.

Bibliography

Bell, Quentin, Angelica Garnett, Henrietta Garnett and Richard Shone. *Charleston: Past and Present*. London: The Hogarth Press, 1987.

Bell, Quentin. *Virginia Woolf: A Biography*. New York: Harcourt, 1972.

Benjamin, Walter. *Illuminations*. Ed. Hannah Arendt. Trans. Harry Zohn. New York: Schocken Books, 1969.

———. *One-Way Street and Other Writings*. Intro. Susan Sontag. Trans. Edmund Jephcott and Kingsley Shorter. New York: Harcourt Brace Jovanovich, 1978.

———. *Reflections*. Ed. Peter Demetz. Trans. Edmund Jephcott. New York: Schocken Books, 1986.

DeSalvo, Louise A. *Virginia Woolf: The Impact of Childhood Sexual Abuse on Her Life and Work*. Boston: Beacon Press, 1989.

Wilson, Jean Moorcroft. *Virginia Woolf: Life and London: A Biography of Place*. London: Cecil Woolf, 1987.

Woolf, Virginia. *The Essays of Virginia Woolf*. Ed. Andrew McNeillie. 3 vols. to date. London: Hogarth, 1987.

———. *The London Scene*. London: Hogarth, 1982.

———. *Moments of Being: Unpublished Autobiographical Writings*. Ed. Jeanne Schulkind. New York: Harcourt, 1975.

———. *A Room of One's Own*. 1929. New York: Harcourt, 1957.

———. *Three Guineas*. 1938. New York: Harcourt, 1966.

———. *To the Lighthouse*. 1927. New York: Harcourt, 1955.

———. *The Waves*. 1931. New York: Harcourt, 1959.

CHEF'S SPECIALS

- ★ **EMPIRE SPECIAL GARDEN** .... 本樓素會 **7.25**
  A splendiferous array of vegetables enhanced by a bed of lotus stems, tasty wood ear mushrooms, glutten of wheat, baby corns, snow pea pods, broccoli & Tomatoes.
- ★ **AROMATIC CHINESE EGGPLANT** .... 五味茄 **7.25**
  Small Chinese eggplant sauteed w. garlic, scallion & pepper in rich aromatic sauce.
- ★ **SLICE PORK SZECHUAN STYLE** .... 蜀湘肉片 **7.95**
  Sliced pork, broccoli, baby corns sauteed in hot black bean sauce.
- ★ **EMPIRE SPECIAL CHICKEN W. SESAME SEEDS** 芝麻雞 **8.95**
- ★ **EMPIRE GINGER CHICKEN** .... 子薑雞柳 **8.95**
  Juicy white meat, shredded string bean and young ginger root threads in Kongpao sauce.
- **WALNUT CHICKEN** .... 核桃雞 **8.25**
- ★ **CURRY FLAVOR CHICKEN** .... 咖喱雞 **8.25**
- ★ **PARADISE CHICKEN** .... 天府雞 **8.25**
  White meat chicken, red pepper and watercress sauteed with hot Szechuan sauce.
- **AUTHENTIC LEMON CHICKEN** .... 檸檬雞 **8.25**
- ★ **GENERAL TSENG'S HISTORIC CHICKEN** 湖南(國藩)雞球 **8.25**
  Diced chicken, waterchestnut, celery, strawmushroom & red pepper sauteed with hot bean sauce.
- ★ **GENERAL TSO'S CHICKEN** .... 左宗棠雞 **8.95**
  Chunks of dark chicken meat, dried red pepper, sauteed with hot Kong-Pao sauce with watercress.
- ★ **GOLDEN CHICKEN W. FIVE FLAVORS** .... 五味雞 **8.95**
- **HONEY DUCK** .... 蜜汁鴨 **10.95**
- ★ **EMPIRE SPECIAL DUCK** .... 本樓鴨塊 **8.75**
  Carefully prepared boneless duck chunks dedded in snow pea pods and red pepper.
- ★ **EMPIRE SPECIAL BEEF WITH SESAME SEEDS** 芝麻牛 **9.95**
- ★ **SZECHUAN PREMIER STEAK** .... 本樓牛柳 **9.95**
  Fancy flank steak, specially cut and marinated with garlic, wine soy and spices, then dry sauteed and garnished with vermicelli.
- ★ **HUNAN FLOWER STEAK** .... 碧蘭牛排 **9.95**
  Succulent beef chunks lightly sauteed with broccoli in hot special sauce adorned w. cherries.
- ★ **CRISPY ORANGE FLAVOR BEEF** .... 脆皮牛
- ★ ~~ SZECHUAN ~~ SAUCE ..... 鹹辣

Virginia Woolf and Her Experimentalist Contemporaries: Mansfield, Richardson and Stein

G. Johnston
After the Invention of the Gramophone:
Hearing the Woman in Stein's *Autobiography*
and Woolf's *Three Guineas*

Rachel Blau DuPlessis contends that Gertrude Stein's work and Virginia Woolf's connect through "intertext," an imagined cut and connected text that "foregrounds a 'feminine' practice of otherness" (100). DuPlessis writes of the texts "Composition as Explanation" and *The Waves*, but readers can also see this "'feminine' practice of otherness" in texts like Virginia Woolf's *Three Guineas* and Gertrude Stein's *The Autobiography of Alice B. Toklas*, partly because these texts redirect our gaze onto women instead of men. In particular, *Three Guineas* and *Autobiography* present a woman's voice, a woman's voice trained in the private arena but heard in the public. I will argue in this paper that Woolf and Stein, in presenting a new voice, react to the new technology of recording sound, and that one way to imagine an intertext between Woolf, Stein, and other modernist writers is to read culture—here, for me, technological culture in the form of the gramophone—influencing the intertext, creating a web of material stimuli.

There is some ambiguity in the attention that *Three Guineas* and *Autobiography* focus on women. Indeed, if one wished to argue against an explicit feminism in these texts, one would point out that both *Three Guineas* and *Autobiography* present their woman's voices through patriarchal textual forms. *Three Guineas*, for instance, presents a sophisticated philosophical argument that fascism and war are caused by patriarchy and the behavior that patriarchy teaches—jealousy, hierarchy, competition. Woolf uses footnotes, a patriarchal textualizing with all the hierarchy and authority that the research form denotes. Simultaneously, however, Woolf undermines this form by reinscribing her philosophical argument in letter form. *Three Guineas*, itself a letter, intertwines its own text with the posited male letter-text: "this letter would never have been written had you [the man writing the letter-writer asking her to help him prevent war] not asked for an answer to your own" (144). Within her response-letter, the daughter of the educated man includes other letters— to her from other women asking for money—and letters that she writes back to them. She imagines these letters for the man as a way of explaining the connections between war and women's oppression.

The Autobiography of Alice B. Toklas also clothes itself in patriarchal form—the autobiography, a genre emphasizing, Carolyn Heilbrun reminds us, accomplishments of the self, something that women have been taught to perceive as "unwomanly" (17). But Stein, too, overturns the form of her text, and presents the "autobiography" from the point of view of another, Alice B. Toklas, a feat causing Cynthia Merrill to call *Autobiography* a "mockery of her genre" (11). Stein's "mockery" has been so successful that her agent and one of her most insightful critics wondered if Alice B. Toklas were in reality the author.[1]

By using these forms, and shaping them to their own uses, Stein and Woolf revalue them. Victoria Middleton suggests that, through form and rhetoric, "Woolf is both using and dismantling the form of a logical argument" (417). Stein does something similar, not with a logical argument, but with perceptions of genre and of boundaries between object and subject. By creating Toklas simultaneously with "Toklas['s]" observations of Stein, *Autobiography* questions subject and object distinctions.

By making radical forays against traditional genre expectations, Stein and Woolf create new voices. The dialogic between "speaker" and audience is new because, by undermining an audience's expectations, the "speaker" confuses the boundary between private and public form and genre. This technique has a parallel in the invention of the gramophone—a voice, recorded in private, could be heard by a large public, and a voice, recorded in public (at a concert, for example) could be heard in the private spaces of the home. The invention of the gramophone, then, can be said to have presented writers of the early twentieth century with a new kind of textualizing that influenced their conceptions of public and private voice. The voice could now be, literally, heard on command.

By isolating the gramophone as a piece of technology influencing literary output, I follow Hugh Kenner's lead, as he shows the influence of the typewriter on Pound, the subway on Eliot: "New ways of writing, then, for new orders of experience; urban experience; Modernism is distinctly urban.... like all live writing it ingests what's around it" (14). When Stein and Woolf present a woman's voice, capture within their era the voice of woman, they enact the gramophone's function. As the gramophone recorded and projected a voice, Stein and Woolf write a woman's voice that speaks outwards to an implied audience. Theirs, however, is not an unresisting appropriation. While they create a literary equivalent of the gramophone, they also modify that mechanical representation, distancing themselves from the mechanical process of stasis while they benefit from the concept of recording.

For the gramophone is not only positive; it has its negative effects. With the gramophone, voice became an object of production, something that could be recorded, mass produced, sold. Voice entered into the capitalist structure. Woolf and Stein, in their texts of the 1930s, ironize that capitalistic production of voice. Woolf, in particular, politicizes the voice, making the patriarchal voicing analogous to the gramophone's production of a recorded voice that does not change. "If" she hypothesizes

> we encourage the daughters to enter the professions without making any conditions as to the way in which the professions are to be practised shall we not be doing our best to stereotype the old tune which human

nature, like a gramophone whose needle has stuck, is now grinding out with such disastrous unanimity? "Here we go round the mulberry tree . . . Give it all to me . . . to me. Three hundred millions spent upon war." With that song, or something like it, ringing in our ears we cannot send our guinea. . . .

Instead, the narrator maintains, "she shall have it on condition that she shall swear that the professions in future shall be practised so that they lead to a different song" (59). Woolf does not condemn the gramophone; after all, she calls only for a "different song." But, by using the gramophone as a simile for public voicing, she exposes three results of the mechanization of voice. First, public mechanical voicing replaces the individual (the poets and artists who Woolf shows singing to each other in earlier eras) with the collective, anonymous, "stereotyp[ing]" tune. Second, the mechanical voicing places the gramophone within the mode of economic materialism and possessiveness that cause war and oppression: "'Give it all to me,'" the machine plays. Third, the mechanical voice keeps readers from questioning the attitudes surrounding the valuing of the gramophone and mass production—attitudes represented by "the old tune" and by the "grinding" of the machine.

Readers can see specific attitudes towards the gramophone's function from its earliest inception. When Thomas Edison first filed for patent of the tin-foil phonograph in 1877, reactions were immediate in thinking about the implications for the invention. A letter in *Scientific American*, for example, hailed the new ability to record "voices of the departed." And the living had the assurance "that his speech may be reproduced audibly in his own tones after he himself has turned to dust" (letter from 17 Nov., 1877, qtd. in Reed and Welch 11-12). The emphasis is on the past, on the voice surviving the grave, on the "old tunes."

Death was not the only absolute overcome by the recording gramophone; so was the uniqueness of performance. "Music can be crystalized . . . . Imagine an opera or an oratorio, sung by the greatest living vocalists, thus recorded, and capable of being repeated as we desire" (Reed and Welch 12). The ability to repeat a performance moves the voice into the realm of mechanical object;[2] it can be "crystalized." The ability to play back a voice "as we desire" recreates the voice as *object* of desire, as object controlled, in time and in production.

In contrast, Stein and Woolf create voices that "speak" outside control of the public audience. Audience, instead of voice, is under control in production because the choice of voice sets up implied dialogue with an audience that never gives an actual response; instead, the voice creates an implied response from the audience. For example, *Three Guineas* creates a temporary audience—a man who has written a letter, "a letter that has gone unanswered," a letter asking a woman how in her opinion war can be prevented (3). Woolf, as she does in *A Room of One's Own* (with Professor von X) imagines "a sketch of the person," and creates him "a little grey on the temples," in the "middle years of life," in "prosperity," and educated (3). Even with this sketch of a specific audience, however, any reader becomes implicated in Woolf's argument that patriarchy causes war. The reader in "the middle years," "a little grey around the temples," educated, becomes a common reader. Even the women who wish to start a women's school—if they start a college that will give degrees, provide lectures, systematize hierarchy—must contend with "the old poisoned vanities and parades which breed competition and jealousy" (35). Since the woman starting the college "must rebuild her college on the same lines as the others" (35), within the patriarchal format, then she too is implicated in the cause of war. Indeed the intersection of voice and implied audience implicates us all.

Stein, while she does not use the gramophone as simile or politicize the gramophone's function, also questions voice. She creates an ironic and reflexive focus upon herself by using Toklas's voice, and she investigates the results of using another's voice instead of her own. *She* is in control of the voice: *she* labels herself genius; *she* accounts for her life in Paris. Stein's ending paragraph of *The Autobiography of Alice B. Toklas* shows her reinterpreting the text's supposed pose. There, "Toklas" states that she "found it difficult to add being a pretty good author" to her other accomplishments, and then casually remarks, "About six weeks ago Gertrude Stein said, it does not look to me as if you were ever going to write that autobiography. You know what I am going to do. I am going to write it for you. I am going to write it as simply as Defoe did the autobiography of Robinson Crusoe. And she has and this is it" (237). Stein deftly repositions herself as controller of the text, while she removes herself from the control of her audience by placing "Toklas" as voice.

Like the daughter voice, the Toklas voice speaks out to an implied audience, but casually—"As I was saying we were all living comfortably together" (4) and "Before I tell about the guests I must tell what I saw" (8). This is a *speaking voice*. Instead of creating a casual and familiar dialogue, however, through imagining another like the grey, middle-aged man, the Toklas voice creates an off-the-set narrative with Stein at center. By creating this voice, directed out to an audience, Stein, though she does not mention the gramophone, enacts some of the gramophone's positive functions: she has kept Toklas's voice fluid and alive (without freezing it), and she has made a voice, as the gramophone has to hearers, available to others after Toklas and she are both dead.

For both writers, using this kind of voice creates an ironic quest—a movement from a naive realism (which can be seen in the recordings of the gramophone) to realism, which includes an understanding of subjectivity. The voice becomes a mimetic creation of sound within a dialogic of audience and text, but it is not placed within the same object-relation economy as is the voice of the gramophone. Instead, it retains a reflecting subjectivity.

To retain and explore subjectivity, Stein and Woolf use the voice to create specularly. "Toklas" specularly creates Stein herself, and the voice recreates Toklas too, through the ear. Woolf, within her political time, creates a collective voice[3], a voice that had been heard rarely—the opinionated woman's voice. *Three Guineas* divides the woman's voice from the man's voice, by posing it through what is clearly a dialogue and then solidifying it through the texts of letters and *Three Guineas* itself. "Let us then ask someone else—it is Mary Kingsley—to speak for us. 'I don't know if I ever revealed to you the fact that being allowed to learn German was *all* the paid for education I ever had. Two thousand pounds was spent on my brother's; I still hope not in vain'" (4). Mary Kingsley "speak[s]" with a voice for the collective "us" and places women as opposed to men—her "paid for" education was only German; her brother's "two thousand pounds."

93

By posing a woman's voice as distinct from a man's voice, Woolf theorizes about that voice. The voice needs theorization because it only exists theoretically. Woolf, creating new space within her time for that voice, articulates its newness—for "when before has an educated man asked a woman how in her opinion war can be prevented?" (3). The voice she presents, the voice of the daughter of the educated man, has never before been heard. For Woolf the connection to feminism is explicit. *Three Guineas* calls for women to have the same rights as men. Exposing the power basis of the gender binary, *Three Guineas* documents the passage of the vote and, from 1919 on, the legality of women entering the work force. Women begin to "voice" political claims for property rights and education.

By creating a new voice, Woolf's text differs from the gramophone recording, since the gramophone captured voices that had already been heard. Woolf changes the gramophone concept of recording voice in two ways. She creates a voice that makes a new viewpoint known. And, in an ironizing move, she creates distance, through use of that voice, from the patriarchal *status quo*. Stein's text differs from the gramophone recording because her text does not stop at recording the voice. Behind that voice is "Toklas['s]" version of Stein. Stein creates a view of herself from the outside. One woman praises another woman publicly—who praises whom is not fully clear; some critics insist that *Autobiography* praises Toklas. Certainly, in both directions, one woman gives autobiographical life to another woman.

Because of the choice of this voice, the voice has become, unlike that in the passive and automatic gramophone, active and controlling. We might, through concepts of activity and passivity in gazing and listening, liken the gramophone to the recipient of the gaze, while Stein's and Woolf's texts redefine their voices. Instead of being objects of an audience's gaze, the voice controls that gaze. Instead of being passive, the speakers of Stein's and Woolf's texts refocus attention onto another. "Toklas" gazes at Stein, a genius and writer. The voice of the daughter of an educated man gazes at war and, through war, the daughter of an educated man—her place, profession, education—and through the daughter, Woolf, herself the daughter of an educated man. Stein and Woolf, the authors, through these created voices of an other, gaze at themselves; the voice of the woman becomes the

Woolf and Her Experimentalist Contemporaries

conduit for the ironic and reflexive gaze. The commodification of the recorded voice that Woolf and Stein revalue, as they have revalued the patriarchal textual form, is thrown into relief in T. S. Eliot's use of the gramophone as part of the machine culture: "When lovely woman stoops to folly and/ Paces about her room again, alone,/ She smooths her hair with automatic hand,/ And puts a record on the gramophone" (ll.253-256). Eliot's presentation of the sound machine and its listener makes the typist as much a machine "with automatic hand" as is her gramophone. Woolf and Stein, in contrast, are concerned with positing a new relationship between what is heard and the listener. Rather than production of the heard being a ticket to a spiritual waste land, Woolf and Stein, influenced by the modern recording, imagine new voices and new relationships between the heard, observed, and listener. The gramophone became, for them, part of the cultural influences through which we can construct an intertext of feminism.[4]

Notes

[1]"I did a tour de force with the *Autobiography of Alice B. Toklas*, Stein recounts, and when I sent the first half to the agent they sent back a telegram to see which one of us had written it" ["Afterward," an interview with Robert Bartlett Hass, *What are Masterpieces* (NY: Pitman Publ. Corp., 1959) 102.] Richard Bridgman, one of the first critics to attempt a critical overview of her work, wrote: "One possibility is sufficiently heretical that no one has dared advance it directly: but there have been hints that Alice Toklas composed her own autobiography" [*Gertrude Stein in Pieces* (NY: Oxford UP, 1970) 209.]

[2]See Walter Benjamin's interdisciplinary study of the impact of technology on art for a fuller representation of the "mechanical reproduction of a work of art" ("The Work of Art in the Age of Mechanical Reproduction," 1936, rpt. in *Illuminations*, trans. Harry Zohn [NY: Schocken Books, 1969] 218) He mentions but does not concentrate on the "reproduction of sound" (219), particularly the phonograph record (see page 221 also). Benjamin's article is especially interesting when paralleled with *Three Guineas*, since Benjamin, too, investigates the connections between Fascism, war, and civilization. Benjamin emphasizes the materialist culture as cause of war rather than patriarchy: "Only war makes it possible to mobilize all of today's technical resources while maintaining the property system" (241).

[3]Lynne T. Hanley makes the collective nature of the voice very clear: "The frame of *Three Guineas* is a letter from *us* in response to a query from *you* as to how to prevent war. Inset in that frame are two letters to women in which the pronoun references vary, but when addressing a man Woolf sharply and consistently divides *you* from *us*" ("Virginia Woolf and the Romance of Oxbridge," *Massachusetts Review* 25.3 [Summer 1984]: 430)

Haller

⁴I thank Jennifer Shaddock and Marianne Cave for their responses to an early draft of and to early ideas for this article. My thanks also to Elise Lemire and Julia Willis for their comments on a near-finished version of the conference paper.

Works Cited

Duplessis, Rachel Blau. "WOOLFENSTEIN," in *Breaking the Sequence: Women's Experimental Fiction*. Eds. Ellen G. Friedman and Miriam Fuchs. Princeton: Princeton UP, 1989.
Eliot, T.S. *The Waste Land, Selected Poems*. London: Faber, 1954.
Heilbrun, Carolyn. *Writing a Woman's Life*. NY: Norton, 1988.
Kenner, Hugh. *The Mechanic Muse*. NY: Oxford UP, 1987.
Merrill, Cynthia. "Mirrored Image: Gertrude Stein and Autobiography." *Pacific Coast Philology* 20.1-2 (November 1985).
Middleton, Victoria. "Subversion and Survival in the Professions." *Twentieth Century Literature* 28.4 (Winter 1982).
Reed, Oliver and Walter L. Welch. *From Tin Foil to Stereo: Evolution of the Phonograph*. 2nd ed.Indianapolis: Howard W. Sams & Co., 1959.
Stein, Gertrude. *Selected Writings of Gertrude Stein*. Ed. Carl van Vechten NY: Random House, 1945.
Woolf, Virginia. *Three Guineas*. San Diego: Harcourt, 1938.

Evelyn Haller
Virginia Woolf and Katherine Mansfield: or, The Case of the Déclassé Wild Child

As critics have pointed out,[1] Virginia Woolf and Katherine Mansfield had overlapping intentions and techniques. Woolf, however, felt antagonism toward Mansfield, seeing in her a woman rival: "the only writing I have ever been jealous of" (*Diary*, 2: 227-228). As a recent study suggests, competition between women is an emotionally and ethically painful subject that has been kept under wraps by feminists.[2] This essay argues that Virginia Woolf made use of her ongoing feelings of antagonism toward Katherine Mansfield as a literary competitor by transferring them to the less unacceptable plane of class consciousness through characterizations in *Between the Acts*.

In this novel the narrator posits the innate superiority of the

Woolf and Her Experimentalist Contemporaries

surreptitious poet Isa Oliver to the vulgar Mrs. Manresa whose name resembles Mansfield. Isa, moreover, is "hot, nerve wired" as she suffers "the rusty fester of the poisoned dart" of jealousy toward the other woman who has her husband Giles in thrall. I suggest, however, that Manresa's sexual encroachment on Isa's territory is a substitution for Mansfield's synchronous occupation of literary territory Woolf preferred to regard as her own. Though this sexual metaphor is more likely to be regarded as an emotional reaction of men, that is, to take a man's territory or his work is to take his woman, sexually charged possessiveness toward territory and work is not a trait limited by gender. What, given Woolf's time and place, would be a less self-incriminating expression of territorial resentment than a direct attack on Katherine Mansfield in Woolf's literary criticism? To attack work similar to one's own would be ultimately self-defeating. Besides, under these circumstances it is the person rather than the work that irrationally receives the brunt of the hatred. Given Woolf's time and place, class consciousness provides such a cushioned vehicle. Moreover, Woolf had already discharged some of her resentment toward James Joyce—merely a male interloper—through class superiority as we can read in her diary where she wrote of *Ulysses*: "An illiterate, underbred book it seems to me; the book of a self-taught working man, and we all know how distressing they are, how egotistic, insistent, raw, striking, and ultimately nauseating" (16 Aug. 1922, 47; 6 Sept. 1922, 49).

Besides being female, Mansfield was also younger than Woolf. Hence, a further suggestive element occurs in the text of *Between the Acts*: the reversal of the six years difference in their ages whereby the older Woolf becomes the younger Isa to the younger Mansfield's Manresa. Surely, the irritation of Mansfield's comparative youth was exacerbated by her habit of referring to herself as a "child." Consider in this light the repeated references to Manresa as "the wild child" stated directly seven times in the text (41, 44, 50, 79, 102, 177).

A chain to Manresa's as well as to Mansfield's origins is provided by an Outline of History Lucy Swithin, who is sympathetic to "savages" in their natural state and sensitive to their beauty (59), carries about with her, a book which suggests H. G. Wells's popular history. "A riot of rhododendrons and humming birds quivered at the mouths of scarlet trumpets" read by

Lucy evokes not only the prehistoric past but lushness. Like New Zealand where Mansfield came from, the neighboring island of Tasmania is lush. Moreover, the pattern evoked for Manresa in the text is that of "a goddess, buoyant, abundant, with flower-chained captives following in her wake... admirable woman, all sensation" (202). She establishes herself as "a thorough good sort" in the eyes and feelings of most people in the vicinity of Pointz Hall.

Nonetheless, kinship between Isa and Mrs. Manresa comes through: the bolster-like bodies, their relative age, their yearnings—acknowledged by Mrs. Manresa, tastefully hidden by Isa. Both are sources of life in the novel: Bart iterates how his daughter-in-law "continues" him while Manresa restores "his spice islands, his youth" (41).

A question, then, of life itself. After a visit to Asheham in August, 1917, Mansfield wrote to Woolf: "we have got the same job, Virginia, and it is really very curious and thrilling that we should both, quite apart from each other, be after so very nearly the same thing. We are, you know; there's no denying it."[3] Woolf would not have been guilty of such plenitude of "verys" even in a hastily written note. And Mansfield's handwriting, in relation to Woolf's was like Manresa's "so huge—so clumsy" (61). Certainly Mansfield lacked the social graces Woolf had acquired during her years at the tea table at 22 Hyde Park Gate.

Similarly, Isa feels aversion for Manresa's techniques for attracting others to her: ogling, the projection of sensuality. But there is much class antagonism in those reactions which have to do with questions of acceptable behavior. Again, "She was over-sexed, over-painted... that old strumpet." (Lady Harpy Harraden is another projection of Woolf's distaste for the type.) Isa's superiority in class shows through her better taste, her more polished manner. Isa does not, for example, cock her thumb. But Manresa's sensuality is riveting, and it is memorable that she is centered during her scenes in *Between the Acts* in a mode that recalls how Jinny is centered in *The Waves*, for example, "Mrs. Manresa in the very center smiled" and "The stout lady in the middle" (78, 79). She calls to others, especially to men: "Follow, follow, follow me" (96). Here is the crux of the matter: "vulgar" and "oversexed" are the dominant aspects of Mrs. Manresa. Recall that Mansfield's bohemian way of life offended Woolf.

Woolf and Her Experimentalist Contemporaries

Moreover, she once observed that Mansfield "stinked like a—well civet cat that had taken to streetwalking" (*Diary*, 1:58). We read of Mrs. Manresa: "Vulgar she was in her gestures, in her whole person, over-sexed" (41). Mansfield had written Woolf "Don't let THEM ever persuade you that I spend any of my precious time . . . committing adultery"⁴; in the novel, Mrs. Manresa emerges from the lush greenhouse with Isa's husband, Giles.

Thus, Woolf's hostilities toward Mansfield could be given a legitimate, or more legitimate, outlet by fixing on Mansfield's vulgarity and commonness. In "Class Distinctions," an unpublished essay in the Berg Collection, Woolf confines her discussion to the question of what is a gentleman while she leaves the question of what is a lady unexamined. Clearly, fewer unwritten rules (as with the British constitution) applied. The question was largely settled through a woman's bloodline or legal affiliations with men. Manresa by these measures would not fare well; nor would Mansfield. Isa would fare better as "Sir Richard's daughter" (16) despite her Irish connections, presumably on her mother's side. Moreover, Isa is safely married to a City man, the son of a retired member of the Foreign Service who is also a landowner.

An element of class distinction represented by Mansfield as well as by Mrs. Manresa is colonial status. Mrs. Manresa "sometimes . . . referred to an uncle, a Bishop. But he was thought to have been a Colonial Bishop only" (40). It is understood that modest status in England counts for more than high status in the colonies. In any case, it is significant that Isa is prevented from hearing further gossip about Mrs. Manresa's grandfather: "some hanky-panky mid-Victorian scandal; malversation of trusts, was it?" because male interruption and contradiction on a nonessential point prevent Isa's would-be informant from continuing (40).

Unlike her husband, Ralph Manresa, "a Jew got up to look the very spit and image of the landed gentry" (40), Mrs. Manresa makes no attempt to pass herself off as other than she is. Nor is she hampered by middle class self-protection as she observes: "It's all my eye about democracy" (102). Moreover, "It was the women of her own class that bored her" (106). Those women return Mrs. Manresa's feelings as one says: "She's a type I don't myself fancy" (159). Not surprisingly, Mrs. Manresa consorts with the lower orders, teaching "the village women *not* how to pickle and preserve; but how to weave frivolous baskets out of coloured straw. Pleasure's what they want, she said" (42-43). As early as *Melymbrosia* and *The Voyage Out*, Woolf had associated attributes she ascribes to Mrs. Manresa to primitive women. Rachel, for example, asks Mrs. Flushing about her proposed journey on the river to the interior: "What d'you think it looks like?... Are there... painted women sitting making baskets...?" (167).

Pleasure's what Mrs. Manresa wants as well as the women with whom she feels she has something in common. She hums a song suggesting sexual availability: "and boys you'll believe me, / I don't want no asking." The last two syllables of Manresa's name—resa—are the Italian word for "surrender" or "delivery."

By making Mrs. Manresa at 45 a decade older than Mansfield at the time of her death at 34, Woolf, in effect, posits a continuing life for her old rival. For the reader, similarities between them show forth as much as differences. One striking difference, however, is Manresa's attraction to childish things—a trait she shares with Mansfield—as well as her iterated claim to being a child, including her insistence: "I'm nothing so grown up as you are" (45). Isa, on the other hand, is mature.

Similarities between Isa and Mrs. Manresa make further sense by way of narrative imagery[5] if we regard them through Ancient Egyptian mythology as Isis and Nepthys, as I argue elsewhere in an argument for the relevance of this mythology to *Between the Acts*.[6] In this light the sexual encounter between Giles and Manresa in the greenhouse—"The door was kicked open. Out came Mrs. Manresa and Giles" (157) or Isa "could feel the Manresa in his wake. She could hear in the dusk in their bedroom the usual explanation. It made no difference; his infidelity—but hers did" (110)—follows Egyptian myth both in story and in representation. Osiris, Plutarch tells us, lay with Nepthys, who resembles Isis and is paired with her in funerary art; the sisters often appear on either side of Osiris on mummy cases in the British Museum. This myth provides an iconographic dimension to Isa and Mrs. Manresa standing on either side of Giles wearing his blood-stained tennis shoes after his dubious victory over the toad-eating snake. But the more salient dimension of Manresa's adultery with Isa's husband is its personal symbolic import for the writer herself: Woolf's literary intention and technique whereby her muse, "the father of her children," as Isa thinks of Giles, could be enjoyed by someone else.

How, then, does one cope with the pain of what feels like betrayal even if a sterner voice would call it envy? If one attacks one's rival—even in disguise—how does one reconcile such an attack with larger issues of justice and "the third emotion" in Woolf's posthumously published novel: peace? The Wellsian dimension of *Between the Acts* provides a perspective—if not an antidote—to the vice or illness of envy, the writer's disease (Friedman). The Wellsian dimension of *Between the Acts* points to injustice inherent in extrapolations of class consciousness or distinction carried beyond light cast by the torch of reason, that inadequate instrument Bart Oliver will carry until its light goes out in the cave. Wells stresses how the English deliberately eliminated the native population of Tasmania by setting out poisoned meat for those who had survived previous depredations. Wells also refers to this atrocity in his *War of the Worlds* as a caution against British assumptions of innate superiority. As the Woolfs knew at the time Virginia was at work on *Between the Acts*, Nazis premised their killing of Jews on their desire for "a certain way of life." British genocide in Tasmania anticipated Nazi attempts to eradicate Jews, an announced intention of Nazi propaganda. As writers and publishers of texts, Leonard and Virginia Woolf were more likely than most people to take Hitler at his published word. Not only had they travelled in Germany after the Fascists had come to power, but they had visited Freud in London after his escape from his apartment in Vienna. The fact of genocide having been perpetrated by the British against native Tasmanians served, I suggest, as a reminder of the limits that must be set even on secret antagonisms, lest, like Blake's poisoned apple, they cause the death of a foe. Woolf, after all, saw in patriarchy and its concomitant will to power the cause of war. Moreover, Katherine Mansfield was removed from the field of battle, as Woolf felt their competition, by tuberculosis, the disease associated with heightened creativity which had also claimed Keats (Sontag). With glittering eyes and febrile cheeks reddened by afternoon fever, Mansfield would have needed less makeup; but she seems to have worn a lot.[7] Part of Mrs. Manresa's coarseness is her excessive use of artifice: "sunset light was unsympathetic to her makeup; plated it looked, not deeply interfused" (202). This Wordsworthian allusion is cousin to a phrase from Mansfield's bread and butter letter to Woolf: "Thank you for letting me see wonderful Asheham. It is very wonderful and it will flash upon my inward eye forever"[8]

At the end of the pageant Mrs. Manresa's eyes "were wet; for an instant tears ravaged her powder" despite her having calmly faced herself in mirrors held by the jerkily dancing children not long before (189). The megaphonic voice with the insistency of a Greek chorus has exhorted the audience not to let "the laying on of paint" protect them. "Or presume there is innocence in childhood. Consider the sheep" (187). Sheep gambol through *Between the Acts* from the sheep bone found in the fishpond that Mrs. Manresa prefers to accept as a relic of "the drowned Lady Ermyntrude" (45) to the sheep Lucy Swithin assumes to be part of an eternal harmony we will one day hear (175). Sheep gambol on the landscape of New Zealand and its neighboring island, Tasmania.

Despite Isa's antagonism toward Mrs. Manresa, she "silently" acknowledges her rival's eye for ornament in "that really adorable little straw hat" (32). (Mansfield had written "shopping hats or committing adultery" as grammatically equal ways she didn't waste her "precious time" in the letter quoted above.) Isa also acknowledges her rival's genuineness when she describes removing her stays to roll on the grass. But, "the wild child's" notion that squatting adds to her charm corresponds to Wells's presentation of the primitive as in his frequent references to squatting places.

Katherine Mansfield's adulthood was, to be candid, lived out in a series of dwellings scarcely removed from squatting places. Though her father was a Wellington businessman who went on to become a director of the Bank of New Zealand, Mansfield herself did not enjoy a share of his material prosperity. Her constrained circumstances were, moreover, exacerbated by her husband J. Middleton Murry's lower middle class parsimoniousness. To what extent Mansfield inwardly acknowledged inferiority at the center of British class consciousness, if she did at all, is difficult to assess. That Virginia Woolf was alert to the probability of such feelings is suggested by her portrait in *The Waves* of Louis's misery not only because his father was a banker who failed in Brisbane, but because he does not sound like the others.

It is unrealistic to expect that Woolf was herself free from what citizens of the United States regard as the blight of class consciousness. More relevant is what she found in her heart and craft to do with it. Lucy Swithin, who incurs Giles' longstanding wrath by her contempt for trade, in speaking of "savages who wished most oddly, for were they not beautiful naked? to dress and live like the English" (47), voices an attitude not far removed from Woolf's own toward non-English people. Recall, for example, Woolf's angering Elinor Wylie by suggesting that all Americans should write like Ring Lardner as well as her ridicule for the Anglo-aping ways of Henry James and "Great Tom" Eliot.

Woolf did acknowledge in her last novel a kind of grudging sisterhood with an old antagonist by praising her life force while also spotlighting the accidental irritations: her vulgarity and what Woolf took to be her exaggerated sexuality (a popularly suspected concomitant of tuberculosis). At the same time, Woolf could gloat with the satisfaction of the survivor, that time had been on her side, that she had outdistanced her rival in volume as well as in experimental audacity; though, perhaps, she remained reluctant to concede that she and Mansfield had worked at "the same job." Katherine Mansfield was for Virginia Woolf a vulgar interloper from Down Under, but one to whom she found it easier to be generous after the passage of decades. Perhaps Woolf was willing to admit that it was really "very curious and thrilling" that they "should both, quite apart from each other, be after so very nearly the same thing." Perhaps Virginia Woolf no longer wanted to deny it. She had privately admitted something of the kind when she wrote of observing audience reaction to a Diaghilev Ballet that was part of a variety bill:

> What a queer fate it is—always to be the spectator of the public, never part of it. This is part of the reason I go weekly to see K.M. up at Hampstead, for there at any rate we make a public of two (*Diary*, 1:222, Nov. 30, 1918).

There, despite an infelicitous repetition of words uncharacteristic of her, Woolf has let us into her innermost mind and heart. How often is one's perspective—never mind one's work—comprehended by another?

Notes

¹See Ann L. McLaughlin, "An Uneasy Sisterhood: Virginia Woolf and Katherine Mansfield, *Virginia Woolf: A Feminist Slant*, ed., Jane Marcus (Lincoln: U of Nebraska P, 1983), 152-161.

²See Evelyn Fox Keller and Helene Moglen, "Competition and Feminism: Conflicts for Academic Women," *Signs* 12 (1987): 493-511. The article opens:
> We undertook this project because we believed that the subject was too important to ignore. We thought that we were cool and detached enough—secure enough, also, in our friendship—to handle it with equanimity.
> We were naive. Although we feel that we have only begun to tap into some of the issues that make this topic so disturbing, we know that we did tap deeply enough into the hidden roots of competition to experience substantial fear—both in what we write about and in our relations to each other as we wrote (493).

³Katherine Mansfield, 14 A.L.S. to Virginia Woolf [Aug 1917 — Aug 1919], Berg Collection 64B5105. In the collection of Mansfield's letters edited by John Middleton Murry, this letter is dated August, 1917 (p. 61).

⁴Katherine Mansfield to Virginia Woolf. Letter cited above in n.5.

⁵See V. A. Kolve's *Chaucer and the Imagery of Narrative: The First Five Canterbury Tales* (1984) for a relevant demonstration of method.

⁶See my "Isis Unveiled: Virginia Woolf's Use of Egyptian Myth" in *Virginia Woolf: A Feminist Slant*, ed., Jane Marcus (Lincoln: U of Nebraska P, 1983), 109-131 and "The Anti-Madonna in the Work and Thought of Virginia Woolf" in *Virginia Woolf: Centennial Essays*, ed., Elaine Ginsberg and Laura Gottlieb (Troy, NY: Whitston, 1983), 93-109.

⁷Ann McLaughlin writes, "Mansfield may have become accustomed to rather theatrical makeup because of her work as a mimic. She supplemented her meager income by giving imitations of well-known people at London parties (160, n. 5).

⁸Katherine Mansfield, Letter to Virginia Woolf quoted above in n.5.

Works Cited

Friedman, Bonita. "Envy, the Writer's Disease." *New York Times Book Review* 26 Nov. 1989: 1, 35-37.

Sontag, Susan. *Illness as Metaphor*. New York: Farrar, Straus, & Giroux, 1978.

Woolf, Virginia. *A Writer's Diary*. Ed., Leonard Woolf. London: Hogarth Press: 1959.

———. *Between the Acts*. London: Hogarth Press, 1941.

———. "Class Distinctions." Unpublished essay. Berg Collection.

———. *Melymbrosia*. NY: NY Public Library, 1982.

"A Rope to Throw the Reader": The Reading of Rhythm in Virginia Woolf

A Discussion moderated by Patricia Laurence with John Briggs; Elizabeth Cabot; Leslie K. Hankins; Beth C. Schwartz; Marilyn Zucker.

This panel explored various definitions and aspects of "rhythm" in the *Diary, Essays,* and novels of Virginia Woolf. The moderator introduced various definitions of "rhythm" in the novel including Virginia Woolf's remarks in a letter to Vita Sackville-West: "Style is a simple matter; it is all rhythm. Once you get that, you can't use the wrong words. But on the other hand here am I sitting after half the morning, crammed with ideas, and vision and so on, and can't dislodge them for the lack of the right rhythm. Now this is very profound, what rhythm is, and goes far deeper than words" (*Letters* 3.247). Observing that the manuscript of *To the Lighthouse* reveals many incomplete sentences, Pat Laurence suggested that when Woolf was not propelled by the right rhythm or "the wave of the mind" that John Briggs discussed, she used a kind of shorthand until she could find it. Various studies of rhythm in the novel (some relating to music) suggest pattern, variation and mystery in this device. The vocabulary—perhaps—for describing certain aspects of the novel is still inadequate: "most words" states Woolf, "are provisional... many metaphorical and some on trial for the first time." Undaunted by the elusive aspects of "rhythm," the panelists explored its varied dimensions using passages from Woolf's texts to ground the discussion.

Marilyn Zucker initiated the panel discussion asking "Why does the conveyance of actual lived-in-the-world rhythm seem incompatible with the movements of Woolf's rhythmic prose?" Dr. Zucker contrasted the incantatory passages of *The Waves* and *Flush* compared to the mixed rhythms of *Orlando* and the unrhythmic, conventionally-narrated *Roger Fry*. She began a discussion of the female voice in writing which Beth Schwartz continued.

Beth Schwartz spoke of rhythm and gender and genre in *The Waves*. By writing to a rhythm, Professor Schwartz claims that Woolf achieved two goals: "First, she begins to fashion a new genre. In the margin of the Holographs, for instance, she writes, 'the author would be glad if the following pages were not read as a book' . . . And second, she creates a genre that is specifically female, having its source in the body and the song of the mother . . . 'the original song' suppressed by oedipal history."

John Briggs discussed "What is a mood wave" in *The Waves*, noting the way it operates at different scales—sentence level, character, overall structure. Professor Briggs cited interesting current theories on the nature of mental states and the neurological operations of the brain, and illustrated how they might work in Woolf's fiction. He asks, as earlier panelists did, what critical language we could develop to describe the elusive states of mind, consciousness and rhythm that preoccupied Woolf, and that would open up rather than close off analysis.

Elizabeth Cabot discussed the creative rhythms of mind of Miss LaTrobe in *Between the Acts*, and the unresolved tensions and rhythms in this last unrevised novel of Woolf's. Professor Cabot views Miss La Trobe, in some ways, as the alter ego of Woolf, and "the pageant and this novel extend the counterpoint between rhythmical and narrative structures that was intrinsic to Woolf's later work." Miss LaTrobe's nervous intensity as an artist is not resolved (personally or artistically) into a harmonious rhythm at the conclusion of the novel.

Leslie Hankins focused on "the rhythms of motion and emotion in Woolf's aesthetics." In a stimulating discussion of "spatial aesthetics," citing the work of the London Film Society, René Clair and Woolf's own essay on "The Cinema" (1926), Dr. Hankins illuminated how Woolf experimented with the intersections between motion and emotion as textual forces, and how this parallelled her interest in film theory. Presenting passages from the *Diary*, bracketed sections from the "Time Passes" section of *To the Lighthouse*, and stills from *Dr. Caligari*, Dr. Hankins argued persuasively about the influence of film on Woolf's "moving aesthetics."

All panelists argued that rhythm is an elusive, unexplored, and exciting dimension of Woolf's work.

John Briggs
Nuance, Metaphor and the Rhythm of the Mood Wave in Virginia Woolf

In "A Sketch of the Past," Virginia Woolf recalled what she described as her "first memory":

> ... in fact it is the most important of all my memories. If life has a base that it stands upon, if it is a bowl that one fills and fills and fills — then my bowl without a doubt stands upon this memory. It is of lying half asleep, half awake, in bed in the nursery at St. Ives. It is of hearing the waves breaking, one, two, one, two, and sending a splash of water on the beach; and then breaking, one, two, one, two, behind the yellow blind. It is of hearing the blind draw its little acorn across the floor as the wind blew the blind out. It is of lying and hearing the splash and seeing this light, and feeling, it is almost impossible that I should be here; of feeling the purest ecstasy I can conceive (75).

Woolf went on to say that she could "spend hours trying to write that as it should be written, in order to give the feeling which is even at this moment very strong in me. But I should fail (unless I had some wonderful luck): I dare say I should only succeed in having the luck if I had begun by describing Virginia Woolf herself." Lyndall Gordon says of this early memory, "Years later, [Woolf] wanted the waves' rhythm to sound all through her greatest books, *To the Lighthouse* and *The Waves*" (43). Whether this memory was of an actual event or was a screen memory cast up out of Woolf's unconscious, the St. Ives image captures in an amazingly concentrated form a vibration that ripples through all her fiction. One of the subtler ways it ripples is through a Woolfian phenomena that might be called "the mood wave."

The mood wave is a constant and recurring narrative rhythm in Woolf's fiction. Typically, a character will begin a rumination in a positive frame of mind about her life; her mood will swell to exaltation or "rapture" (as Woolf sometimes called it), until within a few words or sentences or pages the mood will crash into a discovery of some oppressive dimension of the rumination. Or, if the mood has begun with a depressing insight, the wave rises and swells into ecstasy. Sometimes the mood of a single character rises and collapses in this way for pages.

Take as an example Bernard's final soliloquy (or aria) in the last pages of *The Waves*: Sitting at a dinner table, fresh from a contemplation of "the old brute," "the hairy man" who squats inside him, Bernard begins to rise above his body toward a moment of ecstasy [the wave swells] until he says:

> "When I look down from this transcendency, how beautiful are even the crumbled relics of bread! What shapely spirals the peelings of pears make—how thin, and mottled like some sea-bird's egg. Even the forks laid straight side by side appear lucid, logical, exact; and the horns of the rolls which we have left are glazed, yellow-pated, hard. I could worship my hand even, with its fan of bones laced by blue mysterious veins and its astonishing look of aptness, suppleness and ability to curl softly or suddenly crush—its infinite sensibility" (290).

The Reading of Rhythm in Virginia Woolf

For the next three paragraphs, Bernard reviews his life (once again) and thinks of himself as "a temple, a church" [The mood wave curls and begins to break up but does not crash.] Then, catching sight of himself, an elderly man in the mirror:

"Lord, how unutterably disgusting life is! What dirty tricks it plays us, one moment free; the next, this. Here we are among the bread crumbs and the stained napkins again. That knife is already congealing with grease ..." (292).

[The wave falls.] Bernard laments that "the wave has tumbled me over, head over heels, scattering my possessions. . ."

No need to worry, however; within a page he has regained "the sense of the complexity and the reality and the struggle" [and is riding the swell again].

Amid this rising and crashing of mood, consider Woolf's sentence contained in the up-wave motion where Bernard contemplates his hand. Perhaps the reader is just a little shocked to hear that the hand could "curl softly or suddenly crush." The "suddenly crush" is a kind of crash to the wave of that particular sentence. Woolf's mood waves function at *different scales*: on the level of the novel as a whole, within sections, within sentences. Adherents to the ideas of "chaos theory" might call this *the fractal nature of Virginia Woolf*: Like real waves—which even as they are rising and seem coherent, are, in fact, dissipating and incipient with the very disorder that will soon bring them down—Woolf's mood waves contain wavelets, and wavelets within wavelets, a fractal structure. This rhythmic action—and the rhythmic eddying action within action—imbues her work with its paradoxical atmosphere of both infinite variety and wholeness. The mood wave rhythm is key to Woolf's unfolding of her characters (their lives are composed of such waves) and provides her with a substitution for the conventional plot structure (here the reader turns the page to see, in effect, how the wave will crash, or rise: Woolf's narrative provides the contemplative fascination of the seashore).

Thus, it is evident that from the predominating presence

and pulse of waves in *To the Lighthouse* and *The Waves* to the metaphor of the sea as "growing up" in her first book, *The Voyage Out*, the remembered half-awake, half-asleep moment in the St. Ives nursery must have contained for Woolf an ambience, a nuance or subtle reality which was an endless source of inspiration, in fact, an endless source of novelistic technique. She could return to it again and again from different angles and never exhaust it. In new sentences, new characters, new books she tried new tacks and gave her readers new glimpses of this nuance, which evoked the wavelike movement of consciousness and being itself. This nuance was, for Woolf, a vast hidden reality which she felt it was her task to discover and share with her readers. It was the seed crystal of what she called her "vision."

There are several possible related reasons for Woolf's extensive use of the mood wave rhythm to express her vision. It seems likely that the "hidden reality" Woolf wanted to portray was a single ground experience, neither optimistic nor pessimistic, neither up nor down—neither and yet both—a state of being *beyond* the fluctuations of mood or deep within them. The being beyond mood was possibly what Woolf meant by her concept of the "moment of being." Of the three examples she gave in "A Sketch of the Past" of early "moments of being" in her own life, she said that "two of these moments ended in a state of despair. The other ended, on the contrary, in a state of satisfaction" (83). Her tally suggests that it is not the mood itself that matters, but the way in which a mood—whether positive or negative—punctures the surface of everyday life, shatters for an instant habits of mind and emotion, and reveals the essence beneath. Or perhaps the "being" of such moments lies in glimpsing the mortal fact that thought and perception are forward-going even when revisiting memory—that they are an irrevocable yet recurring process—hence the wave. Or perhaps because language is linear in that we read sentences, paragraphs and pages going from one end to the other, a mood wave rising and falling, swelling and collapsing and swelling again through the narrative is a good and efficient way for an author to express within the linear constraints of language a sense of the nonlinear wholeness of a universe that unites without seam such vast and trivial forces as planetary motion, gravity, water, tides and the little girls in nurseries who lie awake to perceive them. Here, again, one may

The Reading of Rhythm in Virginia Woolf

appeal to the insights of chaos theory which posits that the material universe is in fact not linear process so much as a continuous simultaneous event in which everything causes everything else. In short, perhaps in the mood wave Woolf found a strategy for using the one-foot-in-front-of-the-other simplification of language to express her perception of the absolute simultaneous continuity of life.

The mood wave may also have been a good way for Woolf to describe the subtle movement of her experience of her own creativity, and hence the essence of consciousness itself. Though we have come to think of creativity as a comparatively rare state in human consciousness, some scientists believe it is, in fact, the state that underlies consciousness itself.

At this date, there are a number of neuroscientific hypotheses challenging the popular belief that the brain is a wet-ware computer. Proposing various mechanisms, these several hypotheses (for example, those of Gerald Edelman, William Gray, Paul LaViolette, Karl Pribram, Matti Bergström, and Gerald Holton) focus on what one of the brain theorists calls waves of "emotional nuance" underpinning cognitive activity: Nuance, to use William Gray's term, is not primitive or atavistic brain activity, according to those theories; it is a primary if extremely subtle brain function. In the new perspective, the cerebral cortex is viewed as a limitation as much as an enhancement of conscious awareness. The much vaunted cortex narrows down and inhibits—selects from, simplifies—the range and depth of the primary state. According to the theory developed by Gray and elaborated by Paul LaViolette, consciousness works as follows (Briggs, *Fire* 48-56).

Feelings are basic, Gray says: anger, rejection, fear, loss, joy, astonishment. Between and among them exists a huge variety of possible shades and combinations: nuances. These nuances are products of the fact that sensations and feelings are constantly pouring through our brains in a cascade that comes both from inside the envelope of our physiology and from outside it. Brain regions "below" the cortex circulate this input in a global way. The spinal cord, midbrain and reticular activating system constitute the so-called "reptilian brain" located in the brain stem and governing such basic facets of consciousness as attention and arousal. Around this is wrapped the so-called "old mammalian brain" comprising the limbic system, made up of a number of brain "organs" involved in emotion. The limbic system includes, for example, the hypothalamus, which is known to be the seat of pleasure, and its neighbor, the amygdala, the site of rage. Sites for the visceral functions, heart rate, blood pressure, respiration, digestive activity and hormone levels are also located in the limbic system, hence a literal connection between our emotions and our digestion, between the feeling of love and the quickening heart. The hippocampus, another limbic organ, retrieves long-term memory from storage and turns short-term memories into long-term form. The hippocampus is particularly active during dreaming. The limbic system is also involved in integrating memories from a variety of senses. Thus emotion, which the limbic system controls, includes a complex mix of inner sensations, memories and movements from one state of inner sensation to another.

The neocortex, the so-called "new mammalian brain," is the great outer shell of cells that has evolved above the other two brains and is responsible for the kind of abstraction we associate with high-level (human) thought and perception. Abstracting is our ability to formulate categories, to know that the maple and birch in our backyard, though vastly different entities, are both "trees." The prefrontal part of the cortex is also involved in the emotional responsiveness we associate with intentionality. Individuals who have had connections between the frontal lobes of the cortex and the limbic system severed—a frontal lobotomy—lose creativity and emotional affect; their personalities become flat. LaViolette hypothesizes that the fate of nuance depends on a series of interlocking loops of electrical activity circulating among the reptilian, old mammalian and new mammalian brains.

Imagine young Virginia Stephen lying in the nursery at St. Ives. The movement of the blind and the sound of its cord weight scraping on the floor activate her arousal system, the reptilian brain. Feedback loops coming from the auditory canal to the reptilian brain pass up through the cortex and down into the old mammalian limbic areas, stimulating the release of neurotransmitters that increase her heart rate. The emotional centers of her limbic system are in full swing, drenched with information about her momentary sense of pleasure and pain, the state of her internal chemistry.

The Reading of Rhythm in Virginia Woolf

New mammalian cortical areas are also quite active. A famous series of experiments established that the visual cortex located at the top back of the brain is designed to recognize or abstract certain patterns, like straight lines and circles. Other research suggests that the rest of the cortex is similarly designed. Thus in Virginia's cortex, the angle of the blind, the rhythmic patterns of the waves are being abstracted out and transmitted through the brain as sensory information.

In *The Interpersonal World of the Infant*, Daniel Stern reports evidence that "affective and cognitive processes cannot be readily separated" in an infant, so that even these abstractions originating in the sensory processing parts of the cortex are entirely infused with the electrical activity of the feelings originating in the limbic system. Stern also says that even such basic sensory distinctions as whether something is being seen or heard have not yet been etched in the brain as they will be later on in the child's development. Woolf herself confirms this. She said of her early memories, that if she could depict them, "Everything would be large and dim; and what was seen would at the same time be heard; sounds would come through this petal or leaf—sounds indistinguishable from sights" ("Sketch" 76).

According to LaViolette, raw sense data passes through the thalamus into the limbic system where it circulates around and around in the Papez circuit, a closed-loop network of neurons connecting the limbic organs of the mammalian brain. There they generate what he and Gray call an emotional "theme." Similar to a musical theme, which is composed of an organized pattern of musical notes, an emotional "theme" is composed of a pattern of "feeling tones" or nuances.

The evolving collection of feeling tones or "themes" circulating in the Papez circuit of young Virginia Stephen's subconscious would have included many nuance-laden sense impressions from other days: for example, her relationship to her mother, Julia, associations with the smell of the room, memories of feelings of security and insecurity evoked by the sights and sounds and sensations around and inside her. In "A Sketch of the Past," Woolf noted, for instance, that her mother would come out in a white dressing gown onto the balcony which connected the nursery to her mother's and father's bedroom.

LaViolette proposes that sense data and emotional nuances

physically manifest as neuroelectric waveforms. As these waveforms circulate through the Papez circuit and pass through the hippocampus, they evoke long-term memories having waveforms with similar feeling tone characteristics. These memories, in turn, become part of the evolving nuance "theme." In Woolf's case, the angle of light, the beat of the surf on the beach would have activated memories with similar tags or waveforms, waveforms which might have included the sound of her mother's footsteps or the ghostly sight of her dressing gown in the wind. Together these would circulate and build as a rich "theme" of nuance-riddled sense and memory waveforms. Gray says of "themes," "Wondering is an essential aspect of emotional nuances [and] emotional themes... There is always a questioning, a wondering, an incompleteness...." In the normal course of events, however, this wondering and incompleteness is obscured by the transformation of the "theme" into an organization of thought—into what LaViolette calls an "emotional-cognitive structure."

Woolf wrote that her feeling in the nursery was "due partly to the many months we spent in London. The change of nursery was a great change. And there was the long train journey; and the excitement. I remember the dark; the lights; the stir of going up to bed" ("Sketch" 76). Suppose that the nursery room feeling tone had activated in Virginia Stephen a set of feeling tones involved in the large "theme" of nuances that included her feeling about her St. Ives summers. This "theme," circulating mostly below the level of awareness, would contain countless sensory fragments impregnated with emotional nuance. Over time these nuances constantly would be modified by other nuances, so that the "theme" would vary in a complex way—shifting like sand in an undertow. This subtle shifting of the nuance "theme" is just the kind of movement Virginia Woolf would later depict in her mood waves.

LaViolette suggests that the "theme" circulating in the Papez circuit of the limbic system enters a second loop communicating between a portion of the thalamus and the prefrontal regions of the cortex in the new mammalian brain. This "prefrontal-cortex-dorsomedial-thalmic loop" (PCDT loop, for short) abstracts or filters out certain nuances and amplifies them, and reintroduces them into the Papez circuit: Woolf's feeling of

The Reading of Rhythm in Virginia Woolf

happiness at the sound of the waves would be an example of an abstracted set of nuances. Happiness was only one facet of all she felt that day and only a small aspect of the larger "theme" of things she felt and experienced about her summers at St. Ives. But in the brain a small movement can become rapidly amplified.

LaViolette includes himself among a number of scientists who see the brain as a nonlinear system. In nonlinear systems relatively small events can trigger immense consequences. Nonlinearity operates like the proverbial straw that breaks the camel's back. A system goes along in a fairly stable way until some relatively insignificant element coming at just the right (or wrong) time transforms it. With each cycling through the prefrontal cortex, the idea of happiness at St. Ives might be abstracted and amplified until it suddenly massively transformed the content of the theme. The result would be the thought, "I was happy at St. Ives." This thought, or emotional-cognitive structure, would be an abstraction from various memories and sensory fragments in the circulating "theme" coupled with the accompanying organizing feeling (thought), "I was happy then." The nuances, all the rest of the complex of emotion and perception, are still there, but they now lie in the shadow of this abstraction. "Thoughts are sort of cartoons of reality," says LaViolette. "Once formed they shape the way we perceive the world. When we look at a tree, we're filtering the stream of sense data through a stereotyped thought pattern, the pattern we're accustomed to. As a result, there's a lot of data there that never comes to our consciousness." Gray's and LaViolette's notion that even simple cognition has a complexity of nuance behind it seems validated by research indicating that it is much more difficult to recall facts you learned if you're not in the same mood you were in when you learned them.

Although the newly emergent thought dominates the content of the "theme," as the "theme" continues to circulate the possibility remains that another nuance may become amplified and may reorganize the whole circulating complex into another thought such as, "I wasn't so happy then."

However, the birth of a thought that she was happy or not happy at St Ives is, as we know, not what happened to Virginia Woolf. Woolf apparently didn't (or couldn't) simplify (abstract) her experience into a definite thought. So what she remembered was not a cognition, but the whole complex "theme" itself with all its nuances. She said this memory of St. Ives supported something you could fill and refill, a bottomless bowl. The memory had for her, in Gray's terms, a "wonder" and "incompleteness." The exact emotion she felt could not be defined in thoughts: It was an emotion that contained wonder, fragility, happiness, vastness, security, insecurity—and more. Nuance in the sense that Woolf experienced it was, therefore, a brain state that was not mainly thought but also not mainly feeling, and not mainly perception. It was rather a state in which feelings, thoughts, memories and perceptions were one.

Such a state is difficult to describe and is riddled with paradoxes. Certainly one of the paradoxes here is that Woolf has chosen to express that state with language. One would expect that employing language to think and write about the nuances infusing a childhood memory would tend to convert the feeling tones more quickly into a closed emotional-cognitive structure. Yet in Woolf's case, language seemed actually to enrich her thematic nuances. For example, she claimed that she often pictured the nursery scene to herself as "lying in a grape and seeing through a film of semi-transparent yellow"—a linguistic abstraction that ramifies the nuances of the scene rather than simplifying them. The obvious reason is that her language is metaphoric. Jean Love offers insight into how Woolf came to use language and thought this way.

Woolf, like Einstein, was late in learning to speak and admitted that as an adult, words sometimes seemed like meaningless sounds to her. This suggests that, like Einstein, Woolf retained and, indeed carefully cultivated, the ability to resist formation of the simple cartoons of thought; instead she flooded her brain with the emotion and sense data of pre-thought, what is sometimes called intuition. In fact, in a letter to Vita Sackville-West she described intuition in terms of the rhythm of a deep emotion, and her description fits quite aptly Gray's and LaViolette's idea of the complex of emotional nuance that lies behind cognition. She wrote:

> Now this is very profound, what rhythm is, and goes
> far deeper than words. A sight, an emotion, creates

The Reading of Rhythm in Virginia Woolf

this wave in the mind, long before it makes words to fit it; and in writing ... one has to recapture this, and set this working (which has nothing apparently to do with words) and then, as it breaks and tumbles in the mind, it makes words to fit it (*L* 3:247).

At one level, then, one might say that the mood-wave was the inner pulse of the limbic system itself as it coursed through her brain laden with sense data. But there is clearly another level having to do with language, the point at which the deep mood wave meets cognition (or a kind of cognition) and makes the words to "fit it."

T.S. Eliot had said something similar:

That a poem, or a passage of a poem, may tend to realize itself first as a particular rhythm before it reaches expression in words, and that this rhythm may bring to birth the idea and the image; and I do not believe that this is an experience peculiar to myself. (qtd. in Harding 87)

Woolf said that words (cortex phenomena), which seemed at one moment "opaque" could also suddenly come together in her mind (as metaphor) and, when words did come together, they would become "transparent," as if the objects of experience shone through them. So while for the most part, language is like a flexible, hugely cross-indexed Rolodex to manage the world's complexity, Woolf used metaphorical language as a means to grasp what she said was the painful and shocking "nonreality"— a shadowy world of nuances which she felt lay hidden behind the appearance of the scenes around her. When she tuned in to the rhythm of the mood wave, metaphors emerged with which she believed she could make that nonreality a reality and so take away its power to hurt. By giving the complex of emotional nuance a voice through metaphoric language that others of her species could share, she could find some solace from her feeling that she was, as Jean Love puts it, "the result of a protoplasmic accident."

But, paradoxically, the same rhythm which united her with her fellow creatures also revealed the essential anonymity of individuals immersed in a pulsing, changing sea of nuance at the basis of being. "We can become anonymous through rhythm," she said ("Anon."). So anonymity was a cherished state for her, the source of truth, creativity, individuality and unity, the source of the "common mind."

For an artist, expressing nuance *qua* nuance (and not as a cognitive structure) is the essence of creativity. By focusing on the rhythmic movement of the mood wave, Woolf was able to give nuance and therefore "being" a shape. Her rhythmic juxtaposition of up-waves and down-waves has a dynamic that is the rhythmic analogue of metaphoric juxtapositions uniting apparent logical dissimilars. The mood wave is like the faint fractal lines on the sand which are left behind by retreating of waves of the sea at St. Ives—an inspiring record of the creative joys and depressions Woolf experienced as she labored over her sentences, characters, and stories.

References

Briggs, John. *Fire in the Crucible: The Self-Creation of Creativity and Genius.* Los Angeles: Jeremy P. Tarcher, 1990.
———. *Fractals: the Patterns of Chaos: A New Aesthetic of Art, Science and Nature.* New York: Simon & Schuster, 1992.
Briggs, John and F. David Peat. *Turbulent Mirror: An Illustrated Guide to Chaos Theory and the Science of Wholeness.* New York: Harper Collins, 1989.
Briggs, John and Richard Monaco. *Metaphor: The Logic of Poetry.* New York: Pace University Press, 1991.
Gordon, Lyndall. *Virginia Woolf: A Writer's Life.* New York: W.W. Norton, 1984.
Harding, D. W. *Words into Rhythm.* Cambridge: Cambridge University Press, 1976.
Love, Jean O. *Virginia Woolf: Sources of Madness and Art.* Berkeley: University of California, 1977.
Woolf, Virginia. "A Sketch of the Past" in *Moments of Being.* Edited by Jeanne Schulkind. London: Granada, 1976.
———. "'Anon.' and 'The Reader' Virginia Woolf's Last Essays." Edited with an introduction and commentary by Brenda R. Silver. *Twentieth Century Literature* 25, 3 & 4 (Fall/Winter): 356-438.
———. *The Letters of Virginia Woolf.* Vol. 3. Edited by Nigel Nicolson; Joanne Trautman, assistant editor. London: Hogarth Press, 1975-80.
———. *The Waves.* New York: Harcourt Brace, 1959.

Woolf and War

Andy Delohery and Gail Fay

This panel focused on Woolf's lifelong anti-war message in the context of the war to "liberate" Kuwait which had just been concluded and the victory celebration that followed. The panelists presented a slide show juxtaposing images of patriotic fervor and headlines of the war with passages from Woolf's works.

In the Persian Gulf, the United States becomes the world's policeman. In *Between the Acts*, Woolf offers a satiric view of the English policeman who personifies the established hierarchy. His function is to "give 'em what's due ... Over thought and religion; drink; dress; manners; marriage too," wielding his "truncheon." The squintingly hot, bright trail of an inbound missile over a Saudi Arabian city recalls the "beak of brass, the arid scimitar of the male" that assaults Mrs. Ramsay in *To the Lighthouse*. The soldier attired in his uniform standing firm against the enemy's onslaught brings back Woolf's *Three Guineas'* descriptions of men clothed in the constructs of their office, the bits of feather and gold braid. Endless pictures of boys and men marching in units, bereft of individuality, harken back to *Mrs. Dalloway:* "boys in uniforms, carrying guns."

Hearing leaders in the U.S. Congress orating for national unity against a common enemy we hear Woolf's quandary over whose nation the men are talking about. When the Senator says, "I am fighting to protect our country," Woolf responds, "What does our country mean to me, an outsider?" Woolf's insights have become timeless critiques of the patriarchal hierarchy and how it keeps itself in power. The rules are set by men. Anyone who would succeed must strive within those rules. When they do, they become those men and strengthen the system.

In the atmosphere of jingoism and patriotism stirred up by the Gulf War, who could dare to suggest that there is a better way to resolve the issue than age-old combat? It was good enough for our fathers, so it is good enough for us. The glorification of war, with its carnival-like spectacles of speeches and parades, affects children with the message that war is good.

A general discussion with the audience followed the slide show, with many participants expressing their fear of speaking out against the war and the feeling that the patriarchy described by Woolf has now become neither male nor female. Women have entered the corridors of power from which issue the thunderous, hypnotizing cannon (and canon) fire of patriotism, domination and heroic "leaders."

Intertextualities: Woolf, Dostoevsky, Yourcenar and Weldon

Penny Colburn-McGuire
Interiors: Woolf and Dostoevsky

Virginia Woolf was profoundly influenced by the works of Dostoevsky. She published two essays in 1917 on Dostoevsky entitled "A Minor Dostoevsky," and "More Dostoevsky," evidencing her clear understanding of his genius.

Dostoevsky wrote the most profound psychological novels of the nineteenth century, predating Freud by more than fifty years. His complex characters were drawn through the use of interior monologues, the ancestor of the modern stream of conscious novel.

The Idiot, written in 1873, and *Mrs. Dalloway*, written in 1925, both focus on the psychology of interior lives. The many similarities between these two works demonstrate Woolf's attraction to and use of Dostoevsky's ideas and techniques. She perfected her new form to express the musings, turmoils and reflections of the ordinary mind. As indicated in her essay "More Dostoevsky," she found that Dostoevsky captured ". . .those most swift and complicated states of mind"(85).

As an example, Prince Mishkin and Septimus Smith both

experience a loss of their "physicalness" and are left with a distorted sense of reality which is examined by both authors in a similar way. In addition, Prince Mishkin and Mrs. Dalloway pass through a solitary consciousness where they seem to be only observers.

These two authors took great pains to create a character that was believable and represented a common psyche. Woolf had the benefit of both Freud and Dostoevsky to help her create the psychology of her characters, to help her realize her goal as a writer.

In her essay "Mr. Bennett and Mrs. Brown" Woolf is interested in the "convincingness of the character"(193), and in "Modern Fiction" she wrote that, "For the moderns . . . the point of interest, lies in the dark places of psychology" (290). Both of these ideas she adopted from her reading the great works of Dostoevsky.

Another similarity is their preoccupation with the idea of the soul, for Dostoevsky because of its profound religious implications and for Woolf because of its profound effect on the living. Woolf wrote in "The Russian Point of View" that, "The novels of Dostoevsky are seething whirlpools, gyrating sandstorms, waterspouts which hiss and boil and suck us in. They are composed purely and wholly of the stuff of the soul" (198). She imparted to Mrs. Dalloway a sense that "the unseen part of us . . . might survive, . . . even haunting certain places after death" (231-232), a sense also felt by Prince Mishkin.

Woolf captured the essence of the mind and its hidden realities and presented this hidden reality in her novels. In reading Dostoevsky's work, Woolf discovered his psychological portraits, his ability to make real the darkness of the soul. Woolf recognized and understood this darkness and by understanding it she was able to put it into words, thereby creating her new novel.

In 1923 Woolf wrote in her diary, "one must write from deep feeling said Dostoevsky. And do I? Or do I fabricate with words, loving them as I do? No I think not" (247-248).

Works Cited

Dostoevsky, Fyodor. *The Idiot*. Ed. and trans. Eva M. Martin. London: Dent, 1929.

Woolf, Virginia. *The Diary of Virginia Woolf*. Vol. 2, 1920-1924. Ed. Anne

Olivier Bell. New York: Harvest-Harcourt, 1978.
———. "Modern Fiction." *The Virginia Woolf Reader*. Ed. Mitchell A. Leaska. San Diego: Harcourt, 1984.
———. "More Dostoevsky." *The Essays of Virginia Woolf:* Vol. 2,1912-1918. Ed. Andrew McNeillie. San Diego: Harcourt, 1987.
———. "Mr. Bennett and Mrs. Brown." *The Virginia Woolf Reader*. Ed. Mitchell A. Leaska. San Diego: Harcourt, 1984.
———. *Mrs. Dalloway*. New York: Harcourt, 1925.
———. "The Russian Point of View." *The Common Reader: First Series*. Ed. Andrew McNeillie. San Diego: Harvest-Harcourt, 1984.

Denise Marshall
Dear Reader: Intercepting Romance and Transforming Acculturation in Woolf and Weldon

Virginia Woolf claims that women wrote novels because the novel was a new form malleable and open, unrigidified by centuries of technical assumptions, aesthetic standards, and philosophical baggage. Yet this is not entirely true. The *roman* had lived a fairly chequered life even before women took up its prose format, engendering much controversy in its uses and forms. Whether the romance was realistic or no, that term came to be associated with a fairly particular set of conventions, and those conventions connected to the relationships between men and women. Thus even as women found a form open to them, they found also a form in which for a time Chloe could only like Oliver, and then only as a prospective husband, or tyrant lover, brother, or overbearing father.

Woolf's experiments in the novel moved to change this pattern, and while Fay Weldon prefers to distance herself from the moderns, and from Woolf in particular, she too disrupts this patterning of female development, acculturation and choice by subverting the formulae. Whatever the argument of female development in the so-called mainstream novel, both authors are keenly aware of the popular romance that women readers gobble.

Both confront these fictions of female desire constructing texts that render acculturation, female development, and female "innate characteristics" at the least problematical and at best ambiguous. Such problematizing creates a textual space wherein the authors can expose the mythic dimensions and silent spaces which hover around female growth, and can indict both romance and acculturation via failed sexuality, rotten or no choices, madness and the debilitating entrapment of domesticity.

Perhaps the heaviest accusation both authors make is their excoriating of female ignorance, and the muffling sense of reality that wraps young women in a blanket of confusion and disarray before they can attain the awareness of self. In delineating the effects of acculturation and the affect of the romance plot, Woolf and Weldon divert and subvert cultural norms in ambiguities, grotesqueries, and dis-ease. Using the surface FORM of romance plots served up to girls and women as their developmental niche, these authors process the Cinderellas through refining fires, cracking cultural assumptions and readers' complacent acquiesence. Woolf and Weldon re-contextualize the old culture stories; they transform the romance plot by confounding romance with reality. Thus the grotesque and hilariously surreal inhabit the not-cosy domestic world of their novels. Chaos and disaster erupt in terrifying comic events which change the lives of women. Reading these books is journeying through the parodic multiple universes women inhabit. Even as they expose the cool cruel dilemmas women face, Woolf and Weldon provide support for the leap into the unknown by transforming the pedantic and superior "dear reader" of the eighteenth century novel into the intimate nurturing speech of a woman's network where the dear reader is reader, author, lost soul, learner, and seeker in a community of women who gaze unflinchingly at their culture, and laugh.

Intertextualities: Woolf, Dostoevsky, Yourcenar and Weldon

Judith L. Johnston
"Necessary Bore" or Brilliant Novelist?: What Yourcenar Understood About Woolf's *The Waves*

On the 23rd of February, 1937, Virginia Woolf and Marguerite Yourcenar met to discuss the forthcoming French translation by Yourcenar of *The Waves*. Woolf considered the evening wasted (a "necessary bore"), but Yourcenar wasted none of the insights she gained from Woolf's text. Woolf's analysis of gender politics as well as her formal exploitation of the soliloquy influenced Yourcenar's 1939 novel, *Coup de Grâce*.

Marguerite Yourcenar (1903-1987), a French novelist, dramatist, poet, translator and essayist who lived the last 48 years of her life in the United States, is the first and still the only woman ever elected to the prestigious Académie Française. Best known for her historical novel, *The Memoirs of Hadrian* (1951), Yourcenar is one of the major literary intellects of the twentieth century. Born in Brussels of French parents, she was privately educated in a traditional curriculum. She knew and admired classical Greek and Latin literature, as well as the novels of Yukio Mishima, Henry James, and James Baldwin. She earned a living through her literature, and her list of publications is impressive: ten books of fiction, five books of poetry, six plays, five books of critical essays, and ten translations of literary texts into French—including Virginia Woolf's novel *The Waves*, Henry James's novella *What Maisie Knew*, five Japanese Noh plays, poems of the Punjabi writer Amrita Pritam, James Baldwin's *The Amen Corner*, and two volumes of American gospels, blues, and spirituals. In 1980, the divided vote that elected her to the Académie Française (twenty votes for, twelve against) indicated both the national recognition of her literary excellence and the in-group resistance to admitting an outsider: a female who was neither born in France nor living in France at the time of her election. Her work has earned her a place in world literature.

This brief essay compares Yourcenar's and Woolf's common analyses of gender politics and their different narrative forms of the soliloquy. I define politics broadly, not limited to government, but including all power relationships—at school, in sports, in military and colonial hierarchies, and in families.

125

Narrative forms as well as metaphors and plots may reflect political ideas; contemporary literary analysis can discover interlocking systems of oppression—sexism, racism, colonialism, and classism—in texts once viewed as apolitical.

The Waves is a good example. When I studied that novel in graduate school, the published and accepted criticism viewed the novel as a psychological experiment. Similarly, criticism of Marguerite Yourcenar's novel *Coup de Grâce* has viewed that novel as a study in psychological perversion. Elsewhere, I have argued that Woolf in *Between the Acts* and Yourcenar in *Coup de Grâce* offer readers a political analysis of gender differences (Johnston); here, I argue that Yourcenar understood the political analysis in *The Waves* and used Woolf's insights in *Coup de Grâce*.

In *The Waves*, the reunions of three male characters (Bernard, Neville, and Louis) and three female characters (Rhoda, Jinny, and Susan) are extraordinary precisely because they temporarily break down the exclusionary barriers that separate men's from women's lives. In *Coup de Grâce*, the two male characters, Erick and Conrad, form a bond that excludes Conrad's sister and Erick's lover, Sophie. Erick's narrative absolutely separates the masculine realm of military and political activity from the feminine realm of passivity and passion in which he views Sophie. In both novels, the men formed their bonds at school, which is where Percival becomes a hero to Bernard, Neville, and Louis. Like Percival, Erick is a leader who first rose to power at school, and who is admired by the less aggressive characters. Conrad loves Erick, just as Bernard loves Percival.

As young children, Woolf's six characters lived together; they all learned Latin and Math from Miss Hudson, and they all learned music and exercise from Miss Curry. But once the children are sent away to sex-segregated boarding schools, the barriers between genders are established. At school, the boys learn to read Greek, Latin, and to envy the popularity of bully-boys; the girls learn to practice religion and to envy the popularity of girls who appear attractive in the looking glass. The metaphor of the bully contrasts sharply with the metaphor of the looking glass. Just as the different formal curricula differentiate masculine knowledge from feminine knowledge, so the informal lessons about bullies and looking glass images establish power relationships within separate masculine and feminine worlds.

Intertextualities: Woolf, Dostoevsky, Yourcenar and Weldon

The power of "bully-boys" is acknowledged by Louis, who has already learned to identify his subordinate position within the masculine world: he is the son of a merchant, not the son of a gentleman, and he speaks self-consciously in the accents of a colonial, an outsider.

> "The boasting boys," said Louis, "have gone now in a vast team to play cricket. . . . Now they are boasting. Larpent's brother played football for Oxford; Smith's father made a century at Lords. . . . the names repeat themselves; the names are the same always. They are the volunteers; they are the cricketers; they are the officers of the Natural History Society. They are always forming into fours and marching in troops with badges on their caps; they salute simultaneously passing the figure of their general. How majestic is their order, how beautiful is their obedience! . . . But they also leave butterflies with their wings pinched off; . . . They make little boys sob in dark passages." (206-207)

The power that the "boasting boys" exhibit within the realms of sports and the military includes the sexual rape of younger, less powerful boys.

In Yourcenar's novel, Erick, the dominant leader, is adored by Conrad. Erick refuses sexual intimacy with Sophie, although he visits prostitutes, and he expresses disgust for female sexuality. At school, the relationship between Erick and Conrad included homosexual activity; after World War I, during the civil war in Latvia, Erick sees himself as a Napoleon figure, with Conrad as his subaltern. Erick is a member of the German *Freikorps*, a soldier of fortune, who fights for the Russian aristocracy against the Communist working-class revolutionaries. The dominant-submissive relationships formed within an exclusively masculine world at school continue within the military hierarchy. Similarly, Woolf's "boasting boys," once they become adults, are leaders in cultural institutions. The power of a dominant leader—such as Percival, who grows up to be a colonial administrator in India, or Erick, who chooses to be a soldier of fortune—originates on the playing fields, not from any individual superiority.

Both Percival and Erick demonstrate a leader's power they establish by divisive and exclusionary practices. Both Percival and Erick are associated with bringing order through cutting. In Yourcenar's novel, Erick himself connects his dominance and his eroticism in the image of a knife cutting through ripe fruit. In *The Waves*, when the six gather for a dinner to see off Percival, on his way to India, Neville compares Percival's arrival to a decisive moment in a children's game: paper/rock/knife. A flat open hand signifies paper, a closed fist signifies rock, and extended fingers signify knife. When Percival finally arrives, Neville says, "The reign of chaos is over. He has imposed order. Knives cut again" (260). In the children's game, the knife cuts paper. In the political culture, the one who can divide others becomes the leader. Neville admires Percival's ability to impose order by cutting.

Erick imagines Conrad as a lone horseman, riding to confront death, much as Bernard imagines Percival. But the lone horseman image also applies to Erick himself, telling this story, since he is recovering from a recent wound got while defending Franco in Spain, and he is preparing to reenter any conflict as a mercenary fighting for the side that he thinks will triumph. Conrad views Erick as a hero, but Sophie's perspective makes us see Erick as a bully, a boaster, a liar, and a sadist. Yourcenar understood and extrapolated from Woolf's analysis of the hero Percival and her critique of gender politics. Reading Yourcenar has helped me re-read Woolf's novel.

For a long time, as a reader, I could not understand why Percival was so admired, or why Percival's death was more important to the other characters' consciousness than Rhoda's death. In his final soliloquy, Bernard evokes a fearful and furtive Rhoda, when he remembers "she killed herself" (371). Rhoda was, after all, one of the six; she commits suicide in despair, and yet her death receives only passing attention from Bernard. Unlike Suzette Henke, I do not believe that "Woolf celebrates the tragic heroism of the individual," nor do I agree that "The quest itself is a form of courage" (469). Like John Hulcoop, I see Woolf presenting Percival as an "ambivalent" hero, one who "can easily

Intertextualities: Woolf, Dostoevsky, Yourcenar and Weldon

become a bully or a tyrant" (472), but I do not agree that Bernard is more admirable because he is an intellectual hero.

Bernard's admiration of Percival does analyze the origins of his power over others:

> He is conventional; he is a hero. The little boys trooped after him across the playing-fields. ... Now, when he is about to leave us, to go to India, all these trifles come together. He is a hero. Oh yes, that is not to be denied. ... We who yelped like jackals biting at each other's heels now assume the sober and confident air of soldiers in the presence of their captain. (260)

Using military metaphors, Bernard links Percival's domination of the playing-fields with his leadership in colonial India.

Bernard mistakenly identifies as love of Percival the communion felt by the six friends (262-263). Occasionally in Woolf's novel a communal perspective does unite the six characters, despite their solitary lives, but Percival's departure is the occasion, not the source of their communion. Bernard's last soliloquy embraces the language of the solitary hero, whose heroism is defined by division, by identifying those who are "against us." Bernard feels

> like the proud horse whose rider first spurs and then pulls him back. What enemy do we now perceive advancing against us, you whom I ride now, as we stand pawing this stretch of pavement? It is death. Death is the enemy. It is death against whom I ride with my spear couched and my hair flying back like a young man's, like Percival's, when he galloped in India. I strike spurs into my horse. Against you I will fling myself, unvanquished and unyielding, O Death! (383)

That is the language of heroic tragedy, and it is very different from the language of communion or Susan's language much earlier.

Like Bernard, Susan meditates on death, but she does not confront death as a solitary horseman; instead, she acts to console others in the human community:

> I also make wreaths of white flowers, twisting silver-leaved plants among them for the dead, attaching my card with sorrow for the dead shepherd, with sympathy for the wife of the dead carter; and sit by the beds of dying women, who murmur their last terrors, who clutch my hand. (308)

Susan thinks,

> I cannot be divided, or kept apart. I was sent to school; I was sent to Switzerland to finish my education. I had linoleum . . . . Let me now fling myself on this flat ground . . . . The earth hangs heavy beneath me. . . . I am not a woman, but the light that falls on this gate, on this ground. I am the seasons. (242-243)

Susan's vision is integrated with nature, but, as she ages, she gives up this integrated vision. She gets tired while raising her children, and she sees herself entrapped in a domestic existence: "I have netted over strawberry beds and lettuce beds, . . . I have seen my sons and daughters, once netted over like fruit in their cots, break the meshes" (308). The wreaths and netting are similar images; Susan twists the vines of human consciousnesses together into circles, but she is also a possessive mother who lives rooted in the material world. Susan herself recognizes this: "Yet sometimes I am sick of natural happiness, and fruit growing, and children scattering the house with oars, guns, skulls, books won for prizes, and other trophies. I am sick of the body, I am sick of my own craft, industry and cunning, of the unscrupulous ways of the mother who protects, who collects under her jealous eyes

Intertextualities: Woolf, Dostoevsky, Yourcenar and Weldon

at one long table her own children, always her own" (308-309). Invading the domestic scene are the sons' tools—"oars, guns, skulls," and prize books—which introduce the realms of sports, the military, and school competitions; Susan names no daughters' possessions. Because Susan has been educated by the culture to thrive in the natural world as a mother, entirely within the domestic and agricultural sphere, she has also been excluded from other spheres: the administration of government in India (Percival), the management of commerce in London (Louis). As presently defined, these other spheres are not necessarily desirable, because their power is oppressive—just as Susan's power as a protective mother can be oppressive, as Woolf brilliantly illustrates in her imagery of "netting" thrown over strawberry plants and children. The separate masculine and feminine spheres of power need to be redefined. The six characters feel satisfaction only in brief moments of gender-neutral communion. Percival may have been seeking the holy grail in the chapel perilous, but the solitary quest destroys the communion of the round table.

Yourcenar's novel clearly delineates the separate masculine sphere of power in the military from the feminine sphere of the home; moreover, Yourcenar emphasizes the strong homosocial and homosexual bonds among men within the military, bonds which exclude or belittle women's erotic and political passion. Sophie falls in love with Erick, who refuses to sleep with her. Sophie joins the revolution, but Erick never believes in her political commitment.

Erick's soliloquy, which narrates Yourcenar's novel, cannot be trusted. Unlike Woolf's narrative, which interweaves the six characters' voices, Yourcenar's narrative utilizes only Erick's voice. How does a reader get Sophie's perspective? Erick does quote Sophie occasionally, then denies that what she has said is true. Especially significant is his denial that she could mean the words she uses to curse him—the obscene, unladylike language is not her own, he assumes. Yourcenar provokes the reader to make an active critique of Erick's soliloquy. After Erick's implausible interpretation of events, the reader contradicts his words, correcting his obviously biased history, and even speculating on what Sophie actually said. Yourcenar has involved her reader in a dialogue. Rather than present six different soliloquies, as Woolf did in *The Waves*, allowing her reader to compare the different perspectives, but privileging Bernard as the voice that most often interprets events, Yourcenar presents a soliloquy that challenges her reader to disagree with the dominating voice. Unlike Bernard's final soliloquy, which generally provokes a reader's admiration, Erick's final soliloquy, narrating Sophie's death, provokes a reader's resistance. Erick executes the revolutionary by shooting her in the face; he fails to kill her in his first shot and must shoot a second time. His final comment is: "One is always trapped, somehow, in dealings with women." That assertion compels one to question Erick's interpretation of history.

Yourcenar learned much from translating Woolf's *The Waves*. She and Woolf have similar thematic analyses of the construction of gender politics, and Yourcenar understands the multivocal soliloquy that Woolf employed. Yourcenar, by creating Erick's soliloquy as one dominating voice that a reader must challenge, links the form of the narrative to the theme of domination. Sophie's voice has been excluded from history, but, by arguing against Erick's interpretation, a reader can refuse to be silenced, refuse to be dominated by Erick's heroic perspective on history. Yourcenar's provocation to the reader is a Woolfian strategy. I think Virginia Woolf might have understood it.

Works Cited

Henke, Suzette. "Virginia Woolf's *The Waves*: A Phenomenological Reading." *Neophilologus* 73 (1989): 461-472.

Hulcoop, John F. "Percival and the Porpoise: Woolf's Heroic Theme in *The Waves*." *Twentieth Century Literature* 34 (1988): 468-488.

Johnston, Judith L. "Marguerite Yourcenar's Sexual Politics in Fiction, 1939." in Alice Kessler-Harris and William McBrien, eds. *Faith of a (Woman) Writer*. Totowa, NJ: Greenwood Press, 1988: 221-228.

———. "The Remediable Flaw: Cultural History in *Between the Acts*." In Jane Marcus, ed. *Virginia Woolf and Bloomsbury*. Bloomington: Indiana University Press, 1987: 253-277.

Woolf, Virginia. *The Waves* 1931; rpt. New York: Harcourt, Brace & World, 1959.

Reading at Random

Catherine Nelson-McDermott
Virginia Woolf and Murasaki Shikibu:
A Question of Perception

In her essay "Women and Fiction," Virginia Woolf speaks of the history of women as writers:

> Strange spaces of silence seem to separate one period of activity from another. There was Sappho and a little group of women all writing poetry on a Greek island six hundred years before the birth of Christ. They fall silent. Then about the year 1000 we find a certain court lady, the lady Murasaki, writing a very long and beautiful novel in Japan. (*Essays* 2: 142)

In *A Room of One's Own* this becomes:

> If you consider any great figure of the past, like Sappho, like the Lady Murasaki, like Emily Bronte, you will

find that she is an inheritor as well as an originator, and has come into existence because women have come to have the habit of writing naturally. (104)

How does the Heian court author "Lady Murasaki" come to hold such an important position in Virginia Woolf's assessment of the history of women's writing, and how does Woolf come to know of this classical Japanese author? Whatever her other, rather daunting, talents, Virginia Woolf was not a Japanese scholar.[1] She comes to Murasaki Shikibu and Murasaki's text, the *Genji Monogatari*, through the auspices of Arthur Waley, a well-respected Orientalist and translator who existed rather on the outskirts of the Bloomsbury Group. Waley pops in and out of Woolf's diaries and letters but is generally ignored by her biographers. His connection with Woolf is easily passed over. She, however, seems to have read and been influenced by his translations. Woolf's preface to *Orlando*, however facetious, is suggestive of this tie: "I have had the advantage—how great I alone can estimate—of Mr Arthur Waley's knowledge of Chinese" (7). And of Japanese, I presume, as Woolf reviewed the first book of the *Genji* for *Vogue* in 1925. As late as May 18, 1929, Woolf writes to Vanessa Bell: "In duty to you I went off to Chelsea the other day, first to Mauron's lecture at Argyll House. Then to sit with the MacCarthy's, then back to dine at Argyll House, then home to bed with Waley" (*Letters* 4: 59). As something so "noteworthy" as an affair between the two would not have gone unremarked, I think I may safely assume that Woolf was reading one of Waley's translations, quite likely another of the books of the *Genji*, on which Waley worked from 1925 to 1933. If, as Woolf states, "a woman writing thinks back through her mothers" (*Room* 93), this possible influence is of more than cursory interest. Similarities between the productions of these two writers highlight the possibility of cross-cultural similarities in the ways in which women write their experiences and perceptions into literature. The following is an attempt, in the form of speculation and correlation, to etch in the lines of a link between Murasaki Shikibu's *Genji Monogatari* and Virginia Woolf's *Orlando*.

As with most of Woolf's works, *Orlando* experiences a constant grounding in the senses. To quote E.M. Forster,

> Food with [Woolf] was not a literary device put in to make the book seem real. She put it in because she tasted it, because she saw pictures, because she smelt flowers, because she heard Bach, because her senses were both exquisite and catholic... Our debt to her is in part this: she reminds us of the importance of sensation. (259)

Woolf herself speaks of sensation recall and the process of writing in *Moments of Being*:

> all these colour-and-sound memories hang together ... much more robust ... highly sensual.... [They still make] me feel warm; as if everything were ripe; humming; sunny; smelling so many smells at once; and all making a whole that even now makes me stop...The buzz, the croon, the smell all seemed to press voluptuously against some membrane. (66)

It is an aspect of this feeling which, Woolf states, makes her believe that sometimes when she writes, "The pen gets on the scent" (*Moments* 93). *Orlando*, the text, speaks in this language of physical sensation. Woolf's talent for creating the sensual feeling of the moment for the reader can be found in such passages as that in which, speaking of the "great cloud" hanging over the nineteenth century, Woolf intensifies and particularizes the feeling of the era through an insistence on the concrete and sensual:

> The chill which he felt in his legs the country gentleman soon transferred to his house... Then a change of diet became essential. The muffin was invented and the crumpet. Coffee supplanted the after dinner port... ivy grew in unparalleled profusion.... What light penetrated to the bedrooms where children were born was naturally of an obfusc green, and what light penetrated to the drawing-rooms where grown men

and women lived came through curtains of brown and purple plush. (142-3)

Such passages lead, rather naturally, to Woolf's use of "'pathetic fallacy,' [which technique she carries] to well-known fantastic lengths in *Orlando* when she identifies changes in the landscape with changes in Orlando's state of mind, literary style, and way of life in general" (Gillespie 274). Murasaki Shikibu also speaks in the sensual languages, those of "dress, of calligraphy, of floral and musical preference, of incense concoction" (Field 16). The heightened senses of the Heian courtier, as they are expressed in the *Genji Monogatari*, enable the sensitive reader to see the dew on the *yugao* flower, to actually smell the incense used by the characters and judge of its flavour, to live in the world of the Imperial court, and to gaze at the figure of Genji with the same admiration as does Murasaki. In the *Genji*, "landscape becomes a state of mind . . . . The facial and physical description that modern readers associate with character delineation is absent" (Shirane 121). This may be because Murasaki, too, creates the sensual feeling of the moment, and the juxtaposition of the moment and the character becomes more important than the description of a character's mere physical being. Genji embarks on a fatal elopement with the woman Yugao:

> They drove to an untenanted mansion . . . While he waited for the steward to come out Genji noticed that the gates were crumbling away; dense shinobu-grass grew around them. So sombre an entrance he had never seen. There was a thick mist and the dew was so heavy that when he raised the carriage-blind his sleeve was drenched. (64)

Genji himself is always recognized not by his features but by the distinctively impressive scent which continually wafts from his incensed robes.

This physical "marker" of Genji's presence and importance is an example of the way in which the protagonist is continually lauded in poetic prose by the narrators of both the *Genji* and *Orlando*. Murasaki says that, on the occasion of a celebration, "in particular the young noblemen chosen by the Emperor cut so brilliant a figure that only the lustre of Genji's beauty could have eclipsed their splendour" (158). Genji is known as "Hikaru Genji, or Genji the Shining One" (18); "his beauty astonished everyone" (19). By way of comparison, this is Orlando: "No human being, since the world began, has ever looked more ravishing. His form combined in one the strength of a man and a woman's grace" (86). He has "a pair of the finest legs that a young nobleman has ever stood upright upon; and violet eyes; and a heart of gold; and loyalty and manly charm" (15); "Never was there a woman more fitted for [the] calling [of love and relationships].... a beautiful woman, and a woman in the prime of life" (168).

A beautiful woman with manly charm—the protagonist is not always gender specific. The *Genji Monogatari*, like *Orlando*, gives a carefully structured, unabashed portrayal of a character of ambiguous sexuality who indulges in disguise and intrigue. Genji is often seen clothed as someone he is not. After a brief tryst, he emerges from a lover's room only to be accosted by:

> an old woman who worked in the house.... Seeing a grown man's figure appear in the doorway, 'Whom have you got with you?' [she] asked [Genji's servant], and then answering her own question, 'Why it is Mimbu! what an outrageous height that girl has grown to!' (51-2)

Genji's friends view him in the lamp-light:

> He was dressed in a suit of soft white silk, with a rough cloak carelessly slung over his shoulders, with belt and fastenings untied. In the light of the lamp against which he was leaning he looked so lovely that one might have wished he were a girl. (24)

Indeed, throughout the work, the sheer perfection of Genji's beauty seems "feminine." This impression is intensified by the fact that he casts himself as a mother-figure to the orphaned Murasaki (I'm speaking of the main female character here rather than the author), whom he later makes his wife. Even his sexual orientation is ambiguous:

> 'So be it,' said Genji, 'but you at least must not abandon me,' and he laid the boy beside him on his bed. He was well contented to find himself lying by this handsome young Prince's side, and Genji, we must record, found the boy no bad substitute for his ungracious sister. (46)

The traits of gender and sexual ambiguity are easily recognized in the figure of Orlando, the male writer who wakes up female one fine Augustan morning. Orlando, no matter the designated sex of the moment, fluctuates between male and female: "For it was this mixture in her of man and woman, one being uppermost and then the other, that often gave her conduct an unexpected turn" (118). Orlando's perceived change of gender (as opposed to the actual process of changing from male to female which, of course, occupies a discrete moment in the text) often amounts to little more than a change of clothes:

> Different though the sexes are, they intermix. In every human being a vacillation from one sex to the other takes place, and often it is only the clothes that keep the male or female likeness, while underneath the sex is the very opposite of what is above. (118; see also 138)

The question of male/female relationship leads, through a lateral sidestep, to a telling structural feature of both works. Here is a current critic writing with elegance and insight on the subject of Genji's relationship to women, "The eponymous hero, far from being the controlling centre of the work, is as much constituted by his heroines as they are by him. Yet, for reasons to be seen, he is curiously absent by comparison to his ladies" (Field 17). Here is a critic of some sixty-five years ago, a critic even more elegant than the last (Woolf, from her 1925 review of the *Genji*):

> To light up the many facets of his mind, Lady Murasaki, being herself a woman, naturally chose the medium of other women's minds. Aoi, Asagao, Fujitsubo, Murasaki, Yugao, Suyetsumuhana, the beautiful, the red-nosed, the cold, the passionate—one after another they turn their clear or freakish light upon the gay young man at the centre, who flies, who pursues, who laughs, who sorrows, but is always filled with the rush and bubble and chuckle of life. (53)

Orlando, too, is defined through relationships with women. His/her growth as a character is measured in his response to female figures, especially that of Sasha. From defining Sasha as an object, "a fox, an olive tree" (30), to angrily stereotyping her, a "devil, [an] adulteress, [a] deceiver" (40), to knowing "Sasha as she was" (101), to finally seeing Sasha as a link in the chain of reality, "a girl in Russian trousers" in the "pool of the mind" (204), Orlando's growing perceptiveness defines and redefines itself in ever-widening circles. Orlando is affected by his/her passion for Sasha through to the close of the tale. Sasha occurs as the epiphanal vision, prompting integration of Orlando's selves into the "present moment," but seventeen pages from the close of the work. In *Orlando*, "even minor female characters like the prostitutes Nell, Prue, Kitty and Rose have a serious dignity not bestowed on more prominent male characters" (Knopp 32), and this dignity reflects on Orlando as she interacts with these women in a more significant manner than that to be found in her interactions with the quixotic Shelmerdine. These "adjunctive" characters round out Orlando's character to make a composite picture of women as a whole; as they "like each other," and as they are opaque to men's gaze.

Hero/female interactions continue into the area of character/narrator relationships. Not only is Murasaki Shikibu present in the figure of the major heroine Murasaki (both deriving their name from Genji's mention of a young grass with purple roots [see 98]), but it is Shikibu, in a sense, who makes love most successfully to Genji. Murasaki creates in Genji her ideal male:

> the enchanting boy—the Prince who danced "The Waves of the Blue Sea" so beautifully that all the princes and great gentlemen wept aloud; who loved those whom he could not possess; whose libertinage was tempered by the most perfect courtesy; who played enchantingly with children, and preferred, as his women friends knew, that the song should stop before he had heard the end. (Woolf, "Genji" 53)

An entry from Murasaki Shikibu's diary points to the way in which she relates to the fictional Genji. Murasaki and her friend Lady Saisho are hiding behind a screen at a drunken festival:

> Presently the General of the right came and stood near the pillar on our left . . . I noticed that when the great tankard came his way he did not drink out of it, but passed it on, merely saying the usual words of good omen. At this Lord Kinto shouted: "The General is on his best behaviour. I expect little Murasaki is somewhere not far off!" "You're none of you in the least like Genji," I thought to myself, "so what should Murasaki be doing here?" (*Genji*, Waley's intro. xii)

Orlando is a similar case. The "central relationship is between Orlando and the Biographer" (29), states Sherron Knopp, who goes on to say: "Orlando and her Biographer exist in complementary balance with each other: Orlando all beauty, passion and action; her Biographer—now Keatsian, now Chaucerian, now Shakespearean—all voice and eloquence" (33). Woolf, too, intertwines her own reality and fiction; witness a letter dated Friday Nov. 4, 1927:

Shall I see Orlando next week?
Say yes.
But when?
Let me know in good time.
Was Orlando presented at Court?
  Poor Virginia
  in a
  d—d
  hurry (*Letters* 3: 434)

  The interest of both Woolf and Murasaki in the question of the "truth" of fiction seems a key similarity. The more pertinent portions of a long and highly celebrated discourse by Genji on this subject are as follows:

> There is, it seems, an art of so fitting each part of the narrative into the next that, though all is mere invention, the reader is persuaded that such things might easily have happened and is as deeply moved as though they were actually going on around him. . . . We may indeed go so far as to say that there is an actual mixture of Truth and Error. . . . Viewed in this light the novel is seen to be not, as is usually supposed, a mixture of useful truth with idle invention, but something which at every stage and in every part has a definite and serious purpose. (501-2)

The reader of Woolf is likely struck by the similarity between this and Woolf's search for a line of Truth between biography, fact, and fiction. Woolf speculates whether the method she uses in *To The Lighthouse* may not:

> serve a different use—such as: . . . in some semi-mystic very profound life of a woman, which shall be told on one occasion; & time shall be utterly obliterated; future shall somehow blossom out of the past. One incident

> —say the fall of a flower—might contain it. My theory being that the actual event practically does not exist—nor time either. (*Diary* 3: 110)

"Woolf's interest in biography," as Madeline Moore states, "was only a part of the larger aesthetic question which preoccupied her before and during the composition of *Orlando*: the question of how the dichotomy between fact and fancy affects not only biography, but the novel and poetry, and how that dichotomy might be overcome" (304). *Orlando*, as with the *Genji*, settles the question of "how to create a form that [conveys] the underlying forces of historical process... [and captures] the more evanescent growth of human consciousness and experience" (Silver 360). History and fiction become strangely one; the truth of Virginia Woolf's love for Vita Sackville-West melting into the reality of a historical process; the reality of the societal ambiance of the *Genji*, which thrills historians yet, overlaid with the truth of Murasaki's love for Genji.[2]

Here then I hope I've succeeded in conveying some of the undeniable similarities between the work of Murasaki Shikibu and that of Virginia Woolf. How much of this is influence and how much the similarities perhaps necessarily to be found in the expressions of two brilliant women struggling to bring their creations whole to birth, is difficult to say. Certainly Woolf had read Murasaki with an eye to critical analysis; certainly she was interested in many of the same themes; certainly many of Woolf's works show the intangible and untranslatable quality of *aware* (roughly the "ah-ness" of life, the wonder and sadness of human existence) so vital to the *Genji*; and certainly Woolf's final comment on Murasaki's work is one which seems often applied to the works of Woolf herself:

> not, nevertheless, a star of the first magnitude. No; the Lady Murasaki is not going to prove herself the peer of Tolstoi and Cervantes or those other great storytellers ... Some element of horror, of terror, of sordidity, some root of experience has been removed . . . so that crudeness is impossible and coarseness out of the

question, but with it too has gone some vigour, some richness, some maturity of the human spirit, failing which the gold is silvered and the wine mixed with water. All comparisons between Murasaki and the great Western writers serve but to bring out her perfection and their force. ("Genji" 53, 80)

Woolf, in her own blindly brilliant and yet insecure way, misses the importance of the place she and Murasaki create; a place where, more fortunate than Genji, one "tastes and tries all the queer savours of life" in a search for "something finer," something (perhaps a glimpse of the possibilities of a women's artistic vision) that is not, finally, "withheld" ("Genji" 80).

Notes

[1] Neither was Vanessa Bell, but when she and Duncan Grant "decorated a dinner service for Lord Kenneth Clark in the thirties using the theme of famous women, their designs for the forty-eight white Wedgewood plates formed four groups, each identified by a different design for the outer edge. The plates included ... twelve writers" among which were "Lady Murasaki, Jane Austen, and Charlotte Bronte .... also Virginia Woolf" (Gillespie 198).

[2] It is this "reality" with which Woolf is concerned in such works as *Moments of Being*. See, for example, 122.

Works Cited

Field, Norma. *The Splendour of Longing in the* Tale of Genji. Princeton: Princeton UP, 1987.
Forster, E.M. *Two Cheers for Democracy*. Harmondsworth: Penguin, 1965.
Gillespie, Diane. *The Sisters' Arts: The Writing and Painting of Virginia Woolf and Vanessa Bell*. Syracuse: Syracuse UP, 1988.
Knopp, Sherron E. "'If I Saw You Would You Kiss Me?': Sapphism and the Subversiveness of Virginia Woolf's *Orlando*." *PMLA* 103 (1988): 24-34.
Moore, Madeline. "Virginia Woolf's *Orlando*." *Twentieth Century Literature* 25: 303-55.
Murasaki Shikibu. *The Tale of Genji*. Trans. and Intro. Arthur Waley. New York: Houghton Mifflin, 1935.
Shirane, Haruo. *The Bridge of Dreams: A Poetics of the Tale of Genji*. Stanford: Stanford UP, 1987.
Silver, Brenda. "'Anon' and 'The Reader': Virginia Woolf's Last Essays." *Twentieth Century Literature* 25: 356-441.
Woolf, Virginia. *Collected Essays*. vol. 2. London: Hogarth, 1966.
———. *The Diary of Virginia Woolf*. 5 vols. Eds. Anne Olivier Bell and Andrew McNeillie. NY: Penguin, 1979-1984.

———. *The Letters of Virginia Woolf.* 5 vols. Eds. Nigel Nicolson and Joanne Trautman. New York: HBJ, 1975.
———. *Moments of Being.* Ed. Jeanne Schulkind. Toronto: Triad, 1978.
———. *Orlando.* Toronto: Triad, 1977.
———. Rev. of Arthur Waley's trans. of Murasaki Shikibu's *The Tale of Genji*. *Vogue*. July 1925: 53, 80. Reprinted in: *Literature East and West* 11, no. 4 (Dec. 1967): 424-7.
———. *A Room of One's Own.* Toronto: Triad, 1977.

Lisa Low
Two Figures Standing in Dense Violet Light:John Milton, Virginia Woolf, and the Epic Vision of Marriage

In their seminal text *Madwoman in the Attic*, Gilbert and Gubar argue that the great seventeenth century poet John Milton haunted nineteenth century women novelists, appearing before them not as a sympathetic mentor, but instead as an object of perpetual fear. Virginia Woolf put the dread most succinctly at the end of *A Room of One's Own* when she proclaimed Milton a "bogey" (118). For Woolf, Milton was not only a writer of intimidatingly gigantic stature: his point of view was also exclusively masculine. Like Ben Jonson, Milton had "a dash too much of the male" (107) in him and when he wrote, his masculine vision—a "straight dark bar, a shadow shaped something like the letter `I'"—dominated his writing so much that Woolf had to dodge "this way and that to catch a glimpse of the landscape behind it" (103). In the end Woolf writes, only "money and a room of [one's] own" (4) can substitute a clear blue sky and a view of the landscape for the "large and imposing figure of a gentleman which Milton recommended for my perpetual adoration" (39).

But this paper takes the opposite view. While Woolf sees Milton, and indeed, while Milton is often perceived in general, as the sexist nemesis par excellence, I argue that Milton had feminist sympathies, and that his project in *Paradise Lost* was in many ways similar to Woolf's in *To the Lighthouse*. Both *Paradise Lost* and *To the Lighthouse* represent the race as descending from parental figures of gigantic proportions and both describe marriage in cosmic terms as the single most important aspect of life. Mrs. Ramsay asks herself, for example, ". . .What could be more serious than the love of man for woman?" (100); and similarly, Raphael describes Adam and Eve as personifying "Which two great Sexes animate the World" (VIII, 151). Both describe the race as divided along the Mason-Dixon line of masculine and feminine and both see marriage as having the greatest potential, for happiness as well as despair.

This paper compares the vision of masculinity, femininity, and the relationship between them in *Paradise Lost* and *To the Lighthouse*, suggesting that both are modern epics arranging themselves around domestic figures of colossal importance. In both the survival of the race depends not on the warriors Achilles or Ulysses or Aeneas, but on the successful domestic partnership of male and female. Among the questions which this paper asks are: to what extent does Milton's vision of a partnership between masculine and feminine anticipate Woolf's? Had Milton, in writing what some have described as the first novel, begun to perceive the necessity of turning masculine, epic attention from war to love? Did Milton anticipate what the female novel develops, and nowhere more clearly than in Woolf, that the female is not a subordinate but a partner of epic importance?

Works Cited

Milton, John. *John Milton: Complete Poems and Major Prose*. Ed. Merritt Y. Hughes. Indianapolis: Odyssey, 1980.
Woolf, Virginia. *A Room of One's Own*. New York: Harcourt Brace, 1957.
———. *To the Lighthouse*. San Diego: Harcourt Brace, 1981.

Penny Painter
The Overlooked Influence of John Waller (Jack) Hills on Virginia Woolf

Virginia Woolf's brother-in-law John Waller (Jack) Hills had a life-long influence on Woolf's works, an influence that has been overlooked totally by the critics.

Unlike the feelings she had for her half-brothers George and Gerald Duckworth (which were understandably negative given their sexual abuse of her), Woolf's attitude toward Hills was totally and lastingly positive. It is obvious from all of her journal and letter writing that she considered Hills as a member of the family: He was George's schoolmate, a frequent visitor at St. Ives, husband to Woolf's half-sister Stella Duckworth, lived with Virginia and her family when Stella died, and served as the Stephen family solicitor for many years. In Woolf's last autobiographical attempt, "A Sketch of the Past," she said that Jack "stands in my mind's picture gallery for a type — & a desirable type," and that "Jack's honesty... penetrated to us as children." In "A Sketch of the Past," Jack is the main character in over one-fourth of the pages after his introduction. In Virginia's holographic diary from her fifteenth year, Hills plays a major role; and in her autobiographical "Reminiscences" of 1921, Hills' relationship with Woolf and his romance with her sister Vanessa after Stella's death comprise almost the entirety of the work. Woolf wrote on Jack's death that "for nine years I was intimate with Jack Hills" and that "of all our youthful directors he was the most open minded, least repressive, could have fitted in with later developments."

This paper studies Hills' influence in Woolf's novels, from her *The Voyage Out* and *Mrs. Dalloway* and several short stories where he is the prototype for Richard Dalloway (the careers of the character and Jack Hills are parallel—both Conservative members of Parliament, both involved in tariff and social reform) to Woolf's last novel *Between the Acts*, where actual wording, scenes, place names, and events are taken almost whole cloth from Virginia Woolf's diary written during her fifteenth summer, a few months after Stella died.

The author believes that one reason for the critical misapprehension of John Waller Hills is that Quentin Bell, in his 1973 biography of Woolf, said that "Virginia did not much like Jack Hills." This is not borne out by any of Woolf's writings, and Bell probably feels ambivalence toward Hills because, as Bell has stated, if Woolf's sister Vanessa had married Jack as planned, Virginia's biography "would have been told by someone else."

Also, there are incredible coincidences in the background and family relationship of Virginia's two brothers-in-law, Hills and Clive Bell (who eventually married Vanessa). The author believes that many critics have misread Woolf, thinking she was referring to Bell when in fact she often meant Jack Hills.

Too, Hills has been misperceived as intellectually weak when actually he was a writer of some note, perhaps the English writer of his time on fishing. He wrote many books, and Woolf reviewed at least one of them, *My Sporting Life*, praising his prose and style. He was well-regarded as a statesman, and his obituary in the *Times of London* ran 16 inches.

More work needs to be done on this overlooked influence on the life and work of Virginia Woolf.

Life/Studies: Psychobiography and Virginia Woolf

Judith Lutzer
Woolf and Freud: An Analysis of Invisible Presences

What is a psychoanalyst doing speaking to Woolfians about Woolf? During a recent visit to Monks house I spoke to a pleasant Englishwoman in the Woolfs' sitting room. When I asked her what part of England she was from, she replied, "the Bronx." Not only was she from the Bronx but she had grown up about 3 blocks away from my own childhood home. And we were both struck by the incongruity of Bronx neighbors meeting for the first time in Sussex. On further reflection, I thought that the meeting illustrates one of the appeals of Bloomsbury, that it brings together some of the most unlikely people, in the most unexpected places.

As a psychoananlyst, skeptical of coincidence, I am curious about the increase in literature linking Virginia Woolf with Sigmund Freud. What accounts for the pairing of this unlikely couple? In my talk today, "Woolf and Freud: An Analysis of Invisible Presences," I intend to show that the two writers are linked by their use of the psychoanalytic process to study and understand the workings of the mind. It is the shared process that has tantalized scholars for years, but has resisted interpretation.

The similarities between their work are invisible threads bridging the gap between them. Before examining these threads I'd like to bring to your attention the highly visible threads tying the two figures. Of particular interest is Woolf's ongoing effort to obscure the similarities with Freud and disclaim any formal knowledge of psychoanalysis. As late as 1932 she states, "I have not studied Dr Freud or any psychoanalyst—indeed I think I have never read any of their books; my knowledge is merely from superficial talk. Therefore any use of their methods must be instinctive" (*Letters* 5:36). And later the same year she stresses, "[I] have only a very amateurish knowledge of Freud and the Psychoanalysts; I have made no study of them"(*Letters* 5:91).

The phrase I want to stress is "any use of their methods must be instinctive." I think Woolf was aware of the similarity of her method to Freud's, and feared her work would not be regarded as original. This would clarify her disclaimers of lack of knowledge of psychoanalysis, which I hope to show is highly unlikely, given her intimate ties to the psychoanalytic world.

Take, for instance, her assertion, "my knowledge [of psychoanalysis] is merely from superficial talk." Some of this talk was with psychoanalysts Adrian Stephen, her brother, and Karin, his wife. Surely there was more talk with friends James and Alix Strachey, both analysands of Freud and the English translators of his work. In a 1925 letter to his wife, Strachey refers to a dinner with the Woolfs, where Virginia ferociously attacks psychoanalysis. In the same year Melanie Klein delivered a series of ground breaking lectures from the Stephens' drawing room at 50 Gordon Square, lectures that were translated to English by the Stracheys. Abel (1989) comments that the site of the lectures "dramatized the intellectual home [that] psychoanalysis had found in Bloomsbury" (13).

But it was not only her friends and her brother who were involved with the new science. Her husband, Leonard Woolf, reviewed *The Psychopathology of Everyday Life*, in 1914, shortly after the first of Freud's works was translated into English. "I am ... rather proud," he said in his autobiography, "of having in 1914 recognized and understood the greatness of Freud and the importance of what he was doing when this was by no means common."(*Beginning Again* 167).

Seven years after founding the Hogarth Press on the principle that it would refuse work, "unless we thought it worth publishing or the author worth publishing," (*Beginning Again* 255), the Woolfs took over the International Psycho-Analytical Library and printed close to 70 volumes, including the Standard Edition of Freud's work. "The greatest pleasure that I got from publishing the Library," Leonard said, " was the relationship which it established between us and Freud (*Downhill* 166)."

Returning to the invisible threads, I have found a number of similarities in the work of both authors, threads, which woven together, comprise the psychoanalytic process. In the interest of time limitations today, I will discuss only one of these areas, that of repression: a defensive process by which thoughts and feelings are expelled from conscious awareness. Freud describes repression as "the corner-stone on which the whole structure of psycho-analysis rests"(*Standard Edition* 14:16).

As early as 1894, in "The Neuro-Psychoses of Defense", Freud depicts the repression of "strong emotion", or affect, and how it is separated from its content, or idea:

> if . . . in order to fend off an incompatible idea, he sets about separating it from its affect, then *that affect is obliged to remain in the psychical sphere.* The idea, now weakened, is still left in consciousness, separated from all association. *But its affect, which has become free, attaches itself to other ideas which are not in themselves incompatible;* (SE 3:51-2).

The idea, in other words, remains conscious but without its emotional charge, while the affect is repressed until it reattaches itself to a non-objectionable idea.

If we turn to Woolf's opus, it's illustrative to compare her view of repression with Freud's. As our panel today is focusing on life studies and psychobiography I will confine my examples of Woolf's work to her autobiographical writings. In "A Sketch of the Past"(1976), she reflects,

> In certain favorable moods, memories—what one has forgotten—come to the top. Now if this is so, is it not possible—I often wonder—that things we have felt with great intensity have an existence independent of our minds: are in fact still in existence? And if so, will it not be possible, in time, that some device will be invented by which we can tap them? . . . I feel that strong emotion must leave its trace.(67)

Both Freud and Woolf are discussing how affect, which is not presently experienced, can remain in existence outside of conscious awareness waiting to be called back or reattached to its original idea. You may ask how do we infer the presence of unconscious affect? Delving into her memories of St. Ives, Woolf comes up with the metaphor of "little corks that mark a sunken net"(*Moments* 135), referring to the repressed and its derivatives. The corks are visible on the surface of the water, but the net to which they are attached is submerged and hidden. Compare this to Freud's description,

> It is not even correct to suppose that repression withholds from the conscious *all* the derivatives of what was primally repressed. If these derivatives have become sufficiently far removed from the repressed representative, whether owing to the adoption of distortions or by reason of the number of intermediate links inserted, they have free access to the conscious.(SE14:149)

I think it's clear that both authors are grappling with the same problem—Woolf from the viewpoint of the artist exploring the creative imagination, and Freud as the scientist extracting general principles of mental functioning.

The subject of memory repeatedly comes up in the context of discussing repression. Since memory occupies a privileged position in the work of both Woolf and Freud, it is illuminating to examine how it is effected by repression. Woolf asks ("A

Sketch" 70), "Why have I forgotten so many things that must have been, one would have thought, more memorable than what I do remember? Why remember the hum of bees in the garden going down to the beach, and forget completely being thrown naked by father into the sea? (Mrs Swanwick says she saw that happen.) Woolf questions why the relatively unimportant detail is remembered, while the significant event is forgotten. Freud thought that from about the age of seven, there is a "direct relation between the psychical significance of an experience and its retention in the memory." (*SE* 3:303) However, there is a certain kind of memory, a "screen memory," "one which owes its value as a memory not to its own content but to the relation existing between that content and some other, that has been suppressed (*SE* 3:320)." Screen memories are characterized by a luminous, glowing quality. They are well remembered, but seem to be composed of unremarkable content.

Look at what Woolf describes as "the most important of all my memories"

> It is of lying half asleep, half awake, in bed in the nursery at St Ives. It is of hearing the waves breaking, one, two, one, two, and sending a splash of water over the beach; and then breaking, one, two, one, two, behind a yellow blind. It is of hearing the blind draw its little acorn across the floor as the wind blew the blind out. It is of lying and hearing this splash and seeing this light, and feeling, it is almost impossible that I should be here; of feeling the purest ecstasy I can conceive. ("A Sketch" 64-5)

Examining the content of this description, one might wonder what makes this innocuous, albeit vivid scene, the author's most important memory. It depicts a fairly ordinary moment, highlighted by an emotional charge that permeates the scene and belies its placid surface.

It seems that we're back in the realm of Freud's "Neuro Psychoses of Defense." Here, affect is separated from idea and thus able to remain in consciousness, while the idea is repressed.

Like a trained psychoanalyst, Woolf follows her associations in an attempt to link this considerable affect with its idea. Her first effort, as is often the case, comes up against a resistance. "It was due partly to the many months we spent in London. The change of nursery was a great change. And there was the long train journey; and the excitement. I remember the dark; the lights; the stir of going up to bed ("A Sketch" 65). Even here we encounter derivatives of the repressed which are related to the affect, the excitement, the dark, the lights and the stir of bedtime.

Associations of bed lead to thoughts of her nursery, the scene of the memory, and in her description the content of the material is now enlarged. We learn that the nursery overlooks a balcony which adjoins her parents' bedroom. Perhaps the window, which figures so prominently in the memory, looks out on this balcony. "My mother would come out onto her balcony in a white dressing gown" Woolf says. "There were passion flowers growing on the wall; they were great starry blossoms, with purple streaks, and large green buds, part empty, part full" ("A Sketch" 66). It's a scene of dim, curved, sensuous shapes, of petals, shells, passion flowers, a "globular" picture, "semi-transparent."

It doesn't involve a great leap of imagination from Woolf's luscious and ripe imagery of the natural world, to the female body with its curved and rounded shapes associated to passion, ecstasy and the sexual act. I think Woolf is suggesting a memory of the primal scene, overheard, dimly seen, or perhaps imagined. The interpretation reconnects the affect with the idea or the content, and illuminates the importance of the memory. This is not to suggest that Woolf's memory may not have other functions or meanings as well. Here I'm simply approaching the material from the view point of repression.

Freud, himself, credited the poets with discovering the unconscious before he did. Creative writers, he says "are apt to know a whole host of things between heaven and earth of which our philosophy has not yet let us dream (*SE* 9:8)." The artist "experiences from himself what we learn from others—the laws which the activities of this unconscious must obey. But he need not state these laws, nor even be clearly aware of them... they are incorporated within his creations" (*SE* 9:92—"Jensen's 'Gradiva'" 1907). Here, Freud could be said to support Woolf's assertion that "any use of their methods must be instinctive."

I too think that Woolf's work was original, based on personal analysis and recording of her own inner processes. But I don't think she was unaware of Freud's work, of the ways in which it was similar to her own, nor do I think she could have failed to be influenced by his discoveries. In "A Sketch of the Past," Woolf muses on how she's been influenced by others. "If we cannot analyse these invisible presences, we know very little of the subject of the memoir," she says. "I suppose that I did for myself what psycho-analysts do for their patients. I expressed some very long felt and deeply felt emotion. And in expressing it I explained it and then laid it to rest" ("A Sketch" 80-81).

Woolf and Freud finally met on the afternoon of January 28, 1939. "Immense potential," Virginia Woolf said of Freud, "I mean an old fire now flickering (*Diary* 5:202)." Freud, in a note to Leonard Woolf two days later, said, "Handicapped in the use of your language I think I could not give full expression to my satisfaction of having met you and your lady" (Spotts 244). Instead, Freud gave Woolf a narcissus, the meaning of which remains for us to decipher.

Jane Lilienfeld
"Like a Lion Seeking Whom He Could Devour": Domestic Violence in *To the Lighthouse*

In *Moments of Being* Virginia Woolf acknowledged that *To The Lighthouse* was autobiographical and that writing it had had a positive therapeutic outcome: " . . . I suppose that I did for myself what psycho-analysts do for their patients." (81). In the same memoir, Woolf records several of her half-brothers' incestuous attacks on her (58, 68-9; De Salvo 209-211).[1] While there is no explicit incest material of this sort in *To The Lighthouse*, incest by definition implies abuse, boundary violation, emotional and spiritual assault. As feminist critics of the patriarchal family have long argued, these violations depend on intergender dynamics in which women are ciphers and men are all powerful, a power structure that perpetuates the appropriation of the selves of women and children in service to the powerful adult male (Rapp et. al.; Herman 124-5; Lilienfeld, "Quest"). The patriarchal family dynamic of *To The Lighthouse* results in abusive appropriation of others, and it is within this context that one aspect of the tragedy of Mrs. Ramsay and her children can be clearly seen.

An essential element of the Ramsays' marriage in *To the Lighthouse* is emotional and spiritual battering. The Ramsays' transactions have the specific patterning analyzed by feminists such as Susan Schechter and Del Martin who study domestic violence in the contemporary white middle class and working class family. Consider the argument in Book 1, chapters 5 through 8. There the husband verbally assaults his wife for the simple reason that her assessment of the weather disagrees with his. Not one critic has focused on this scene as a study of a classic battering relation. Nor has any critic remarked on Mrs. Ramsay's behavior from this perspective. She does not confront her husband. She does not get up and leave, taking her little boy with her. She sits still, bows her head as if to accept her husband's behavior and only chastises him in thought. Her anger is directed less at him than at herself in the form of self pity. Suddenly her husband reappears and apologizes, as is typical of one aspect of the battering cycle. For having acted out, the batterer feels strengthened and refreshed by the fact that—to the batterer—the problem is temporarily assuaged. Usually soon after the assaultive behavior, the batterer will apologize, insist s/he is sorry, swear never again to behave so and will become loving (Martin 259; Porterfield 16-7; Hoye; Cloud). At her husband's apology, Mrs. Ramsay acknowledges neither his verbal abuse nor her inability to confront it. Instead, appearing to accept his apology, she thinks, "She was not good enough to tie his shoe strings, she felt." (Woolf, *Lighthouse* 51).

As is clear from looking closely at the several paragraphs in the first part of the argument, the actual site of abuse in *To The Lighthouse* is Mrs. Ramsay herself. The central intelligence narrates the scene by reporting Mrs. Ramsay's indirect interior monologue. The tortured denial process by which she reacts to her husband's abuse indicates that she as a self who can name, reject or protect herself and her son against violation is not only absent, but has never been allowed to live.

Chapter 6 begins with Mr. Ramsay's shame that William Bankes and Lily Briscoe have seen him fantasizing: "He shivered; he quivered. All his vanity, all his satisfaction in his own splendour, riding fell as a thunderbolt, fierce as a hawk at the head of his men through the valley of death, had been shattered, destroyed" (Woolf, *Lighthouse* 48-9). This mocking view of Mr. Ramsay as the grandiose hero of his imaginary life is an example of the methods characterizing him in Book One. His internal voice is always parodied. This comedic approach replicates the contradictions between that which he is personally and that which he receives because of his gender and his role as patriarchal late-Victorian upper middle class father (Roberts). Personally he is an immature man with few social skills, little self knowledge, an obsessive, immobilizing dependence on his wife's mothering, and a deep sense of personal inferiority; that is, personally he presents one classic profile of an adult male batterer as analyzed by Del Martin (46-7). But socially he is a well-known intellectual, a professor, the father of a prosperous family who, because of his social role, wields almost totalitarian power over it. The contradiction has a curious result. Mr. Ramsay has no independent voice which does not render him ridiculous. Thus the vicious and threatening meaning of much of his reported behavior is undercut by his silliness and is muffled by the narrative method. His violence occurs only obliquely or in metaphors.[2]

In Chapter 6, Mrs. Ramsay protects her husband from experiencing his feelings. Like so many other late-Victorian families, the Ramsays find themselves forbidden to discuss feelings. Particularly taboo are men's feelings of weakness and fear (Houghton). "Not for the world would she have spoken to him, realizing . . . that he was outraged and anguished. She stroked James's head; she transferred to him what she felt for her husband." (Woolf, *Lighthouse*, 49). The family systems theorist Murray Bowen characterizes such transfers as "triangulation," those communications between marital partners which depend on an exchange of another person as object (Bowen 478, 234-40, 372-6).

Participating in the triangulation, after he has nursed his

hurt feelings, Mr. Ramsay hits James so subtly and seemingly playfully that his intent is hidden: "as his turn came round again, at the window he bent quizzically and whimsically to tickle James's bare calf with a sprig of something." (Woolf, *Lighthouse* 49).

While appearing not to notice that the boy is being struck lightly, Mrs. Ramsay suddenly offers herself as the object of Mr. Ramsay's swats. She mentions the trip to the lighthouse by announcing that she is knitting stockings to be taken on the journey there tomorrow. Her husband "snapped out irascibly": "There wasn't the slightest possible chance that they could go to the lighthouse tomorrow." Courageously his wife challenges him, "How did he know? . . . The wind often changed." (Woolf, *Lighthouse* 50).

In trying to establish what precipitates male battering in white middle or working class homes in America and Britain, contemporary researchers like Leonore Walker and the Dobashes discovered that seemingly minute or meaningless occurrences would set off the abuse (qtd. in Martin 259; Schechter 209-16). Viewed rationally, these often made no sense—the dinner was late, the house wasn't clean, or they were nagged—that is, their opinions were questioned. Mr. Ramsay's behavior follows this classic pattern in abuse.

> The extraordinary irrationality of her remark, the folly of women's minds enraged him. He had ridden through the valley of death, had been shattered and shivered; and now, she flew in the face of facts, made his children hope what was out of the question, in effect, told lies. (Woolf, *Lighthouse* 50)

That which Mr. Ramsay thinks he is furious about and that which he is actually furious about may be quite distinct. As a white middle class male raised in Victorian England, he knows that women are rendered illogical by their biology, a belief supported by most informed medical opinion of his day (Gorham 85-90). Mr. Ramsay's grandiose fantasy of himself as a doomed thinker equivalent to the Five Hundred who rode into the cannon at Balaclava is as irrational as any idea he thinks his wife may have. What Mr. Ramsay is furious about in his wife (and son) is that which he fears and despises in himself.

Mr. Ramsay's reaction to what he experiences as his wife's questioning his sagacity and his envy of the bonding between her and James escalates into direct abuse. Mr. Ramsay curses his wife. "He stamped his foot on the stone step. 'Damn you,' he said. But what had she said? Simply that it might be fine tomorrow. So it might." (Woolf, *Lighthouse* 50). Almost no direct, attributable dialogue occurs in *To the Lighthouse*. Yet the typography marks this curse as spoken aloud, making it all the more powerful.

Although his may appear as a mere childish tantrum, contained within emotional and verbal violence of this sort is the implicit threat of physical violence, feminist theorists of battering assert. An unpredictable, irrational temper expresses a violent refusal of self control which could certainly erupt into physical acting out. As Susan Brownmiller argued about rape and as contemporary feminist theorists argue about verbal violence, expressions of uncontrollable rage make clear the physical force implicit behind all social control of women (Schechter 216-234; Porterfield 50).

Mrs. Ramsay's reaction indicates that not only is she herself the target of abuse, but that the abuse of her is the conduit to abusing the child.

> To pursue truth with such astonishing lack of consideration for other people's feelings, to rend the thin veils of civilization so wantonly, so brutally, was to her so horrible an outrage of human decency that, without replying, dazed and blinded, she bent her head as if to let the pelt of jagged hail, the drench of dirty water, bespatter her unrebuked. There was nothing to be said. (Woolf, *Lighthouse* 51).

Where is the word "I" in this passage? Where is the recognition that "I" was beaten verbally? Where is the vision that a little child witnessed this attack? Where is the knowledge that

Mr. Ramsay was pursuing power over other people, not truth? Silenced.

Nevertheless, even though the absent self cannot name its own violation or the child's, encoded in this passage is a recognition of brutality. What can be acknowledged as assaulted is the Victorian middle class system of separate spheres by which the man was given the whole external world to rule. "[T]he thin veils of human civilization" emblematize more than the middle class Victorian division of labor; they encode the furniture covers the Victorians draped over chairs and tables and the truths about the body—and by extension the clothes torn in rape.

Her body language indicates victimization: she bent her head the way an animal in a fight with a bigger animal indicates subservience. Why is there nothing to be said?

As I have argued in my published essays, Mrs. Ramsay, now fifty, in a narrative set in 1909, was raised as an upper middle class Victorian woman ("Mother Love"; "Spear Plants"). Girls of her class raised in Victorian England were socialized to believe that their primary duty in life was sacrifice of self to the needs of others, parents first, and then the men of the family. As numerous Victorian autobiographies of both men and women of Mrs. Ramsay's social class make clear, Victorian children were routinely used as objects to meet their families' needs, a practice not constructed by that culture as abuse. (Gosse 42-3, 109, 135-9; Mill 25, 35; Houghton). Although this is thought by some scholars to have changed about 1860, as revealed by Victorian children's literature, other scholars believe such literature to be wish fulfillment rather than proof that such use of children by middle class parents had ceased (Silver).

In Murray Bowen's analysis, middle-class Victorian methods of rearing girls had impaired Mrs. Ramsay and appropriated her core self (Bowen 200-3, 306).[3] Such a person has a great deal of trouble recognizing abusive behavior. It is not cowardice or lack of intelligence which partially blinds Mrs. Ramsay; her upbringing has insured that she will lack the tools to name what is happening. Thus Mrs. Ramsay is unable to argue back directly in conflictual situations. The middle class Victorian rules of propriety rigidly demarcated as acceptable only certain feelings: duty, optimism; feelings themselves were suspect, suppressed and denied (Houghton). Certainly, women of her class and upbringing did not argue; anger was unacceptable in women (and children). Access to anger and the ability to act on it are weapons that demand a core self and high self esteem—the very qualities most harmed in suffering the abuse that oppression brings. Mrs. Ramsay's behaviors as an adult in her marriage and mothering suggest that for her the process of being raised in the traditional Victorian family resulted in what she experienced as severe boundary violation.

To me, Mrs. Ramsay's response to her husband's seeming apology is as tragic as her response to his temper. "Very humbly ... he said that he would step over and ask the coast guards if she liked. There was nobody whom she reverenced as she reverenced him" (Woolf, *Lighthouse* 51). An oppressed person with no options other than remaining in place cannot challenge power without directly threatening his or her own existence.

Idealization rather than rage is Mrs. Ramsay's response. Quickly this turns to a martyr's self pity to mask rage at both herself and her husband:

> She was quite ready to take his word for it, she said. Only then they need not cut sandwiches—that was all. They came to her, naturally, since she was a woman, all day long with this and that; one wanting this, another that; the children were growing up; she often felt she was nothing but a sponge sopped full of human emotions. Then he said, Damn you. He said, It must rain. He said, It won't rain; and instantly a Heaven of security opened before her. There was nobody she reverenced more. She was not good enough to tie his shoe strings, she felt. (Woolf, *Lighthouse* 51)

The key word is "natural." This is the voice of a woman whose conviction that she must give all and take nothing has reached the point of self immolation. Far from amusing like descriptions of The Angel in the House, this passage as it proceeds becomes a tragic voice, a cry from the heart, a cry from a woman so taken out of her right to have an independent self not indentured to the needs of others that she has been almost annihilated as a free standing functional human agent ("Professions" 278-9). But that part of her consciousness which knows the truth transforms the pure water of her well back to the filthy water of her husband's curse. Her body is the sponge which absorbs it.

At no point in her summary of the conversation does Mrs. Ramsay's core self appear. The reader sees Mrs. Ramsay denying experiences which the reader has witnessed. The summary reproduces in language that which Mrs. Ramsay is forced to choose as action. Mr. Ramsay's behavior is paramount; her response only to be imagined, never stated. Anger seems absent. Idealization takes the place of acknowledged feelings.

It is no accident that Mrs. Ramsay's idealization of her husband ends in her vision of herself as his obsequious servant. In a Victorian middle class marriage of the kind that her parents would most likely have had, a wife had the legal status of property. Mrs. Ramsay does not have the sensibility of a young woman coming of age in 1909, but that of woman whose identity was formed during the height of the Victorian era. Thus Mrs. Ramsay treats herself and is treated by her husband as her husband's servant. As servants in the middle class Victorian home were expected to do, she worked hard to obliterate any trace of her true self to put his needs first.[4]

Mrs. Ramsay sincerely loves and admires her husband. Her adult identity resides in her role as a married woman. She is not in a position whereby she can allow herself to recognize the emotional violence consistently directed against her and her children which is one aspect of her complicated marital partnership.

For both partners, Mrs. Ramsay's response of veneration is an effective alternative to the knowledge of abuse and powerlessness. Idealizing her husband protects her from having to admit the reality of a situation to which she has no realistic social, emotional or perhaps economic alternative. Idealizing Mr. Ramsay protects him, too, and protecting him from negative emotions is a primary goal of her life as a Victorian wife. Rather than raging, which is as unladylike as it is unimaginable to her, Mrs. Ramsay reweaves the veil which her husband's behavior has rent.

Throughout the interchange between his parents, little James has stood silent. So intent is Mr. Ramsay on imposing his will and Mrs. Ramsay on surviving that James is eradicated from their consciousnesses, though not perhaps from the reader's. Current family theory speculates that children who witness verbal violence against a parent experience themselves as violated (Bradshaw 20-1). As Mrs. Ramsay is impacted by her husband's infantile temper, James thus becomes a direct recipient of his father's rage. He is powerless to protect himself or his mother. Unfortunately, just like the girls who blame their mothers rather than the male perpetrators for incest, James experienced his mother rather than his father as abusing him, for he remembers this transaction not as abuse of the mother by the father but as his own abandonment by the mother (Woolf, *Lighthouse* 277-8; Jacobs).[5] Coupled with his father's obvious belief that women are to be harassed until they accede to male desires, this misinterpreted memory helps explain why the motherless James becomes a hostile and selfish adolescent whose contempt for mother and sister far exceeds that of his own father. And so the cycle continues....

I thank Susan Hoye, Counselor, Respond and Kate Cloud, Director, Respond, Somerville, MA for sharing their insights about the principles of intervention, analysis, and therapy in patterns of male battering. My thanks to Sally O'Leary, R.N., M.A., Boston, MA for training me to apply Bowenian system theory to feminist analyses of dysfunctional family systems.

Notes

[1]"I can remember the feel of his hand going under my clothes; going firmly and steadily lower and lower. I remember how I hoped that he would stop; how I stiffened and wriggled as his hand approached my private parts too. I remember resenting, disliking it—what is the word for so dumb and mixed a feeling? . . ." (Woolf, *Moments of Being* 69).

[2]In *To the Lighthouse*, Mr. Ramsay's irrational and explosive rage is characterized by martial metaphors: "She saw his anger fly like a pack of hounds into his eyes, his brow, and she knew that in a moment something violent would explode..." (144). His sexuality is equally menacing. His son perceives Mr. Ramsay as "lean as a knife, narrow as the blade of one" (10). His rapacious love is the sword of death, a relentless "scimitar" which smites the wife "again and again" (59). Similarly, a comforting image of his love has menacing overtones, as when his mental nearness to his wife's mind becomes an action resembling a raised hand, as ready to strike as to cherish (184). Even his hunger for human contact is violent, for he is "like a lion seeking whom he could devour" (233).

Psychobiography and Virginia Woolf

³There is indeed a Mrs. Ramsay who is not the perfect Victorian middle class wifely ideal, but she appears rarely, in the safety of silence and solitude: "She could be herself, by herself... This core of darkness could go anywhere, for no one saw it" (Woolf, *Lighthouse* 95-6).

⁴" [In the Victorian middle class marriage] [a]t the worst the wife was reduced to the status of a slave, at best she was permitted to hold the rank of head servant" (Harrison 6).

⁵For a Freudian reading of this scene rather than one based on theories of incest and abuse in the dysfunctional family, see Abel 52; 65-66.

Works Cited

Abel, Elizabeth. *Virginia Woolf and the Fictions of Psychoanalysis.* Chicago: University of Chicago Press, 1989.
Bowen, Murray. *Family Therapy in Clinical Practice.* London: Jason Aronson, 1990.
Bradshaw, John. *Healing the Shame that Binds You.* Florida: Health Communications, Inc., 1988.
Brownmiller, Susan. *Against Our Will: Men, Women and Rape.* New York: Simon and Schuster, 1978.
Cloud, Kate. Personal Interview. 18 Feb. 1990.
De Salvo, Louise. *Virginia Woolf: The Impact of Childhood Sexual Abuse on Her Life and Work.* Boston: Beacon Press, 1989.
Gorham, Deborah. *The Victorian Girl and The Feminine Ideal.* Bloomington: Indiana UP, 1982.
Gosse, Edmund. *Father and Son.* New York: Norton, 1973.
Harrison, Fraser. *The Dark Angel: Aspects of Victorian Sexuality.* New York: Universe Books, 1978.
Herman, Judith and Lisa Hirschman. *Father-Daughter Incest.* Cambridge: Harvard University Press, 1981. Hoye, Susan. Telephone Interview. 9 Feb. 1990.
Houghton, Walter. *The Victorian Frame of Mind: 1830-1870.* New Haven: Yale UP, 1963.
Jacobs, Janet L. "Reassessing Mother Blame in Incest." *Signs.* 15 (Spring 1990): 500-14.
Lilienfeld, Jane. "'The Deceptiveness of Beauty': Mother Love and Mother Hate in *To the Lighthouse.*" *Twentieth Century Literature* 23 (1977): 345-76.
———. "Flesh and Blood and Love and Words: Lily Briscoe, Stephen Dedalus and The Aesthetics of Emotional Quest." *New Alliances in Joyce Studies.* Ed. Bonnie Kime Scott. Newark: University of Delaware Press, 1988. 165 - 178.
———. "Where The Spear Plants Grew: The Ramsays' Marriage in *To the Lighthouse.*" *New Feminist Essays on Virginia Woolf.* Ed. Jane Marcus. Lincoln: University of Nebraska Press, 1981. 148-69.
Martin, Del. *Battered Wives.* New York: Pocket Books, 1983.
Mill, John Stuart. *Autobiography.* New York: Bobbs Merrill, 1957.
O'Leary, Sally, R.N., M.A., Personal Interviews. 9, 16-17 March 1990.
Porterfield, Kay. *Violent Voices.* Florida: Health Communications, Inc., 1989.

Roberts, David. "The Paterfamilias of the Victorian Governing Classes." *The Victorian Family: Structure and Stresses.* Ed. Anthony Wohl. London: Croom Helm, 1978. 59-81.
Rapp, R., Ross, E., Bridenthal, R. "Examining Family History." *Feminist Studies* 5 (Spring 1979): 174-200.
Silver, Carole. Telephone Interview 1 July 1990.
Schechter, Susan. *Women and Male Violence.* Boston: South End Press, 1982.
Woolf, Virginia. *Moments of Being: Unpublished Autobiographical Writings.* Ed. Jeanne Schulkind. Sussex: University of Sussex Press, 1976.
———. "Professions for Women." *The Virginia Woolf Reader.* Ed. Mitchell Leaska. New York: Harcourt, Brace, Jovanovich, 1984. 276-82.
———. *To the Lighthouse.* New York: Harcourt, Brace & World. 1927.

Louise DeSalvo
Virginia Woolf, Incest Survivor

The following paper was written by Professor DeSalvo based upon a transcript of her talk at the conference.

I am today not going to deliver a prepared lecture, but, instead, I am going to give a talk, and I want to say why. My decision is, in one sense, based upon a politics. Since the time I wrote my book on Virginia Woolf as an incest survivor, I have been talking to incest survivors throughout the United States, England, and Canada, sharing the life stories of scores of women and men and how their experience replicated or differed from Woolf's. During that time, I have felt, increasingly, that reading a prepared document about Virginia Woolf and incest is incompatible with what I have learned from incest survivors. Incest survivors, in recovery, are reaching for a language that honestly describes what they have experienced without obscuring it, blunting its effect, or denying it. What they require from the people they meet and talk to, what they require from their lovers, families, friends, and therapists, is an acknowledgement that what they have experienced really happened, that they haven't made it up. I am now convinced that the language of contemporary critical discourse cannot possibly be used to describe a work of literature that conveys the experience of incest survivors without obscuring its pain or the heroism of the act of writing about it.

Once the word "incest" is typed on the page, and delivered as part of a discourse that is a critical analysis of a work, the reality of what happens to children's bodies abused by incest gets lost in the locution. Once you begin using the language of "lit-crit speak," the reality of incest—its effect on the psyches, on the bodies of real people who have been abused, inevitably gets lost. I believe this is so because those who employ contemporary critical discourse, obscure the relationship of the work of literature to the life of its writer and to experiences of other people in the world. Denial is the burden that incest survivors labor against throughout their lives. To employ a criticism that is an act of denial, is to collude with the silencing of those who have been abused, rather than to help explode that silence.

Contemporary literary criticism is a manic denial of the *experience* of human beings who have suffered, and who have written about their suffering to understand it. Setting themselves up as superior to the experience described on the page, believing that they know more about the work than the writer who penned it, many contemporary literary critics, while thinking themselves radical, protect themselves from feeling the pain of the uttered word. They do this by dipping into a standard grab bag of literary critical terms, and using them, no matter what the work is about. Instead of beginning with the work, instead of trying to figure out what the author is trying to tell us, and then trying to find a language appropriate to describing the unique experience in the work they are reading, these critics pull out their heavy artillery, the "in" literary critical terminology, and they aim it at the page, despite what the page is about.

Whether the work is about incest, or about lust, or about war, or about pleasure, the language that critics use to describe it sounds very much the same. The effect of using this homogenized language on every work that a critic encounters suggests that one work of literature is very much like another. It is not the work that cues the response, but rather the mode of criticism that cues the response. Instead of entering a dialectic with the work, instead of entering a responsible relationship with it, instead of listening to the pain the work expresses, with empathy and humility, instead of trying to understand how the work is a unique expression of a unique experience, the critic batters the work into shape to fit the discourse that s/he is using to explain it.

I believe much of contemporary literary critical discourse is an act that is hostile to the work, rather than in sympathy with it, an act that tries to tear down and destroy what the writer has very carefully constructed. Instead of "reconstructing" the experience of the writer through the work, the critic deconstructs, and, in so doing, destroys that which s/he would understand.

I read contemporary literary critical discourse as an act that abuses the work. I believe we must not use it to discuss literary works exploring incest, child abuse, and sexual violence. Contemporary critical discourse does not break a silence. Its language obscures, rather than reveals. It struts and postures, engages in linguistic wordplay, and asserts power over the work. It behaves in relationship to the work much as the incestuous parent behaves in relationship to the child. It commits a violation.

It took me about fifteen years to find a language appropriate to describing Virginia Woolf's life as an incest survivor. It took me about fifteen years to write the words "Virginia Woolf was a sexually abused child. She was an incest survivor" straightforwardly, without pomp and ceremony, on the page. Although they are the first words that appear in my book, they were among the last words I wrote. Writing those two very simple sentences was so very difficult, I now understand, because, like many critics, I did everything that I could to protect myself from the pain embedded in the reality that those words convey. If I treated Woolf's novels as texts to be deciphered, rather than as experiences to be understood, I would never have to relive the trauma that she experienced. Much as I tried, I was not able, for many years, to name Virginia Woolf's experience as sexual abuse. Nor could I link her experiences—her suicidal wishes and acts, her self-doubt, her unwillingness to eat enough to sustain life—with her being an incest survivor.

What got in the way, first, and for a very brief time, was a

Psychobiography and Virginia Woolf

seductive literary critical movement that rewarded those who learned its language. What was equally pernicious yet equally confounding was the way in which other biographers of Virginia Woolf spoke about her experience. Quentin Bell, author of the first, "official" biography of her life, to his credit, discussed Woolf's abuse. Yet he described her response to incest as if she were overreacting to it. Had she been healthier, psychologically, he claims, the incest would not have affected her as profoundly as it did. Her neurosis, her "madness," in his view, caused her breakdowns. Her problems were not a set of sequelae to what had happened to her, they were due to the defects in her psychic makeup. Other biographers followed Quentin Bell's lead.

The view of Woolf as insane, rather than as reacting to the problematic experiences in her life—her childhood suffering in a dysfunctional family, her witnessing the violent treatment of her half-sisters Laura and Stella, her neglect, her abuse—is extremely difficult to dislodge. We would all like to believe in a simplistic universe like the one Quentin Bell describes in which some people are born crazy, and others are born sane. That soothes us and comforts us and absolves us of responsibility for our actions as parents and as caregivers. The idea that people in Woolf's life were directly responsible for causing her to become neurotic, responsible for her breakdowns, her suicide attempts, her life-long lack of faith in herself, her sorrow, her suffering, is an idea that is difficult to swallow. If Woolf's half-brothers, if her parents were agents of suffering, then so can we be.

My early work on Virginia Woolf used the comfortable distorting lenses of a late-Freudian theory of personality. In this view, reports of incest are viewed as wishes, not as descriptions of actual happenings. Although I always believed that what Woolf said happened to her, really happened to her, I saw her neurosis as separate from her experience. This theory, as others have argued, blames the victim rather than the abuser. Not until I read the groundbreaking work of Judith Lewis Herman on incest (*Father-Daughter Incest*) did I understand the ways in which Woolf's response to her experience coincided with that of other survivors.

Until I read historical accounts of incest survivors, I did not understand that Woolf's "coming out" as an incest survivor in the '20s in an essay that she read to the Memoir Club was extraordinarily brave. Nor did I understand that Woolf's desire to relate her experience as an incest survivor and her lifelong suffering from depression was brave, singular and prophetic. She might well have been the first incest survivor to have done so. I did not understand that, in writing "Sketch of the Past," which she wrote late in her life, she was able to explore how her parents and half-brothers had harmed her, exploding the myth of the idyllic late-Victorian family. In writing a history of her family in the context of Victorian mores, she presaged the contemporary discipline that studies the history of childhood, pioneered by Alice Miller, that studies the ways in which families raise their children, and the relationship between childrearing and historical experience.

A distortion that I had to overcome was that Woolf's experience inside the Stephen family was anomalous, that, as a child, she was bathed in a protective love. The most ardent supporter of this view is Lyndall Gordon, who paints a picture of an idyllic Stephen family except for a few problematic incidents. We all want, in times of strife, especially if our own households were compromised, romantic fantasies about a perfect family that exists somewhere out there. Contemporary documents do not support this view of the Stephen family at all. Leslie Stephen's own letters to his wife portray a family riddled with problems, from before the time of Julia's death. Laura was abused and neglected. Most biographers downplay Vanessa's suffering, her life-long battle with depression and portray her, inaccurately, as a serene Madonna, untroubled by anything that came her way. A tragic moment, I think, in Vanessa's life occurred when she, herself a victim of incest, had to care for Virginia after their father's death. It was she who put a stop to her sister's exploitation by telling the family physician about what was occurring. She shovelled whatever ill effects she suffered under the rug to care for her sister, find a new home, pack up the household. Both women, not just Virginia, were severely damaged. Both were heroic.

The notion that the Stephen family, *except for* the abuse of two daughters (Virginia and Vanessa), was otherwise well-functioning is ludicrous and dangerous. A family in which any child is abused is, by definition, a seriously dysfunctional family.

Evidence about incest is always difficult to find, after the fact. If you read that Woolf's incestuous experience began when she was six years old, and then reemerged in her adolescence, in the wake of her mother's death, you need to ask what happened to her meanwhile, if there is no evidence that it continued. Literary scholars think that all the evidence that we have is all the evidence that existed. In the case of incest in a famous family, it is likely that evidence has been destroyed. The evidence that exists is, in all likelihood, a fraction of what once existed. Dr. Sue Shapiro, at work on a biography of Clara Thompson, and a psychoanalyst specializing in the treatment of incest survivors, has stated that we should hypothesize incest or abuse as having occurred, when a certain set of symptoms—addictive behavior, self-mutilation, anorexia, suicide attempts—is present.

Only when I read the work of people who studied incest, who studied childrearing, did I begin to realize that Woolf's life could be understood in relationship to her experience as an incest survivor. Only when I read the "speak-out" documents of survivors such as Louise Armstrong (*Kiss Daddy Goodnight*) did I understand that Virginia Woolf's novels were attempts to understand what had happened to her, and to repair the effects of the damage to her psyche. The patterns of language and imagery in Woolf's work echoed that of other survivors. The language of incest survivors, by necessity, simultaneously explains and hides. To tell the truth about incest is dangerous: you run the risk of being labelled a liar, or crazy, as Woolf was called crazy. Listening to how survivors described their experience taught me how to read the words of Virginia Woolf.

What Virginia Woolf accomplished was to write one of the first coherent narratives about the effect of incestuous abuse. We have yet to discover the number of men and women who have been so abused, but the numbers are staggering. Diana E. H. Russell, in *The Secret Trauma* reported that 38 percent of the women she studied described at least one experience of sexual abuse before the age of eighteen, 28 percent before the age of fourteen. Judith Lewis Herman's most recent work, described in Janet Hawkins, "Rowers on the River Styx" (*Harvard Magazine*, March-April 1991, 43-52) shows that *one* such trauma can result in significant, lifelong changes in the psyche. The effect of sexual abuse, Herman now believes, is best understood as a "post-traumatic stress disorder," akin to that suffered by Vietnam veterans. Only recently, have researchers begun to understand that "the traumas of civilian life and the traumas of war ... are the same" (Hawkins 50). The outgrowth of this insight is that treatments developed for Vietnam veterans work in the rehabilitation of incest survivors (Hawkins 50). Although the disorder is amenable to treatment, *if* the therapist understands its origin, untreated, it is serious, often life-threatening, and long-lasting. "The evidence is strong and growing," according to Herman, "that trauma can and does cause biological changes: `The startle response, irritability, nightmares, flashbacks, hypervigilance and hypersensitivity—all these must relate to some sort of alteration in a person's reactivity, in their autonomic nervous system'" (Herman quoted in Hawkins 50). Addictive behavior, Dr. Bessel van der Kolk has discovered, is often an attempt at "self-medication" (Hawkins, 50).

If we teach, many of our students, men and women, sitting in our classrooms, will have been victims of this kind of violence. Many of our students who have suicidal tendencies, who have fantasies of self-mutilation, who abuse themselves, who are drug abusers, who are alcoholics, are unacknowledged victims of post traumatic stress disorders, victims of sexual violence. In the years since my book was published, my journey has included visits into the corridors and hallways and church basements, into public and private spaces where people try to recover. Theirs is not the language of "lit-crit speak" that denies and distorts. They talk about the damage to their psyches and the damage to their bodies that incest causes. (Readers of this essay who, themselves, suspect they are survivors, or who know a survivor, often can find a support group through local Rape Crisis Centers, Incest Survivors Anonymous [although many of these groups are difficult to contact], Adult Children of Alcoholics, or Alcoholics Anonymous; the latter can be particularly helpful in locating support groups. Ellen Bass and Laura Davis's *The Courage to Heal* [New York: Harper & Row, 1988] is an extremely helpful manual for survivors.)

Finding out that Virginia Woolf, too, was an incest survivor means a great deal to survivors. She is a fellow traveller, one of many, who entered the painful and solitary journey of insight and understanding. Woolf is one of many survivors, who, by virtue of their stories, compelled the psychoanalytic establishment to change their views about the effect of incest.

Since incest survivors often suffer in silence, they often resort to hiding behind the facade of telling a story to communicate their abuse. My hope is that we can hear these stories, for only in hearing them, and in acknowledging them, does the incest survivor traverse the terrible isolation that this abuse entails.

As painful as this journey has been for me, I am deeply grateful to Virginia Woolf for having forced me, through her heroic journey through her work, into understanding her experience as an incest survivor. I no longer see works of literature as sets of signs and symbols, unrelated to human experience and human suffering. That change has enriched my life, my teaching, and my writing.

The last thing I did in preparing for this talk was to go back and reread the series of notebooks that I kept while working on this book. One entry, in particular, reminded me of the pain that the work had entailed. It read, "I just sat down and cried and cried, and I couldn't stop crying. I couldn't stop crying because I was writing about Laura [Stephen]. When will the pain that Laura must have suffered leave me?"

Feeling pain is the risk we run if we climb into people's lives to try to understand them. The pain of Virginia Woolf, as an incest survivor, is one that never leaves me. The pictures of her as a child, as an adolescent, looking frightened and unhappy, are with me always. Alice Miller believed that understanding pain, reliving it, in our own lives, and in other people's lives, is necessary if we wish to lead lives that are not mired in depression and despair. For Alice Miller, the opposite of depression is not happiness, but rather, vitality. Paradoxically, understanding Virginia Woolf's pain has been a tremendously empowering and enriching personal journey for me. Her courageous work stands as an important example of the healing power of language for incest survivors.

Roger Poole

A Phenomenological Reading of Certain Photographs*

It is a great disappointment to me that I am not able to be here today. The fact is, that I am involved in the busiest week of the British academic year and, as you hear these words, I will be marking final examination papers in batches of 60 at a time!

But Mark Hussey has very kindly invited me to say a few words through the good offices of Vara Neverow-Turk, and there are one or two thought processes going through my mind which I would like to suggest to you today. They are thought processes largely provoked by a reading of Louise DeSalvo's recent book, and if Louise is in the room, I would like to extend a ghostly trans-Atlantic greeting to her, and thank her for providing me with some answers to questions that have been worrying me for some time.

Louise DeSalvo's book *Virginia Woolf: The Impact of Childhood Sexual Abuse on her Life and Work*, opens up a horrifying world. Roald Dahl once said that no-one who has been to a British public school can quite get over, in later years, the luxury of being able to sleep in a bed without having his back to the wall, and on the evidence presented by Louise DeSalvo, it would be reasonable to suppose that Virginia Woolf in later years could never quite adapt to the thought that she would not suddenly be cornered by George Duckworth, and forced into some degrading act with him.

Indeed, 22 Hyde Park Gate, the childhood home of the Stephen girls, is little less than a nightmare. It is a "patriarchal" world of violence and terrified repression. Louise DeSalvo operates a totalizing method that is not unlike that of the practitioners of the Geneva School of phenomenological criticism, in that she attempts to co-incide completely with the consciousness of her chosen writer, entering a world, attuning herself to it, and learning how to interpret every part of it in terms of every other part, the "life" being expressed in the "work" and vice versa.

---

*Paragraphs 3-8 appeared in Modern Fiction Studies, copyright 1991, by Purdue Research Foundation, West Lafayette, Indiana 47907. Reprinted with permission.

Psychobiography and Virginia Woolf

Was the old, self-pitying Sir Leslie Stephen simply unaware of the outrages being committed against the young women under his roof, or did he, in some malign "ideological" way, even connive in it, or think it was "good for them?" The wild and emotional J. K. Stephen, for instance, was allowed constant access to Stella Duckworth, even though he was often quite out of control and acting in a menacing way. It would appear from his poetic reverie "The Last Ride Together" that Stella had been, at some point in their tempestuous relationship, submitted to anal rape. And what grim suffering lay in wait for Stella with Jack Hills, as sex-obsessed as J. K. Stephen had been? Stella was married on 10th April 1897. On their honeymoon, Jack turned out to be "a tiring lover," and by the 19th July she was dead. The official account was "peritonitis." Jack, bereaved, then went on to terrify Virginia with the urgency of his sexual needs. And what repeated and humiliating oppression lies behind Virginia's short sketch TERRIBLE TRAGEDY IN A DUCK POND? Apparently no more than a witty exercise in reporting about three young people who had been tipped out of their punt while on a moonlit trip on the lake, it nevertheless offers an entire symbolic code for decipherment, a series of signifiers pointing (for these are the happy days before Lacan) to a series of signifieds.

Virginia Woolf, promising to send a copy of the story to her friend Emma Vaughan, emphasizes: "Do you see? You must read my work carefully—not missing my peculiar words." What peculiar words? Well, the endlessly repeated "duckweed" for one, an obvious play on Duckworth. But why this play on the name? What is associated with it? "The reason for her death by drowning is that she is shrouded in green weed, in `duckweed,' in `slimatica.' The green carpet of duckweed has `closed over its prey;' but although the surface of the pond seemed unruffled, below it, however, someone was dying."

The movement in phenomenological criticism is from text to text, from assonance to assonance, and always using hypothesis (there can be no proof) but I do find DeSalvo's sudden intuitive sideways movement both deft and convincing. She relates a note in Mitchell Leaska's edition of *Pointz Hall* to the duckweed fantasy, a note to a line from Swinburne's "Itylus," "Swallow, my sister, O sister swallow." This bit of serendipitous cross-referencing allows DeSalvo to press on to her point: "Women who have been sexually abused often refer to their feelings of being smothered, of not being able to breathe. In many cases these images become connected to having been forced into oral sex."

But the terror of all terrors at Hyde Park Gate was the terror about falling foul of Sir Leslie. The most horrific chapter in a horrifying book is, for me, the opening one, about Laura, Laura who simply didn't fit into the pattern. She wouldn't or couldn't read. This Sir Leslie found "intensely provoking" and he set out to break Laura's will. Of course, the full powers of a patriarch in his own house, exerted against one small child, cannot but be successful. Laura was moved into a distant part of the house and in 1887, is finally "sent to the country to live apart from the family." Laura died in 1945, "still confined to the asylum." Why had she deserved this fate? What had she done? Nothing—except to get across the power of the Father, the Paterfamilias.

Reading Louise's book, and becoming more and more convinced that real damage had been done to Vanessa and Virginia and to Stella, and more and more convinced, too, that the Jeffrey Masson and Alice Miller way of correcting Freud's wilful refusal of the evidence is the only way to go, I have begun to reflect upon the photographs that Louise reproduces in her book.

One photograph in particular stands out as worthy of special attention, and that is the one showing Stella Duckworth holding up a bunch of grapes, with George Duckworth intimately caressing her from the left hand side of the photo, and Jack Hills tickling her affectionately from the right. (The photos follow p. 222. I refer to the second to last page of photos, the lowest on the right.)

I have known this photo for a long time, of course, but it was when I saw it again in the context of the "duckweed" chapter (especially pp.255-261) that I began to ask myself: What was the duplicitous slyness about the photo that gave it its particularly subversive quality?

Without doubt, that "subversive quality" is its character of icon. It is a carefully posed photo, which refers to many Medieval and Renaissance paintings of the Fall. Temptation is its theme, and it is (as usual, of course) the woman who is implicitly being blamed for the imminent Fall. Instead of an apple, though, there are grapes—an even more romantic and exotic form of Eastern temptation. The photo is taken in a highly artificial setting, a conservatory in which exotic fruit are forced (the grape vine is heavily laden) and which reminds the reader of Renaissance texts of Tasso's magic garden of Armida, where "Nature imitates Art, for a joke" (per scherzo) in *Gerusalemme Liberata*. Armida is the seductress, of course. Spenser's Acrasia, also a seductress, in her "Bowre of Blisse" in *The Faerie Queene*, is modelled upon Tasso's original temptress. Both conceptions are doubtless modelled upon Homer's Circe, who turned men, through lust, into pigs. The whole iconography of the photo is highly literary.

The woman holds up the forbidden fruit, and the quality of her look is what needs examining. She is, firstly, deeply complicit: she is complicit with the photographer; with the two men who play their ancillary roles in this mini-drama; and with the naked sexual innuendo of the pose itself—the invitation to sin.

She is, secondly, ironic: she ironises (with her smile) the complicity with the photographer; she ironises the two men at her sides; and she ironises the sexual innuendo of the pose itself. Instead of reading: "the invitation to sin" her smile says "isn't this a joke?"

And yet, there is, thirdly, a certain tragic dimension to her smile. Complicit, yes, ironic, yes, but isn't there, in those clear eyes, an appeal for remission, isn't there a certain kind of suffering, isn't there a quality of worldly-wise experience which throws into doubt her iconic virginal status?

"After such knowledge, what forgiveness?" (T.S. Eliot)

And the two men themselves—there's something fishy about them too. George Duckworth's hold on Stella is both possessive and knowing. I have commented in *The Unknown Virginia Woolf* (NJ: Humanities Press International, 1990, p. 112) on the extreme possessiveness of his stance next to Virginia (two pages earlier, top right). In this photo with Stella, he is both confiding, confident, confidant and seducer. His attitude is one of patronage: "here's my little girl, and what a good girl she is too!" Jack Hills, whose extraordinary antics Louise DeSalvo has documented in the book, appears to be fingering the grapes, (a light blur on the photo indicates movement), but he too, has this possessive, knowing, patronizing attitude to his bride-to-be. He too is tempted by the proffered fruit, he too is preparing to enjoy it.

But that future tense ("preparing to enjoy it") is belied by the temporality of the photo (the icon). The time, the tense, implied here, is the past, not the future. These two men have enjoyed the fruit, rather than are preparing to enjoy it. They are "past-masters" (if the pun may be allowed) in the game of seduction. That Stella should be (iconically) trying to persuade them into temptation, doubles the irony of the icon, for it is precisely she that has so visibly been seduced (in the past). Such a complicity of gestures, in the mini-drama being played out by the three protagonists, can only be a product of experience, of "knowing each other so well"—which is what the icon is definitely telling us. These three people do "know each other so well"—too well, one might surmise, if one were to look again at that penetrating glance from Stella: who would willingly have foregone the experience which came too early, the experience which Louise DeSalvo suggests has to do with "duckweed."

I can only offer these rapid suggestions for confirmation or disagreement. If there are those who have an insight as a result of these unguarded remarks, well and good. If there are those who think I am pushing things too far, I shall not attempt to insist on my case.

I would merely add this: let the doubters look at the expression on Vanessa's face in the "family group," showing an intensely despondent Sir Leslie Stephen and an almost despairing Julia Stephen, in the family photo on the fourth page of photos (following p. 232, second photo down). Like the photo of George, hand in pocket, laying claim to an almost annihilated Virginia (opposite) this photo has long fascinated me. Vanessa's face shows amusement (Thoby has obviously just cracked a joke), irony, enjoyment, and maturity.

But the knowingness of that smile is far too advanced for a girl in her early 'teens, in "circa 1894-95." It is the smile of a fully grown woman, and indeed of a fully grown woman of great experience.

Put that "Mona Lisa" smile of knowingness next to the triple layers of knowledge in the icon of Stella, George and Jack, and one is sent yet farther into the belief that Freud did irreparable damage to psychoanalysis when he decided that his female patients' stories of early molestation were all nothing but a neurotic fantasy.

Virginia Woolf Seeking Other Worlds With New Language, Vision and Ritual

Patricia Cramer
Notes from Underground: Lesbian Ritual
in the Writings of Virginia Woolf

In my talk this afternoon, I would like to talk about Virginia Woolf as a lesbian writer.[1] Because all lesbian writers are not, of course, the same, I place Woolf within a particular tradition of lesbian writers. Although these writers significantly differ among themselves (due, for example, to differences in race, class, and historical context), the commonality by which I group them is that defining a lesbian or woman-centered identity and eroticism is a central preoccupation of their work. This particular lesbian tradition has been defined by Judy Grahn in *The Highest Apple* to include Sappho, Emily Dickinson, Amy Lowell, H.D., and Gertrude Stein—and among contemporary lesbian writers—Judy Grahn, Pat Parker, Audre Lorde, Olga Broumas, Adrienne Rich, and Paula Gunn Allen. While women, like Woolf, writing before the lesbian feminist movement could not adopt the identification "lesbian" in precisely the same ways as contemporary writers, nevertheless, all the writers in this grouping adopt the homoerotic self as a center from which to oppose patriarchal values and to reimagine self and community. Beginning with *The*

Voyage Out, where Rachel Vinrace avoids marriage through her early death, Woolf consistently favors women who resist heterosexuality. Through her beloved spinster characters, she works to create a female identity grounded in indifference to heterosexual norms; with Mary Datchet, Lily Briscoe, Eleanor and Sarah Pargiter, and Miss LaTrobe, Woolf explores the special point of view and creative gifts of these outsiders to heterosexuality.

This use of the lesbian as metaphor and vantage point has been variously defined by feminist critics. Mary Carruthers says that among contemporary lesbian feminist poets, lesbian "encapsulates a myth of women together and separate from men"; "the essential outsider"; "erotic connection"; "radical internal transformation"; and "social redemption" (294-5). Monique Wittig describes the lesbian in her work as an "axis of categorization from which to universalize" (qtd. in Farwell "Lesbian Literary Imagination" 117); Marilyn Farwell defines lesbian as a space of sameness opposed to hierarchical difference in western narratives ("Heterosexual Plots" 102); and Adrienne Rich describes the lesbian in literature as a matrix: the *"primary presence of women to ourselves and each other . . . which is the crucible of a new language"* ("Power and Danger" 10). Woolf's homoerotic self-identification is central in these ways, providing a lens through which to assess her society, and an erotic consciousness shaping her narrative, metaphoric, and spiritual politics.

As Woolf's most overt celebration of lesbian sexuality, *Mrs. Dalloway* is our best key to the link between Woolf's lesbian identity and her writing. Woolf wrote *Mrs. Dalloway* during the beginning of her love affair with Vita Sackville-West. She began *Mrs. Dalloway* in 1922, and the book was published in May 1925 (Bell 2: 98;108). Vita and Virginia met in 1922, and by February 1923 Virginia had recognized the "sapphic" implications of Vita's interest in her: "She is a pronounced Sapphist, & may, thinks Ethel Sands, have an eye on me, old though I am" (*Diary* 2: 235). By January 1925, Vita's feelings were decidedly reciprocated: "My aristocrat . . . is violently Sapphic, and contracted such a passion for a woman cousin, that they fled to the Tyrol, or some mountainous retreat together. . . . To tell you a secret, I want to incite my lady to elope with me next" (*Letters* 3: 155-56). A diary entry on September 15, 1924 indicates how much Vita was on Virginia's mind as she composed this novel: "Here I am peering across Vita at my blessed Mrs. Dalloway; and can't stop, of a night, thinking of the next scene. Vita, to attempt a return, ... strides on fine legs, in a well cut skirt, & though embarrassing at breakfast, has a manly good sense & simplicity. . . . Oh yes, I like her" (*Diary* 2:313).

Written during the early stages of their love affair, *Mrs. Dalloway* records the emotional reorientation and joy of Woolf's coming out experience. Like her contemporary Gertrude Stein's posthumously published *QED*, *Mrs. Dalloway* belongs within a narrative convention indigenous to lesbian literature and life: the coming out narrative. Coming out narratives are oral as well as written traditions—rites of passage by which a lesbian affirms herself. Coming out may happen with her first sexual experience with a woman, or simply be that moment when she accepts her sexual and emotional preference for women. Coming out narratives repeat elements common to this convention: retold like rituals, coming out narratives explain how we came to be lesbians, and name coming out as a turning point for seeing the world in a new way. At the core of the coming out narrative is the newly identified lesbian self which becomes a focal point for redefining one's life—especially the past. Virginia and Vita apparently exchanged coming out stories as indicated by Vita's journal entry on the 29th of September 1928: Vita writes, "Virginia told me the history of her early loves—Madge Symonds who is Sally in *Mrs. Dalloway*" (qtd in Bell 1: 61). I like to think of Virginia and Vita alone in Paris engaged in this favorite lesbian ritual: disclosing those early signs of homosexuality within the story of coming out.

The similarities between Richard Dalloway and Leonard Woolf, and Peter Walsh and Clive Bell suggest that Woolf may have adopted the persona of Clarissa in order to reevaluate her own heterosexual history in the light of her coming out experience. While repeatedly juxtaposing Sally's kiss with Peter's horrible intrusion, Clarissa questions her key life choices: her rejection of Peter and her marriage to Richard. At first, Clarissa vaguely understands her preference for the less sexually demanding Richard as a self-protective defense of something she calls "priceless"—perhaps "solitude" or "dignity" (181) she surmises. But earlier it's Sally's kiss which she calls "infinitely precious" (53) and later it's Septimus who "hold[s] his treasure,"

(281) "the thing there was that mattered" (280) most. Adrienne Rich defines the coming out experience "as the beginning of naming, of memory, of making the connections between past and present and future that enable human beings to have an identity" (qtd. in Penelope xvi). Coding Clarissa's homosexual awakening in ways typical of lesbian writers of her generation, Woolf portrays Clarissa's reassessment of her past through her word choices. Connecting what was "precious" about Sally's kiss with the "treasure" Septimus died for, Clarissa understands that the "priceless dignity" which she preserved in a marriage without sexual passion is the sanctity of her sexual and emotional preference for women. At the end of the novel when Clarissa identifies with Septimus on the basis of their homosexuality, she changes her life narrative from a tale of heterosexual failure to a story of homosexual resistance and compromise.

Coming out narratives focus on the empowerment and ecstasy of coming out and this self-realization underlies Clarissa's self-affirmation when she recognizes her affinity with Septimus and reenters the party, revitalized. However, despite the joy of self-realization, Clarissa also must face what she has thrown away by denying her homosexuality. Miss Kilman is a reminder of the economic and emotional deprivation threatening lesbians and the limits of our choices in a patriarchy where heterosexualty is compulsory. *Mrs. Dalloway*, in fact, presents the three characteristic endings in coming out narratives written before 1969 in the fates of its three homosexual characters: the ending in marriage and suppression of homosexual feelings (Clarissa); loneliness and ostracism (Miss Kilman); and suicide (Septimus).

Since at least Gilbert and Gubar's *Madwoman in the Attic*, feminist readers have become accustomed to seeking subplots in novels by women which encode less socially acceptable levels of meaning—like the rage enacted by the madwoman figures in nineteenth century novels by women. As Christine Froula notes in her analysis of female initiation in *The Voyage Out*, one of Woolf's primary tasks was to create new plots where marriage and motherhood are not the only stories for women. Like the coming out narrative in *Mrs. Dalloway*, these subversive subplots are usually homoerotic and woman-centered. For example, Jane Marcus suggests that in *Night and Day* the real love story is the lesbian subplot between Katherine and Mary (*Languages of Patri-*

archy xiii.) In *The Years* gynocentric knowledge is transferred between Eleanor, Sarah, and Peggy, and in *Between the Acts*, the lesbian artist La Trobe momentarily reunites the matriarchal family—Isa, Lucy, and Dodge.

Woolf's gynocentric plots oppose social and novel conventions by presenting symbolic and narrative realities common to women. By creating representations of women's lives, she aims to create an audience and a sisterhood of women who recognize patterns of female experience embedded in her novels. The goal of coming out narratives is not only self-affirmation but creation of lesbian community. By sharing stories, lesbians invent lesbian identity and community based on common experiences and create models for others. In keeping with this coming out tradition, Virginia Woolf's record of her coming out experience in *Mrs. Dalloway* is a gift (like Septimus' to Clarissa) to lesbians seeking historical models and explanations for their sexual attractions for women. But Woolf's lesbian figures speak not only to lesbians, but to other women as well. For example, Peter's violent intrusion on Clarissa and Sally is paradigmatic of the prevalence of male sexual violence in women's lives. Under the spell of Clarissa's self-questioning, other women in the novel (and among her readers as well) begin to share Clarissa's developing consciousness. For example, Mrs. Dempster and Rezia think about the connections between marriage, war, and rape. This myth-making process is also apparent in Woolf's representations of her characters against a background of human types: for example, the tyrant fathers, heroic sons, and dead or diminished mother/goddess figures throughout her novels.

Woolf's method of connecting the individual and collective in this way is a narrative convention common to lesbian writers. In *The Highest Apple*, Judy Grahn defines this method as "mythic realism." In mythic realism, "female subjects [are] portrayed realistically on one level, yet with deep connections to a communally held myth at the same time" (87); "the result is art based on our creative consciousness and collectivity" (87). Narrative written in this way, Grahn notes, shares with gynocentric rituals the goal of personal transformation for the purpose of community making. Woolf abhorred egotism and preferred what she calls in *A Room of One's Own* the "common life" (117). In *A Room of One's Own*, she makes it clear that our ability to create and live within this collectivity is necessary for women's full creative expression. The communal aims in Woolf's plotting led me to call her narrative method "ritual" rather than narrative—because "ritual" describes the dynamic and transformative goals of Woolf's story telling.

While mythic realism helps to understand some of Woolf's structural devices, Jane Harrison's ritual theories help clarify the mystical and erotic elements of Woolf's narrative politics. According to Harrison, rituals express the beliefs and dreams of the community; inspire group participation by which the group is created and renewed; and rituals aim at personal transformation—an enlargement of self from isolated ego to the group (*Ancient Art and Ritual*). Harrison particularly admired the matriarchal fertility rites which preceded heroic narratives and encouraged other writers to return literature to its earlier social or group orientation (*Ancient Art and Ritual* 245-52). These fertility rites which Harrison admired were structured on a two part rhythm of blame and praise—the exorcism of evil and the induction of good (*Prolegomena* 7-8). This dynamic juxtaposition of good and evil parallels Woolf's practice of contrasting patriarchal and matriarchal values and methods; thus, Woolf's repetitive documentations of the evils of male domination can be viewed as a kind of ritual exorcism of evil within the ritual pattern described by Harrison.

The second part, which is the emotional basis of the ritual, aims at what Harrison calls the "magical inducement of fresh life" (*Themis* 546). Harrison stressed the emotional basis of ritual, insisting that rituals are essentially reenactments of emotions considered central to the life and coherence of the group (*Ancient Art and Ritual* 47-49). Harrison also used words like "enhancement" and "releases from self" (*Ancient Art and Ritual* 242) to describe ritual renewal—language which very closely matches Woolf's descriptions of lesbian love and visionary ecstasy. Harrison linked the emotional basis of fertility rituals with vegetation cycles and the need for food. However, as the following discussion of the simultaneity of Woolf's expressions of female sexual arousal, spirituality, and creativity will show, Woolf very specifically grounds the erotic and emotional bases of the induction phase of her narrative rituals in the lesbian body.

Woolf repeatedly describes the renewal and enhancement

which Harrison links with fertility rituals in language suggestive of lesbian love. In her letters and diaries, Woolf describes Vita's effect on her as a kind of magical revitalization: a special intensity which enlivens, renews, and transforms. Virginia described her feelings for Vita shortly after their return from Paris in 1928: "Well, somewhere I have seen a little ball kept bubbling up and down on the spray of a fountain: the fountain is you; the ball me. It is a sensation I get only from you. It is physically stimulating, restful at the same time I feel suppled and anointed now—." (*Letters* 3:540) Her favorite word for Vita is "glowed" (*Letters* 3: 229); in December 1932 she writes that Vita's departure "takes away; a lamp and a glow, and a shady leaf and an illuminated hall from my existence" (*Letters* 5: 141). On Vita's return she writes, "Lord how nice to see the shops pink again" (*Letters* 5:180). Perhaps the best illustration of Woolf's association of her lesbian sexuality with creative renewal is in a diary entry which links her feelings for Vita with her most sacred emotions: "Two nights ago, Vita was here and when she went, I began to feel the quality of the evening—how it was spring coming; a silver light; . . . I had a tremendous sense of life beginning; mixed with the emotion, which is the essence of my feeling, but escapes description. . . . (*Diary* 3:287).

In her novels, Woolf frequently uses the same language to describe female sexual arousal and those "unreasonable exaltation[s]"(*The Years* 382) common to her visionary and artist female characters. This suggests that the "divine vitality" (9) which attracts Peter and others to Clarissa is grounded in her homoeroticism. For example, in one of her "moments," standing on the threshold of her drawing room Clarissa compares her feelings to "waves which threaten to break, but only gently split their surface" (44). This imagery for Clarissa's moment of being matches the imagery for her response to women, similarly described as "some pressure of rapture, which split its thin skin" (47). Clarissa is described as "kindling all over with pleasure at the thought of her past with Sally" (261) and she wants to "kindle and illuminate" (6) at her party. Because Clarissa's parties are her artwork, Woolf equates lesbian sexuality and female creativity here.

Woolf's woman-identification shaped many of her metaphoric as well as narrative choices. Her codes for female sexual arousal place her firmly within a lesbian literary tradition which rewrites men's conventional associations of women as fragile and vulnerable flowers by using flowers instead as images of female sexual power. Both Priscilla Pratt and Paula Bennett have discussed Emily Dickinson's use of land and gardens to image the female body, decoding flowers—especially the rose and lily—as symbols of female sexuality. Both discuss flowers as vaginal and the preponderance of pellet or stonelike objects as clitoral imagery. In reviewing the lesbian poetic tradition, Judy Grahn identifies the rose as a common image for lesbian eroticism—symbolizing "the vulva with its birthing sexual creative and menstrual/intuitive powers" (*Highest Apple* 93). Woolf compares Vita to blossoming flowers in a letter written November 19, 1926: "The flowers have come, and are adorable, dusky, tortured, passionate like you—." (*Letters* 3:303); describing Vita to Vanessa, Woolf thinks of "the roses flowering; and the garden full of lust and bees, mingling in the asparagus beds" (*Letters* 3: 275). Recalling the "perfection" of Vita's body, Woolf thinks of "pellets which perhaps may unfold later" (*Diary* 2:306).

In *Mrs. Dalloway*, flowers, especially roses and lilies, are frequently associated with Clarissa and Sally. Clarissa "loved her roses" (182) and Sally, who "often went to her garden to get from flowers a peace which men and women never gave her" (293) calls Clarissa "a lily—a lily by the side of a pool" (294). Sally remembers Clarissa most clearly with her "hands full of flowers" (287). Clarissa's favorite memory—Sally's kiss—is associated with flowers. Clarissa remembers

> the most exquisite moment of her life passing a stone urn with flowers in it. Sally stopped, picked a flower; kissed her on the lips . . . And she felt she had been given a present, wrapped up and told just to keep it, not to look at it—a diamond—something infinitely precious, wrapped up, which, as they walked (up and down, up and down) she uncovered, as the radiance burnt through, the revelation, the religous feeling. (52-3)

Virginia Woolf Seeking Other Worlds

In this passage, the precious, wrapped, hard object suggests the clitoris and the "up and down" which uncovers this "diamond" suggests clitoral stimulation.

This is not the only time Woolf refers to a precious, wrapped object in this way: later, the "thing that mattered" which Septimus recalls for her is *"wreathed* [my emphasis] about with chatter" (280), and in *The Years* Sarah counters the phallic power of her father by forming her body into a vulva-like chrysalis: in opposition to her father "pirouetting up and down with his sword between his legs," Sara lies like a "chrysalis wrapped round in the sharp white folds of the sheet" (*The Years*: 144).

A more explicit link between flowers and lesbian eroticism occurs in Woolf's orgasmic description of the feelings aroused in her by proximity to women she admires: Clarissa describes her response to women as

> a sudden revelation, a tinge like a blush which one tried to check and then, as it spread, one yielded to its expansion and rushed to the farthest verge and there quivered and felt the world come closer, swollen with some astonishing significance, some pressure of rapture, which split its thin skin and gushed and poured with an extraordinary alleviation over the cracks and sores! Then for that moment, she had some illumination; a match burning in a crocus; an inner meaning almost expressed . . . the hard softened. (47)

In Woolf's passage, the clitoral and labial imagery in match and crocus are obvious, and the pattern of expansion, rush, rapture and splitting of surfaces is common in Woolf's descriptions of her lesbian feelings. Here, revelation is imaged as female orgasm; elsewhere, Clarissa's visionary ecstasies are again grounded in the aroused vulva: "moments like this are buds on the tree of life, flowers of darkness they are, she thought (as if some lovely rose had blossomed for her eyes only)" (43). There are numerous examples of this sameness of language for spiritual and sexual ecstasies in Woolf's other novels as well.

In *The Years*, Miss Craddock's and Kitty's mutual attraction is similarly coded in flowers, and like Sally and Clarissa, Kitty and Miss Craddock's intimacy is disrupted by men. Excited about Kitty's arrival, Miss Craddock thinks, "She's coming!" (*The Years* 144). However, when Kitty begins to respond to Miss Craddock's warmth, her teacher remembers Dr. Malone, and averts Kitty's gesture of intimacy by saying, "Look at my flowers." Kitty touches Miss Craddock's flowers, "tenderly" and then she remembers Chuffy's damp hand on her knee (*The Years* 65). This pattern representing the arousal of sexual and emotional intimacy between women checked by a male intrusion suggestive of rape shows that Woolf saw male sexual violation as a curb on her sexual feelings for women and not a cause, as some have suggested, of her lesbian identification. Looking for causes of lesbianism assumes heterosexuality as the norm, and Woolf's paradigmatic repetition of women loving women interrupted by male intrusion suggests the priority of her homoerotic connections.

Woolf understood and repeatedly represented male sexual violence as the core and origin of patriarchy. In the war of images Woolf wages in her writings, she repeatedly counters patriarchal images with images which empower women. And at the core of her counter-mythology she fosters a lesbian based model of female eroticism and relationship as a spiritual, sexual, and cognitive base for a new paradigm for culture. In *Mrs. Dalloway* this occurs, for example, when Clarissa compares the "purity, the integrity of her feeling for Sally" (50) with Peter's egotistical self-centered love affairs. And when Clarissa ritualistically recalls her delphiniums, sweet peas, lilacs, roses, and carnations as a counter-magic against the war state, there's far more than just the beauty of flowers that she is "calling up" (*Ancient Art and Ritual* 79).

In this counter-mythologizing within the subplots of her novels, Woolf creates what Adrienne Rich has described as a transformational poetics ("Power and Danger" 8) aimed at recreating community through poetry, ritual, and narrative. Woolf constructs her "dream of a common language" in metaphors rooted in the female body—speaking a language of female fantasy and sexual desire. By connecting her individual characters with her communal, gynocentric symbolic system, Woolf aims to transform not only our personal and political consciousness, but our collective unconscious as well. By using the language of lesbian love to express her creative vision, she places her lesbian identification at the center of her narrative politics. Perhaps this is what Woolf is telling us in *Between the Acts* when she reincarnates her spinster/artist figures as the more overtly lesbian La Trobe—the lesbian behind the village ritual—as well as Woolf's life work.

Notes

1. For discussion of Woolf's relationship to Vita Sackville-West, see Cook, DeSalvo, Knopp, Trautmann.

Works Cited

Bell, Quentin. *Virginia Woolf: A Biography*. 2 vols. New York: Harcourt Brace Jovanovich, 1972.
Bennett, Paula. *Emily Dickinson: Woman Poet*. London: Harvester, 1990.
Carruthers, Mary. "The Re-Vision of the Muse: Adrienne Rich, Audre Lorde, Judy Grahn, Olga Broumas." *The Hudson Review* (Summer 1983): 293-322.
Cook, Wiesen Blanche. "'Women Alone Stir My Imagination': Lesbianism and the Cultural Imagination." *Signs* 4.4 (1979): 195-214.
Desalvo, Louise. "Lighting the Cave: The Relationship between Vita Sackville-West and Virginia Woolf." *Signs* 8.2 (1982): 195-214.
Gilbert, Sandra M. and Susan Gubar. *The Madwoman in the Actic: The Nineteenth-Century Literary Imagination*. New Haven: Yale UP, 1979.
Farwell, Marilyn R. "Heterosexual Plots and Lesbian Subtexts: Toward a Theory of Lesbian Narrative Space." *Lesbian Texts and Contexts: Radical Revisions*. Eds. Karla Jay and Joanne Glasgow. New York: New York UP. 91-103.
———. "Toward a Definition of the Lesbian Literary Imagination." *Signs* 14.11 (1988): 100-18.
Froula, Christine. "Out of the Chrylalis: Female Initiation and Female Authority in Virginia Woolf's *The Voyage Out*." *Tulsa Studies in Women's Literature* 5.1 (1986): 63-90.
Grahn, Judy. *The Highest Apple*. San Francisco: Spinsters Ink, 1985.
Harrison, Jane. *Ancient Art and Ritual*. New York: Henry Holt & Co., 1913.
———. *Prolegomena to the Study of Greek Religion*. Cambridge UP, 1903.
———. *Themis: A Study of the Social Origins of Greek Religion*. Cambridge: Cambridge UP, 1912.
Jensen, Emily. "Clarissa Dalloway's Respectable Suicide." *Virginia Woolf: A Feminist Slant*. Ed. Jane Marcus. Lincoln: University of Nebraska Press, 1983. 162-79.
Knopp, Sherron. "'If You Saw Me Would You Kiss Me': Sapphism and the Subversiveness of Virginia Woolf's *Orlando*." *Publications of the Modern Language Society* 103.1 (1988): 24-34.
Marcus, Jane. "Thinking Back Through Our Mothers." *Art and Anger:*

Reading Like a Woman. Columbus: Ohio State UP, 1988. 73-100.
———. *Virginia Woolf and the Languages of Patriarchy*. Bloomington: Indiana UP, 1987.
O'Brien, Sharon. *Willa Cather: The Emerging Voice*. New York: Oxford UP, 1987.
Penelope, Julia and Susan J. Wolfe. *The Coming Out Narratives*. Watertown, Massachusetts: Persephone Press, 1980.
Pratt, Priscilla. *"Then Sunrise Kissed My Chrysalis": Figurations of the Erotic in the Poetry of Emily Dickinson*. Dissertation. February 1991. University of Minnesota.
Rich, Adrienne. "Power and Danger: The Work of a Common Woman." *The Work of a Common Woman: The Collected Poetry of Judy Grahn 1964-1977*. New York: St. Martin's Press, 1978. 7-21.
Trautmann, Joann. *The Jessamy Brides*. University Park: Pennsylvania State UP, 1973.
Woolf, Virginia. *The Diary of Virginia Woolf*. 5 vols. Ed. Anne Olivier Bell. New York: Harcourt Brace, 1977-1984.
———. *The Letters of Virginia Woolf*. 6 vols. Eds. Nigel Nicolson and Joanne Trautmann. New York: Harcourt Brace Jovanovich, 1980.
———. *Mrs. Dalloway*. New York: Harcourt, Brace and Jovanovich, 1925.
———. *Moments of Being*. New York: Harcourt, Brace and Jovanovich, 1976.
———. *A Room of One's Own*. New York: Harcourt, Brace and Jovanovich, 1929.
———. *The Years*. Harcourt, Brace and Jovanovich, 1937.
Zimmerman, Bonnie. *The Safe Sea of Women: Lesbian Fiction 1969-1989*. Boston: Beacon Press, 1990.

Merry Pawlowski
Virginia Woolf's *Between the Acts*: Fascism in the Heart of England

During the final decade of her career, Virginia Woolf moved most provocatively toward the expression of a feminine and feminist voice in her texts. Due to the increasing momentum of this change, we find a kinship between Woolf as theoretican and contemporary French and British feminist thinkers. Such an alliance is explained in part by the deep disturbance so many women share in the face of Freudian theory and fascist, patriarchal ideology; and we find the change fully blossomed in Woolf's last text, *Between the Acts*.

Woolf's textual practice as she reached the end of her career demonstrates how a writing woman might differ from and revise, rather than imitate, the social, cultural, and artistic texts written by men. This practice resulted in Woolf's problematizing the possibility of unification, creating a discursive method which disrupts conventional linear discourse, a discourse inadequate for the feminine voice.

Woolf confronted and revised within the field of her writing the discourses of patriarchy as she searched for the place, language and history of women in her late texts, and she anticipated the work of current feminist and postmodern theorists who have acknowledged the slipping away of meaning and being through the sieve of language. Very noticeable among the multiple subtexts of Woolf's *Between the Acts* is Freud's *Group Psychology and the Analysis of the Ego*, and the war brewing in Europe collected into the massive images of the "Fuhrer" and "Il Duce." Woolf felt impelled to confront Freud's work in her determination to voice feminine experience. Woolf also knew herself as a woman, particularly in terms of a fascist ideological abstraction of woman, to be defined by the standards of her society as an outsider to power, both seeking and trapped by the ties and restraints of family and society, always as an "other." It is this social concept and Freud's psychoanalytical theories which concerned Woolf in her reading notes during the gestational period of *Between the Acts*, notes in which Woolf associated Freud's view of mankind with the war gathering in Europe. As a result, Woolf questions the evolution of society from its very beginnings to the present day of writing her novel, and she finds that woman's image and voice has been inscribed as lack. Two motions emerge in the discourse of *Between the Acts*: one to uncover this inscription of woman as absence and the other a struggle to replace it with feminine presence.

Led by the intensity of her reading of Freud to consider the unraveling of the fabric of society in time of war, Woolf uncovers fascist ideology as it has shaped English history in *Between the Acts*, paying close attention to the compliance of women in their own oppression. Woolf also recognizes in her text that women must transcend a preoedipal attachment to their mothers in the formation of their own egos, in essence, "killing the Angel in the House." Having done this herself in *To The Lighthouse*, Woolf is free in *Between the Acts* to attempt or suggest the discursive reconstruction of the feminine ego in the search, not for unification, but for equal balance in society.

Such a balance creates a narrative which seeks to be "other" than narrative, a text at once recognizing and refusing itself by masquerading as a play within a play and yielding to the metonymic shifting and continuous deferral of meaning in the prose poems uttered by Isa throughout the text. Such a motion carries within it its own negativity—a negativity at the heart of the conflict between language and vision, the definitive conflict of Woolf's mature phase. Woolf engages a complex philosophical and psychoanalytic system in her discourse as she disassembles the notion of centering and sameness which coincides with the belief in a transcendental ego. In terms of that male-defined philosophy of ego, one of the most important boundaries Woolf chooses to chart in her last text is the boundary between man and woman, seeking for woman both a voice and a place.

Woolf, in *Between the Acts*, chooses a path that is most destructive to conventional patriarchal language, a language she saw as excluding women from power and expression while upholding the horrors of fascist oppression. Her path insists, rather, upon vision, image, and sound which can only approximate, not reproduce, what she sees. Approximation, after all, is all that is possible for those who have been denied the power of language. Woolf pushes language to the point where it fails; and we are then forced to read her texts in a new way, not in "the formal railway line of the sentence . . . ," but in the way people think and dream, "all over the place. . . "[1]

Between the Acts sums up Woolf's textual practice as antinarrative, but the question remains whether this novel succeeds in writing a new (non)plot for women or providing a vision of society in the future which offers optimism and hope. I do not insist that Woolf escapes the trap of the old plot, the battle between the sexes here, but I am not sure she intended to do so. I do hope to argue, however, that this, of all Woolf's late texts, is not only her most important theoretical revision of masculine, dominant culture as she saw it, but also her greatest technical innovation in the establishment of an essentially different feminine discourse, dismantling fascism, psychoanalytic theory, and a philosophy of unification in one blow.

Note

[1] Letter to Jacques Raverat, a painter and friend with whom Woolf had many exchanges about the differences between form in painting and writing. *The Letters of Virginia Woolf, Vol. IV: 1923-1928*, ed. Nigel Nicolson (New York: Harcourt Brace Jovanovich, 1977) 136.

Penelope Cordish
Virginia Woolf's Mountain Top—
That Persistent Vision

In a diary entry of November 23, 1940, Woolf adumbrates a book which she did not live to write: "I shall brew some moments of high pressure. I think of taking my mountain top—that persistent vision—as a starting point" (*Diary* 5:341). The goal of this paper is to ascertain what the "mountain top" means to Woolf and just how "persistent" and significant it is in her oeuvre and consciousness.

The mountain-top perspective, which she elsewhere terms "looking out at peace from a height" (*Diary* 5:187), is observable in Woolf's texts as early as the ascent of Monte Rosa in *The Voyage Out* and as late as "The Symbol" holograph dated March, 1941, which is either her last or penultimate short story. Drawing on instances throughout the canon, such as the ascent of Monte Rosa, Bernard's "moment . . . on the turf somewhere high above the flow of the sea," and Kitty Lasswade's climb to the crest of a hill in *The Years*, I define the common properties of the elevated view for Woolf as a vast vision of the whole perceived by the mind/soul freed from the constraints of time, space, and personality. This distanced, general view in which peace and rest are found is an aesthetic one of order, proportion and rhythmic pattern. So, in a paradigmatic scene, Kitty, thinking "all passes, all changes," climbs, we are told, "higher and higher" toward the crest of a hill:

> Suddenly she saw the sky between two striped tree trunks extraordinarily blue. She came out on the top. The wind ceased; the country spread wide all round her. Her body seemed to shrink; her eyes to widen. She threw herself on the ground, and looked over the billowing land that went rising and falling, away and away, until somewhere far off it reached the sea. Uncultivated, uninhabited, existing by itself, for itself, without towns or houses it looked from this height. Dark wedges of shadow, bright breadths of light lay side by side. Then, as she watched, light moved and dark moved; light and shadow went travelling over the hills and over the valleys. A deep murmur sang in her ears—the land itself, singing to itself, a chorus, alone. She lay there listening. She was happy, completely. Time had ceased. (*The Years* 300—all references to Woolf's fiction and essays are to the Hogarth Press editions.)

Such "moments on top" have a place within the larger context of Woolf's belief in the simultaneous validity of dual perceptions of existence which are the products of viewing life from radically different perspectives. In *To the Lighthouse*, Woolf encapsulates these seemingly conflicting points of view in a diagrammatic image: "...the waves shape themselves symmetrically from the cliff top, but to the swimmer among them are divided by steep gulfs, and foaming crests" (*To the Lighthouse* 244) Here the perspective of the swimmer is the necessarily foreshortened one of the self-conscious individual, actively engaged in time and immersed in the "innumerable perplexities" of existence. In the process of reading a text by Woolf much of the time/space is spent viewing indeterminate existence from this perspective. "Such is the complexity of things" that a Woolfian character—or reader—is always "being made to feel violently two contradictory things at the same time." From the vantage point of the cliff top, however, the "waves shape themselves symmetrically"; the rise and fall, ebb and flow, light and shade of existence are revealed as patterned and rhythmical factors of a greater whole: "All is resolved . . . into simplicity."

In the early novels, these dual perspectives often exist side by side in philosophical and formal tension. Such tension is manifested, for example, in the two distinct narrative points of view in *Jacob's Room*, one limited by particularity—"ten years' seniority and a difference of sex"—and the other capable of ranging through vast continuations of time and space from the vantage point of the heights that border and contain Jacob's brief life, Dods Hill on the one hand, and the Acropolis on the other.

During 1925 through 1929, however, Woolf works out a "theory of fiction . . . about perspective" which resolves this tension and accommodates both ways of envisioning human life (*Diary* 2: 50). "Reality," she posits, in "Phases of Fiction" is something that various authors "put at different distances" Thus the new novel predicted in "The Narrow Bridge of Art" will offer both the "up close to life" perspective of prose and the more general and distanced one of poetry. Modern fiction, then, will require a new perspective; according to Woolf, "this unnamed variety of the novel will be written standing back from life, because in that way a larger view is to be obtained" (*CE* 2: 224). In "Notes on an Elizabethan Play," Woolf is even more specific in her designation of the proper distance and position for the ideal novelistic point of view—one that is, in fact, about the height of a mid-sized summit:

> Our contention merely is that there is a station, somewhere in mid-air whence Smith and Liverpool can be seen to the best advantage; that the great artist is the man who knows where to place himself above the shifting scenery; that while he never loses sight of Liverpool he never sees it in the wrong perspective. (*CE* 1:55)

During the same period in which she was composing these

theoretical essays, Woolf was also putting her new theories concerning perspective into practice within the content and form of her experimental novels. Invisible, impersonal, and unobtrusive, the unique narrator which Woolf introduces in *Mrs. Dalloway* is most markedly a point of view, a perspective on existence. "Standing back from life," it perceives the whole, contains and composes all the isolated and searching consciousnesses of the characters. Passing from mind to mind, each with its subjective and partial knowledge, this narrator assembles the more than "fifty pairs of eyes" that Woolf claims are needed to get round experience. Relating all in past tense indirect discourse, the narrator, as J. Hillis Miller has demonstrated, collects all the individual, "close-up" perspectives without comment, yet in its synthesizing, over-arching view (often associated with the sky) are revealed similarities and repetitions which together weave the patterned texture of the novels (Miller, in *The Shaken Realist*, 100-127).

More than the sum of the particulars it collects, this narrative vision alone persists throughout long spaces of darkness and absence, such as "Time Passes," which would be otherwise "unseen by anyone." It is this creative perception Woolf claims that "perceives pictures, knife and fork, also men and women .... And further goes from mind to mind ... and from body to body, creating what is not mind or body, not surface or depth, but a common element in which the perishable is preserved, and the separate become one" (*Pointz Hall Transcript*, Berg Collection, 57-58).

The perspective from on high—this impersonal vision of wholeness in which all particulars are assembled in a formal order—is the realm in which Virginia Woolf's unusual narrator resides perpetually and to which her characters ascend occasionally. At the crest of her career, the novels of 1925-1929, *Mrs. Dalloway*, *To the Lighthouse*, and *Orlando*, all build to climactic conclusions in which the protagonists themselves achieve moments of vision while at actual heights: upstairs window, cliff or hill top. In such symbolic conclusions, the perspective of the character literally and figuratively ascends to approach that of the narrative perceiver; the dual perspectives of the novel converge. The accomplishment of the protagonist's vision, the achievement of the narrator's perception, and the completion of

Virginia Woolf Seeking Other Worlds

the author's creation all take place concurrently in a remarkable oneness of effort. The whole is assembled; the self realized; the past recovered; the vision achieved; all concluded in recollection, reunion and revivification.

The weight of these conclusions, with their triumphant moments of completion, rests upon a single (usually female) figure, a seeker and seer, who, standing on some high station, assembles, summarizes, and integrates everything within herself and her vision of wholeness. In the course of the novels, it becomes increasingly evident that this solitary figure is, for Woolf, the prototype of the artist and that the view from on high is one of aesthetic vision and creative process.

Fittingly then, the act of reading true literature, for Woolf, also metaphorically raises the reader to this transcendent perspective. Thus, in "The Window," Mrs. Ramsay reads a Shakespearean sonnet: "and so reading she was ascending, she felt, on to the top, on to the summit. How satisfying! How restful!" Moreover, in *A Room of One's Own*, the would-be writer must pass a similar test; she must make the reader feel, "as she went on writing, as if one had gone to the top of the world and seen it laid out majestically beneath" (140-141).

More importantly for Virginia Woolf the artist, the constructive act of writing itself, which alone brings about the "synthesis of [her] being" (*Diary* 4:161), is symbolically and emotionally associated with the view from on high:

> There are very few mountain summit moments. I mean looking out at peace from a height. I made this reflection going upstairs. That is symbolical. I'm 'going upstairs' now, when I write Biography. Shall I have a moment on top? Or when I've done Roger? (*Diary* 5:187)

The composing of Roger Fry's life in particular and of art in general is her reply to the fact of formlessness and death.

In the diary, she recalls the fear that came to her of death at Fry's funeral: "I felt the vainness of this perpetual fight with our brains and loving each other against the other thing; if Roger could die." Why not, as she says elsewhere, "acquiesce and resign?" (*To the Lighthouse* 219-220). This is the question which haunts Virginia Woolf's writings, personal and fictive, and in reply to which she writes her novels. The answer lies, for her, in the transcendent power of art:

> But then... the other thing begins to work—*the exalted sense of being above time and death which comes from being again in a writing mood*. And this is not an illusion, so far as I can tell. (*Diary* 4:245, emphasis added)

It is not surprising then, that Woolf should choose to create her fiction in a room with an elevated view: "From some higher station I may be able to pull it [*The Waves*] together—at Rodmell, in my new room" (*Diary* 3:268). Nor does it come as a shock that her diary record of a wonderous experience of what Mark Hussey terms "reality" should contain mountains in its imagining: "Then... I see the mountains in the sky: the great clouds; and the moon which is risen over Persia; I have a great and astonishing sense of something there, which is 'it.'" (*Diary* 3:62).

In the last section of Woolf's next novel, *The Waves*, Bernard, the aging writer, like the protagonists before him, is left "to sum up" and so to recount the novel. "On a turf somewhere high above the flow of the sea," he, too, attains a transcendency in which seeing "the world ... without a self," he recaptures the beginning: "the house, the garden, the waves breaking. The old nurse who turns the pages of the picture-book had stopped and had said 'Look. This is the truth!'" (204).

Such a "moment on high" concludes the three novels that precede *The Waves*; now, however, the vision of wholeness is strikingly penultimate. "Blindness returns," selfhood and temporality reassert themselves. "Always it begins again." "The vision," Bernard realizes and regrets, "must be perpetually remade." The mountain top itself is only the momentary crest of a wave, participatory rather than transcendent. Still, the novel ends on a note of valiant acceptance of the rising and falling rhythm of life and of the perpetual effort it requires. (207-211)

In the last decade of Woolf's life, the incessant repetition of

Virginia Woolf Seeking Other Worlds

"building it up" anew apparently becomes increasingly frustrating and exhausting. Her next novel, aptly named *The Years*, takes five years to finish and its conclusion leaves her dangerously close to suicide. On June 11, 1936, she writes in the diary "to say at last after 2 months dismal and worse, almost catastrophic illness—never been so near the precipice to my own feeling since 1913—I'm again on top" (*Diary* 5:24).

Moreover, as the world moves, in Leonard Woolf's words, "downhill all the way" to the chaos and disintegration of world war, the realities of life and art seem increasingly divorced from each other, as do artist and audience. In these years, Woolf's mountain top motif itself undergoes a strange yet predictable alteration. The summit is no longer a "mid-air station" from which the pageant of existence can be viewed to best advantage, but a frozen death-like realm of solipsistic escape. She writes in the diary of a desire "to write a dream story about the top of a mountain . . . . About lying in the snow; about rings of color; silence; . . . and the solitude" (*Diary* 5:95). When the image of looking out from a height reoccurs at the ambiguous conclusion of her last novel, *Between the Acts*, the vantage-point belongs now not to the seer or artist, but to a prehistoric being seeing nothing but darkness: "It was night before roads were made, or houses, It was the night that dwellers in caves had watched from some high place among rocks" (*BTA*, 256).

Finally, in "The Symbol," which is probably one of the last two stories Woolf wrote in March of 1941, an elderly English woman sits on a balcony of a hotel in the Swiss Alps writing a letter in which she ponders the symbolic nature of a mountain. As she writes, she watches a party of young men, one of whom she knows, climbing up the slopes of the mountain. Instead of reaching the summit, however, they silently disappear into a crevasse as if into the abyss. The pen falls from the writer's hand, and a drop of ink struggles "in a zig zag line down the page." Late that night after the bodies have been recovered, she attempts to go on writing: "The old cliches will come in very handy. They died trying to climb the mountain . . . They died in an attempt to discover . . . There seemed no fitting conclusion" (Dick, *The Complete Shorter Fiction* 284). As Lyndall Gordon comments, "instead of transmuting grief into art, art in this final story—literally the act of writing—is arrested by the prospect of mortality" (*A Writer's Life*, 179).

Octavia Wilberforce, Woolf's friend and doctor, visited her on March 12 and reported that Virginia, who had just finished a story, was feeling "desperate — depressed to the lowest depth." (Gordon 279) Sixteen days later, Virginia Woolf drowned herself.

Virginia Stephen Woolf, herself the child of a famous Alpine mountain climber and celebrant, was indeed her father's daughter. It has been noted that the name of the proprietor of the inn in this last story, "The Symbol" recalls that of Leslie Stephen's Swiss guide, Melchior Anderegg (Gordon 279). What is more, in *The Voyage Out*, Woolf transports Monte Rosa from Switzerland, where Stephen climbed it during his *first* Alpine expedition in 1858 (Maitland 83), to the South American site of her *first* novel. In a sense, the daughter metaphorically meets her father on his own turf and claims at least as much effort required for her task as he did for his. In his essay, "A Bad Five Minutes in the Alps," Leslie Stephen, the agnostic Victorian, asserts his only remaining faith—"in playing out the game." So, too, Virginia Woolf, the atheistic Modern, asserts, as long as she can, her belief in the transcendent possibilities of art by means of her "mountain top—that persistent vision."

Time, Embodiment and the Problem of Separation in the Novels of Virginia Woolf

Amanda Grant
Life Without Boundaries

Critics often discuss how Virginia Woolf writes about the past and the present but few explore her use of the future as an individual segment of time. Her characters are not only influenced by her use of time as a narrative technique but their lives are actually interrupted by the future more than the past. Woolf writes extensively about the simultaneous existence of past experience and the certainty of future happenings, particularly death, as an inherent part of her characters' lives. Her novels demonstrate that the experience of time differs, for although a moment may be only a split second to a character, it may last an eternity to the reader and the characters often define this uneven progression in their thoughts.

The particular significance of the future is manifested in three different forms throughout Woolf's writing. The impact of the future is not only obvious in the structure of books, but also its effect on the past and present. The future balances on a thin line between nostalgia, a slow yet simultaneously speedy progress in the form of regression, and nightmare. Woolf's characters often turn into the very children, in old age, that they are so nostalgic about. They creep backwards to youth as they physically become immersed in age.

Woolf is extremely conscious of how thoughts of the future impact on life, especially in *To The Lighthouse* where the Ramsay family and Lily Briscoe are constantly affected by the dread of future prospects. Past memories also impact the lives of Woolf's characters as they realize that the people and places in the past have not changed but their memories of the past have been transformed. The future brings change that is often feared since uncertainty changes what is known. Regardless of how much of the past we understand it is impossible to determine future events, or comprehend the present. Woolf implies that it is terrifying to realize one is in the present moment because that means life is one more part history and one less part future experience. The future tears us further away from youth which is so treasured and makes us look at ourselves as it becomes the past, just as the audience in *Between the Acts* is forced to stop time and view themselves, and Mrs. Ramsay, in *To The Lighthouse*, watches her party become a memory even before it has ended.

Death permeates Woolf's writing as an impending future event. In *Jacob's Room* the death of Jacob Flanders is expressed both as a memory and a future event in the lives of the characters. Woolf blends the past and future to illustrate through memory the happenings in *Jacob's Room*. She takes a memory and allows the reader to see that the future is described, which in fact is the present just as Jacob speaks as a child in the past, about occurrences in his future, which are the present of the book. The imminence of death as part of the future is also clearly demonstrated in *Between The Acts* where Woolf strongly emphasizes that the future will exist when the past is forgotten.

In *Mrs. Dalloway* Woolf shows how people exaggerate past occurrences and feelings in their memories. She believes no matter how well you know someone, the effect of memories is to change the way you think you knew them and frighteningly, even the way you thought you knew yourself as a child. This is the nightmare of the future and the regression into childhood as we age.

Virginia Woolf emphasizes the way a memory can be refashioned with the passage of time. In *To The Lighthouse* she uses the analogy of painting, and emphasizes that each observer views a work of art differently, particularly with the passage of time. Nothing is ever the same in memories as it was during the actual experience and similarly our reactions to memories in the future will be ever-changing. Our memories, we are to understand, are not accurate. We do not remember things as they were but we change them, exaggerating qualities which stand out and repressing others.

The relationship of the past, present and future are constantly in the forefront of Virginia Woolf's writing. There is an element of relativity as perspective depicts varying situations shaped by time. As Woolf explains in "A Sketch of the Past," the present is nothing without the experiences of the past and anticipations of the future. Using her characters, Virginia Woolf transports her readers through the passages of time by her all-encompassing use of yesterday, today and tomorrow.

Kathy Brady
Time, Space and Silence

Is it experience perhaps—repeated shocks each unfelt at the time, suddenly loosening the fabric? breaking something away? Only this image suggests collapse and disintegration, whereas the process I have in mind is just the opposite. It is not destructive whatever it may be, one may say that it was rather of a creative character. ("Reading" 25)

One of the most compelling and problematic paradoxes of human existence is our concept of time. Time is our omnipotent adversary, one that we slice into discrete linear segments (days, hours, minutes, and lifetimes) which become a shield against our fear of obliteration and death. Our collective obsession to control and dominate time—to see it as a construct instead of constructive—ultimately results in fragmentation and loss of self. In the novels of Virginia Woolf, time simultaneously inhibits and enables, punishes and rewards, obscures and reveals. The fabric of conventional chronological time is "loosened," something "breaks away," a process of creation, not destruction. Through some of her characters, Woolf reveals a timeless and timely vision in which traditional boundaries of the future, present and past are indistinguishable and all-inclusive. These characters from *Between the Acts, Mrs. Dalloway, To The Lighthouse*, and *Jacob's Room* derive strength from a wellspring of ambivalence, powerful and positive, which they embrace thus allowing them a fluidity of mind and body that transcends time, space, and language.

Characters like Lucy Swithin, Mrs. Ramsay and Lily Briscoe, Betty Flanders and Clarissa Dalloway, embody holistic alternative time. Each of them has access to other times, other spaces, other voices. Time for them, creates and is created, enveloping, empowering and enlightening. Like Lucy Swithin, who "was given to increasing the bounds of the moment by flights into past or future" (9), these characters create opportunities for transcendence through non-linear time. Singularity of space and time is dangerous and limiting, and Woolf's vision is one in which "multiplicity becomes unity which is somehow the secret of life" (*Jacob's Room* 131).

Conversely, characters like Giles Oliver and Dr. Bradshaw, Jacob Flanders and Mr. Ramsay, exist in worlds distinguished by delineation and classification which preclude multiplicity. Like Mr. Ramsay, who strives to reach "R" (himself) in alphabetical order, they are impaled on the skewer of time by social and intellectual pursuits.

The power of Virginia Woolf's vision is that it acknowledges the nuances of time's endless spectrum. Although some of her characters are more receptive and connected to alternative holistic time, it would be a mistake to think that some of them "have it" and some of them don't. Even characters imprisoned by conventional time and space experience timeless moments, hear other voices, feel other spaces; some sustained and some fleeting. In *Beauty and Sadness*, by Yasunari Kawabata, a character notes that, "Time flows in the same way for all human beings; every human being flows through time in a different way" (164). When the husk of time splits, it reveals illuminations and daily miracles, connecting and disconnecting us, each of us perceiving it differently, and yet the same.

Hungry to Talk: A Roundtable Discussion of Teaching *To the Lighthouse*

Beth Rigel Daugherty and Mary Beth Pringle, with Marcia McClintock Folsom; Nancy Topping Bazin; Sally Jacobsen; Katherine Hill-Miller; Susan Yunis

The seven panelists barely notice their salads and soups at a pre-roundtable lunch. They busily scribble notes on napkins and folders as the questions, comments, and suggestions fly. Intrigued by what others say they have tried, they are already planning how they might teach Woolf's novel *next* time. At this meeting and the later roundtable discussion, people are hungry to talk about teaching Woolf's *To the Lighthouse*.

"How do you manage to get slides of Impressionist and Post-Impressionist art?"

"Have your students' responses to Mr. and Mrs. Ramsay and to Lily changed over the years?"

"Have you read . . . ? What do you think of . . . . ?"

"I *love* your idea about teaching *To the Lighthouse* with other family chronicles by women. What other books have you considered using?"

"Have you ever thought about . . . ?"

"Do your students resolve their own work/family tensions as a result of reading *To the Lighthouse*? And how do they work through those issues? In journals? Or . . . ?"

They fill a large classroom on Saturday evening at 5:00 p.m. As the panelists briefly discuss their approaches to teaching *To the Lighthouse,* the space begins to feel less academic with its rows of desks bolted to the floor and fluorescent lights glaring overhead. Instead, it feels more communal. There's a place set for everyone and platters laden with ideas get passed around. The supposedly plain boiled beef and prunes of pedagogy taste pretty fine sometimes.

Kathy Hill-Miller stresses the importance of keeping the novel accessible to students whose reading experience in many cases has stalled at Stephen King. The novel, she tells those gathered, helps students achieve self-definition, an important concern for traditional age students. Because we often define ourselves against the expectations of parents, Kathy notes, we need to come to terms with these familial expectations. Her class analyzes both the Ramsays and their house guests and what they expect of each other. Students note that characters free themselves when they give up extraordinary attachments to others.

In the context of an undergraduate seminar on the Bloomsbury group, Susan Yunis introduces Woolf's experimental novel by showing slides of Impressionist and Post-Impressionist paintings. Focusing on revolutionary techniques of late nineteenth-century art, Susan shows her students how an artist's angle of vision can distort the human figure, how the subject can be both content and "creator" of art, how paintings of the period gradually shift their focus from an external subject to the process of perception, and how this process of perception may distort the world being looked at. Susan also illustrates the modern period's loss of solid outlines and its placement of human effort at the margins. After this slide show introduction, students, she says, *see* what Woolf is doing in her novel.

Sally Jacobsen hopes her students will appreciate *To the Lighthouse's* humor through understanding the way Woolf tells the story. She introduces stream of consciousness and shows students how to determine whose stream of consciousness they are in. Then Sally compares the comedy of manners in *To the Lighthouse*—juxtaposing "everybody's interior thoughts about everybody else"—to the drawing room humor in Austen, Brontë,

Hungry to Talk

and Molière. Sally also shows her students how funny Woolf's "intrusions" into her stream of consciousness are: her "arch exaggerations" and gentle spoofs comment on the action, as when Mr. Ramsay reflects on the progress of his career using letters of the alphabet.

For Nancy Topping Bazin, *To the Lighthouse* articulates the choice Woolf had to make and the choice her students, mainly female, still feel they must make: that between meaningful work and a happy family. The resulting tension, so well delineated in Mrs. Ramsay and Lily, demonstrates for students the implications of each choice, raises questions about having it all, and gets at the spiritual dimension of work.

In her undergraduate classes at Wheelock College, Marcia McClintock Folsom frequently contrasts the first and third sections of the novel—respectively their crowded vs. empty feel, their fast vs. slow pace. In a Radcliffe Seminar for adult women, she instead teaches Woolf's novel with four contemporary family chronicles by American female writers (Pauli Murray's *Proud Shoes: The Story of An American Family,* Sara Lawrence Lightfoot's *Balm in Gilead:The Journey of a Healer,* Maxine Hong Kingston's *The Woman Warrior: Memoirs of a Girlhood Among Ghosts,* and Kim Chernin's *In My Mother's House: A Daughter's Story*). Doing so, she tells us, shows the collaborative nature of the American autobiographies compared with Woolf's solitary creation and the Americans' recent confrontation with anger compared with Woolf's modernist, fictional displacement of it. All five works, though, reveal the effect a divided heritage has on daughters.

Using what she learned from a class in contemporary American women's memoirs, Mary Beth Pringle plans to use Mary Catherine Bateson's *Composing a Life* as a "map for reading *To the Lighthouse*" the next time she teaches the novel to upper-level undergraduates and graduate students. Bateson's memoir, because it *is* memoir, has an immediacy for students that can help them "bridge the distance between now and then, us and them." Both Bateson and Woolf use indirection, she says, to define a female quest motif and to portray a unity "based on achievement as well as caring" underlying the improvisational, quilted surface of women's lives.

In Beth Rigel Daugherty's twentieth-century literature class for freshmen and sophomore English majors, students read E. B.

White's "Once More to the Lake," write about their memories of summers and parents and places, and then share those memories in classroom discussion. From there, it's a short step to Woolf's 1905 Cornwall diary in *A Passionate Apprentice* and to snippets from her "Sketch of the Past," diaries, and letters. The power of memory, she says, links students' lives to Virginia Woolf's, which makes *To the Lighthouse*, though still difficult, more real to them.

As usual, way too much food is prepared for the meal and questions of several types, prepared by the panelists for each other, never get asked. Panelists want to know more about duplicating approaches in their own classes, about resources, and about student assignments, Other questions concern student reactions to approaches and to aspects of the novel, and further questions focus on passages in the novel or on extending approaches in new directions. For example, Kathy wants to know how Beth ties the idea of memory to Lily's completion of her painting at novel's end. "Where can I obtain copies of pictures of Talland House and the Godrevy Lighthouse?" Sally plans to ask Beth. Susan to Kathy, "Do you have any writing assignments for your students that encourage them to explore their own separation from their parents and their parents' expectations?" Nancy to Mary Beth, "If you have any males in your class, how do they respond to the gender difference you describe in male vs. female quests?" Mary Beth wants to know how Sally handles it when a student reads Mr. Ramsay as a sympathetic character surrounded by cold fish. Sally plans to ask Marcia, "Do you think Woolf's archness in portraying other characters' anger—James wanting to take an axe to his father in the opening pages, Tansley's rage at Lily—was a socially acceptable way of handling her own?" Kathy would have asked Susan, "Off the subject of *To the Lighthouse*, but I'm interested. How do you fit Forster into the 'experimental' picture? This has always been my problem in courses on the Bloomsbury Group. His novels are so apparently conventional, at least in terms of technique."

Although we are running out of time, questions about working-class characters, a lesbian sub-text, journals, and "misreadings" do get aired. Even after the session ends, conversations continue in the aisles, amongst the panelists, and between the panelists and audience members for so long that Mary Beth

Hungry to Talk

and Beth almost don't get a bite to eat before Eileen Atkins' performance of *A Room of One's Own*!
We should get together more often. . .

For fuller discussion of several of these approaches, consult the forthcoming MLA volume, *Approaches to Teaching Woolf's To the Lighthouse*.

VIRGINIA WOOLF MISCELLANIES
Pace University, New York
Saturday, June 8, 1991

A Reading of

MRS. DALLOWAY AND THE AEROPLANE

from the novel by Virginia Woolf

adapted by David Bucknam and Lisa Peterson
music by David Bucknam

Clarissa Dalloway......................Randy Danson
Mrs. Coates...................Claudine Cassan-Jellison
Septimus Warren Smith................Alan Heinberg
Mrs. Dempster...............................Alma Cuervo
Mr. Bowley..John Jellison
Maisie Johnson.............................Jennifer Rosin

*

Lisa Peterson and David Bucknam collaborated on an adaptation of Virginia Woolf's *The Waves* which was produced by New York Theater Workshop last spring. It was the recipient of two Drama Desk nominations.

Leonard and Virginia Woolf Working Together

Wayne K. Chapman
Leonard and Virginia Woolf
Working Together

To regard various activities Leonard and Virginia Woolf undertook together between late 1915 and 1920 involves an ideal of social cooperation that arose in response to international disorder. To expropriate Virginia Woolf's phrase from *Three Guineas*, a work of later date, it was largely a matter of "men and women working together for the same cause" (102). If she was the more brilliant writer, he was the more prolific, dedicating most of his writing to making ends meet for both of them. In autumn 1915, when she was fairly recovered from her nervous breakdown of 1913 and the devastating relapse of February to June 1915, she remarked: "Leonard is writing so many different books—one for the morning, another for the afternoon" (*Letters* 2:68). In six months she added: "Leonard is as usual writing away at about 6 books, and he has now trained himself to compose straight on to a typewriter, without a mistake in sense or spelling" (2:83). If she was by then well enough to envy his talent, energy, or coordination, she assisted his projects because she believed in his work. His dedication to write a great "History of

Diplomacy," as she called it, was wholly admirable—had not the Webbs intruded with the distractions of the Fabian Research Bureau. Before her relapse of February 1915, she worried about overwork. Although she fretted about his wearing himself thin, she thought it "absolutely essential" that his history should be "superbly good" (*Diary* 1:22). Consequently, after her recovery, she became far more involved with the "webspinning" of public affairs than critics generally allow—and possibly more than she herself cared to acknowledge.

As a research aid, Virginia Woolf helped gather materials for work commissioned by the Fabian Society and appearing, in 1916, as Part II of Leonard's "History of Diplomacy," *International Government: Two Reports*. Her contribution was limited to the penultimate chapter, on the "Internationalisation of Commerce, Industry and Labour," with traces elsewhere. She wrote out short synopses on "The International Telegraph Union" and on "The Universal Postal Union," no doubt abridged from sources in the British Library or elsewhere. The book was influential at the Foreign Office when England's position on the League of Nations was worked out.

In Virginia Woolf's view, this was not the "masterpiece" Leonard's *Empire and Commerce in Africa* (1920) was to be, his next important contribution to political thinking at the time, on international commerce and colonial affairs. But neither did she have as much of herself vested in its making as she did in the later book, a large project with a pressing deadline. Hence she began an extensive index for the factual data he collected. Only one of her responsibilities in the project, she filled out hundreds of five-by-eight-inch cards for this system, which amounted to a resource that helped him with Part I of the African study as well as projects that soon followed—e.g., the pamphlet, International Economic Policy (written for the Labour Party in 1919), and his book, Economic Imperialism (which in 1920 compared the undeveloped countries of Asia and Africa in relation to the European states). She took on the added task of examining dozens of books on loan to him from the London School of Economics, and was entrusted to take notes on works by French authors and on such English authorities as P. L. McDermott's British East Africa and Uganda (1893). This was hard work and complemented the research Alix Sargant-Florence was engaged to do among Consular Reports and Board of Trade Blue Book reports on East African shipping and trade after the Anglo-French Treaty of 1888.

Janet M. Manson
Leonard Woolf, the League of Nations Society and the Journal *War and Peace*

This paper is about Leonard Woolf's work (assisted by his wife, Virginia) to promote international peace through the League of Nations Society and the journal *War and Peace*. His work was directly in line with projects he had undertaken, with Fabian sponsorship, on international cooperation—projects which had just led to publication of his treatise on supernational councils for the prevention of war, *International Government* (1916). He made his case for a point of Weltpolitik on which he, Cambridge mentor G. Lowes Dickinson, and other members of the League of Nations Society differed with their counterparts of the American League to Enforce Peace. The point was not merely intellectual (as between rival viewpoints on a settlement which had begun to look increasingly likely), though it was substantially theoretical in those days because there had never been international cooperation of such kind before, affecting national dominion and security. The matter at issue was of such consequence that Woolf's (viz. the Woolfs') analysis forecast the state of affairs that would precipitate the fascist take-over in Germany, due to an overly punitive peace settlement, and eventually the Second World War. The matter was addressed implicitly to the passionately anti-imperialist, idealistically pacifist intelligentsia of the Bloomsbury persuasion. Leonard Woolf made his case for "practical politics" (with his wife's help) to a covert audience, with whom he was warmly sympathetic.

The result, in manuscript, is a most interesting document (now in the Woolf Papers at the University of Sussex). One can easily imagine the unease of its principal author (Leonard Woolf) as he made his way between two seemingly antithetical poles of thought. Certainly, the idealistic viewpoint was tangibly embodied in his secretary, Virginia Woolf, who, probably in more than one sitting (due to her health), took the entire twenty-one pages of dictation in longhand. Labeled simply "In'l Re'ns" by her, the work was extensively revised, as one judges by the typescript fragment her husband did not destroy, and renamed "The Enforcement of International Law" (cf. his signed introduction to "Shall the Nations Enforce Peace?", the January 1917 special issue of *War and Peace*).

As a conference paper read to the Society of Friends in October 1916, "The Enforcement of International Law" would have placed Leonard (and Virginia) Woolf in the center of the intellectual and political debate over British foreign policy during the war and over the formation of foreign policy on the creation of a "League of Nations." As a member of the Fabian Society and the League of Nations Society, both of which promoted the League concept, Leonard Woolf participated in discussions with intellectual and political leaders who, with him, were then hammering out what became the British position on the League. In addition, he had joined the Union of Democratic Control (or U.D.C.), an influential political opposition organization founded by Labour Party leader James Ramsay Macdonald, Norman Angell (a leading pacifist and the intellectual nucleus of *War and Peace*), Liberal Party M.P. Arthur Ponsonby, and political activist Edmund Dene Morel. U.D.C. members were strongly supportive of a League, and many of them, especially Cambridge philosopher Dickinson, economist J. A. Hobson, Angell, and Ponsonby, joined forces to work on the League concept with Lord James Bryce (historian, jurist, and diplomat) in the so-called "Bryce Group." In this context, the hitherto unidentified manuscripts, "In'l Re'ns" and "The Enforcement of International Law," demonstrate an uncommon meeting of the minds of Leonard and Virginia Woolf.

Jean Moorcroft Wilson
Leonard Woolf: The Pivot or Outsider of Bloomsbury?

Virginia Woolf did not include her husband Leonard in her 1920s definition of Bloomsbury and it is true that he was absent from a vital period of its development betweeen 1904 and 1911. Leonard himself felt exiled at this time and when he returned it was to rejoin a group which had already established certain rituals and relationships. His novel *The Wise Virgins* (1914) reveals a strong sense of isolation from what is clearly a parody of the Bloomsbury Group. It also shows a pronounced awareness of his Jewishness, a further factor which distinguishes him from the other members.

Leonard was, by temperament, an outsider: in addition he differed temperamentally from most of Bloomsbury. His earnestness contrasted sharply with their more relaxed, at times even frivolous attitude. He was practical in a way that many of them were not and possessed a certain hardness, which he describes as a "carapace" formed in youth to protect his "naked soul."

Leonard's character was to some extent shaped by his circumstances, which again distinguish him from the rest of Bloomsbury. His father's early death plunged his family into relative poverty, necessitating scholarships and the need to work for a living, unlike, say, Clive Bell, Maynard Keynes, Desmond McCarthy, the Stracheys, or the Stephens (most of whom had private incomes). Leonard's lack of money and Jewishness combined to exclude him from the socially secure positions enjoyed by the other members of the Group.

Perhaps Leonard's most striking difference from the rest of Bloomsbury, however, lies in his political activities, which had been sparked off by his seven years absence in Ceylon. He underlines the difference between his own and the Group's attitude toward politics when he records their discouraging remarks about the book he agrees to write on the First World War. Undeterred, Leonard himself worked quietly but effectively behind the scenes on such major problems as equal opportunities for women, the prevention of war, and the dismantling of the British Empire. To set him even further apart from

Bloomsbury, Leonard was far more to the left than the rest of the Group, whose politics, if they had any, were usually of the gentler Liberal variety.

However, Leonard was also pivotal to Bloomsbury in a number of ways. He was at Cambridge as a founding member in 1899 and proved a vital link with the philosopher, G. E. Moore, who had a powerful influence on the Group's outlook. Leonard was not only a member of the prestigious "Apostles," whose freedom of speech undoubtedly had an effect on Bloomsbury, but also of every other significant Bloomsbury-related group, the Midnight Club, the "X" Society, as well as the "1917" and the Memoir Club.

When Roger Fry shocked the British public with his Post-Impressionist Exhibitions, in true "Bloomsbury" style, Leonard was there at the second exhibition as Secretary. He also patronized Fry's Omega Workshops and, like Fry, tried to help the artists of Bloomsbury by commissioning work from them.

By marrying Virginia, Leonard was certainly central to the Group, because without his support she would quickly have ended her life and without Virginia there would probably have been no enduring fame for Bloomsbury. He did more than keep Virginia alive, however. As her diaries show, he also advised her constantly on her work and she relied heavily on his judgment.

Leonard was also important to the Group in his own right: without his impressive achievements it would lose some of its identity. The most striking of these was the founding of the Hogarth Press, which among many other books, published all but the first of Virginia's works, and in circumstances which favored her experimentalism. Leonard published works by other writers and painters of Bloomsbury, as well as giving them a chance, in the political journal he edited, to review or be reviewed.

Above all, Leonard contributed another dimension to Bloomsbury. His political activities and deep commitment to social problems lend the Group a seriousness, *gravitas*, or depth it might otherwise have lacked. He had a breadth of vision that the rest lacked. Both literary and political, appreciating art as well as action, he was in effect, Renaissance Man.

The Rhetoric of Virginia Woolf's Feminism

Pamela L. Caughie with Anne Callahan
Virginia Woolf and Postmodern Feminism

"Without you, I'm nothing."
(Sandra Bernhard)

[*The special effect this paper was intended to create at the conference can best be experienced by reading it aloud to a group, imagining that you have approached the podium just after I have been introduced. At the conference, Anne Callahan played you, that is to say, she assumed the role of "I."*]

"Here then was I (call me Mary Beton, Mary Seton, Mary Carmichael or by any name you please—it is not a matter of any importance) . . ." (*Room* 5). So begins Woolf's narrator's story of how she came to write the lecture she is now going to deliver. Compare Woolf's widely acclaimed opening with my own appropriation of it: Here then am I (call me Pamela Caughie, Anne Callahan, Virginia Woolf or by any name you please—it is not a

215

matter of any importance).

Why is Woolf's effort to undercut the authority and the specificity of the speaking subject endorsed by so many feminist readers as the appropriate rhetorical stance for a feminist practice, while my own effort to flaunt the figurality of my being and the fictionality of my authority might well be dismissed as irresponsible, if not scandalous, by many feminists? "That's the problem with you postmodernists," I can hear Susan Bordo say, "'[you] refuse to assume a shape for which [you] must take responsibility'" (144). What, then, is the difference between Woolf's and my rhetorical situations—that is, the relationship among speaker (I), audience (you) and subject (women and fiction, or rhetoric and feminism) that informs each of our discourses? Who can say "I" in these two essays? In other words, specifically, Judith Butler's words, what are "the rules that regulate the legitimate and illegitimate invocation of that pronoun," "I" (*Gender Trouble* 143). And since for a woman, saying "I" is always an act of impersonation, Butler's question can be refined: what are the rules that govern a woman's legitimate and illegitimate impersonation of another woman?

But, you may say, we asked you to speak on the rhetoric of Woolf's feminism. What has that got to do with impersonation and postmodernism?

I will try to explain. Originally I was invited to speak at this conference on the subject of my book, Virginia Woolf and postmodernism. Then I was moved to this panel on Woolf and rhetoric. I found this shift somewhat ironic since recently many feminists have argued the incompatibility of feminism and postmodernism so that my effort to bring them together in this paper might seem to be mere rhetoric. Indeed, postmodernism is said to reduce truth to rhetoric, reality to discourse. At the same time I was pondering this relation between postmodernism and rhetoric, I came to realize that I would not be able to deliver this paper in person. Yet I continued writing in the first person singular, knowing that when the speaker said "I", she would not be speaking in her own person but assuming the persona of another woman. By adopting that personal pronoun, I was opening up a space for female impersonation, engaging the speaker in a performance, and creating the potential for

The Rhetoric of Virginia Woolf's Feminism

misrecognition by the audience. Was my use of the "I", then, legitimate? As I contemplated my subject position, it occurred to me that these very questions of the legitimate and illegitimate use of the pronoun "I", and the legitimate and illegitimate assumption of femininity, are those Woolf pursues in *A Room of One's Own*.

Thus, the question of who can say "I" in these two discourses—Woolf's and mine—became caught up with the question of who can claim to be a speaking subject in the discourses of postmodernism and feminism. If we agree with Woolf's statement that "'I' is only a convenient term for somebody who has no real being," then we might well ask, as Woolf seems to, the postmodernist question par excellence: "What difference does it make who's speaking?" (Foucault).

Of course, this very question has divided postmodernists and feminists. The difference between postmodernism and feminism depends upon whether this question is taken rhetorically—What *difference* does it make who's speaking?—or literally—What difference *does* it make who's speaking? According to many feminists, this question as raised by a male postmodernist implies that it doesn't matter whether the speaker is male or female, real or fictional, authentic or spurious; for the speaking subject is merely a function of discourse, a discursive construction. This conclusion follows from the postmodernist deconstruction of the Enlightenment subject, the Cartesian concept of a unified, autonomous, individual identity behind the authorial voice. The inauthenticity of such a subject position, so we are told, leads postmodernists to a denial of subjectivity altogether, and ultimately to a refusal of reality, history and responsibility. Postmodernism is seen as incompatible with feminism precisely because its deconstruction of subjectivity means that it lacks a theory of agency necessary for political action (Hutcheon; Bordo; Waugh). While feminists may share the postmodern critique of the Enlightenment subject, they identify this subject position as masculine. Rather than reject all subjectivity as a "humanist ideal," they offer instead an alternative concept of the subject, one based on women's experiences, as "relational," "collective" and "historically specific" (Waugh; Bordo). The difference between postmodernism and feminism, then, would seem to lie in the difference between equally clichéd masculine and feminine concepts of the "I".

Similarly, the difference between Woolf's and my rhetorical situations would seem to hang on that letter "I." Clearly Woolf's "I" is a fiction. Its personas, the three Marys, are characters in a narrative, the Ballad of Mary Hamilton, and Mary, as in Mary Doe or Mary Roe, has traditionally served as a fictitious name to protect an anonymous identity. Thus, the identity of Woolf's "I" is *immaterial*, in both senses of incorporeal ("'I' is only a convenient term for somebody who has no real being" [*Room* 4]) and unimportant (for who's speaking is "not a matter of any importance"). Where Mr. A's "I" is individual and personal, Woolf's "I" is said to be collective, anonymous and depersonalized (Marcus; Meese; Furman). If it doesn't make any difference who's speaking, it's because the speaker is seen to represent women as an anonymous collectivity.[1]

In contrast, the "I" in this paper would seem to refer to some*body*: Pamela Caughie the writer, Anne Callahan the performer, or Virginia Woolf the subject of this discourse. These women are not fictions but real beings; thus, the identity of the "I" in my discourse is hardly immaterial. To claim that what we call this "I" does not matter would be an illegitimate use of the pronoun "I," a misappropriation of another's identity. Although the "I" in my essay, as in Woolf's, can stand for many different women, it is neither collective nor anonymous. You want to know, I'm sure, who wrote this paper, whom to make responsible for this performance, whom to thank or whom to blame.

But this distinction between Woolf's "I" and my own rests on a referential use of language, not a rhetorical one. When Woolf's persona claims that "I" has no real being, she is not necessarily asserting the subject's anonymity but rather denying the pronoun's referentiality. Indeed, the rhetorical force of that "I" derives from the concept of subjectivity being enacted in this discourse. In other words, Woolf's "I" does not represent female subjectivity as an anonymous collectivity; it personifies the feminine subject position as a conceptual anonymity, for "[women] remain even at this moment almost unclassified" (*Room* 89). In fact, to argue that Woolf's "I" presents women as anonymous and collective, to argue, that is, for an alternative concept of subjectivity rooted in women's experience, is to buy into the concept of women in patriarchy. When Woolf's persona writes

The Rhetoric of Virginia Woolf's Feminism

of women writers who adopted male pseudonyms, she says "they did homage to the convention, which *if not implanted by the other sex was liberally encouraged by them* . . . that publicity in women is detestable. Anonymity runs in their blood" (*Room* 52—my emphasis). So when we come upon the line, "It is one of the great advantages of being a woman that one can pass even a very fine negress without wishing to make an Englishwoman of her" (52), we needn't take this literally, as if Woolf herself agreed that women lack men's desire for fame. Instead, we can attend to the rhetorical effect of this use of the personal pronoun. "One" next to "woman" jolts; for "one", like "I", conventionally signifies that unified, self-sufficient, masculine subject of Enlightenment thought. It is an illegitimate use of "one". As such, this sentence does not tell us what women are like; rather, it reclaims "one" for a female subject position, and for the title of Woolf's essay: *A Room of One's Own*. [This argument, by the way, is the speaker's, specifically Anne Callahan's.] Yet at the same time the rhetoric of Woolf's essay reclaims *one* as specifically feminine rather than generically masculine, the grammar of the title places *one* in the genitive position. As object of the preposition, *one* skirts the subject position once again. [*This* argument, by the way, is the audience's, specifically Eleanor Skoller's.]

Thus we might argue, as Woolf's persona seems to, that the truth of women, like the truth of fiction, lies not in some correspondence to real experience but in the conventions that govern the relation between the masculine and the feminine. For women are to men as fiction is to life: they function as distorting mirrors (*Room* 35, 74). Those personal pronouns that place woman in the subject position undermine the mirroring relation between self and other, between male and female subjectivity. Woolf's essay does not attempt to define the difference between male and female subjectivity; rather, her rhetoric establishes the rules by which the personal pronouns can be intelligible when assumed by a woman (Butler 143).

Rhetorically speaking, "I" marks the site of female impersonation, flaunts the imitative status of femininity and parodies the self-reflexive status of Enlightenment subjectivity. This is not to say that women are fictions, or to set up a choice between "I" as historical agent and "I" as rhetorical construct—that is, between feminist and postmodernist concepts of the subject. Rather, it is to deny the opposition between history and rhetoric, fact and fiction. When Woolf's persona claims "I" has no real being, when she refers to her story of Judith Shakespeare as "found out or made up," she does not necessarily mean that it doesn't matter whether "I" is real or fictional, whether her version of history is true or false. Instead, she frees writing from the fact/fiction opposition, and subjectivity from the true/false opposition, acknowledging the mediated nature of reality, history, subjectivity. Woolf's concept of female subjectivity is an *effect* of her rhetoric, not simply the subject of her essay.

But, we are told, "women rarely possess men's healthy love of rhetoric"—or so claims the anonymous contributor to the *New Criterion*, as quoted in *A Room of One's Own* (78). And indeed, feminists' suspicions of postmodernism's rhetoric would seem to confirm this received notion of gender difference. If women *do* bear a different relation to rhetoric than men, Dominick LaCapra may help us to understand why: "Rhetoric has often been in the scapegoated position of the radically 'other'—sometimes elevated as the marginal hope of language or more frequently debased as its common whore. It is usually contrasted with logic or science, which may assume the figurative position of legitimate 'wife' of the mind" (16). Women could hardly bear a *healthy* relation to rhetoric; for to embrace rhetoric, they would have to assume an illegitimate subject position—the common whore not the legitimate wife. Once again, what is irresponsible, illogical and debased is represented as feminine. In his chapter on rhetoric and history, LaCapra opposes this representation of rhetoric but says nothing against this figuration of the feminine. In their insistence on the priority of history over rhetoric, many feminists reject this representation of the feminine while accepting the debased view of rhetoric. What both critiques ignore is the identification of women and rhetoric as both are conventionally represented.

Female impersonation acts out this identification. The act of impersonation enables a woman to claim the subject position without reducing female subjectivity to a mere fiction, and at the same time, without renouncing women's fictive status as mere rhetoric. The double status of the "I" characterizes female impersonation. In Woolf's essay, "I" is both the character and narrator of her story, both agent and object of the representation

The Rhetoric of Virginia Woolf's Feminism

of a woman writer. In my essay, each "I"—the writer's and the speaker's—is at once subject and audience of the other's performance; for I write for Anne Callahan, and I speak for Pamela Caughie.

Where, then, does all this leave "you," the audience? If you interpret Woolf's "I" as a collective voice, as many feminists do, if you interpret her discourse as a collaborative narration that shares authority with her audience (Marcus; Meese), then you take the "I" literally, not rhetorically. A literal reading turns Woolf's collective, depersonalized, relational "I" into an argument for women's collective, depersonalized, relational identities. It thereby neglects the performative force of Woolf's rhetoric. When Woolf's "I" challenges the audience, "it is for you to seek out this truth," in the fiction she is about to construct, and in the fictions already constructed about women (*Room* 4), "you" also become both agent and object of the representation. If you collaborate in this production, then, it is by inhabiting the site of female impersonation. Like Kathy Acker's impersonation of Erica Jong, like Cindy Sherman's impersonation of Marilyn Monroe, like Sandra Bernhard's impersonation of Nina Simone—indeed, like Anne Callahan's impersonation of Pamela Caughie—Woolf's impersonation of the three Marys implicates her audience in the construction of female subjectivity and parodies the identification of women and rhetoric as illegitimate without denying the truth of that representation.

Thus, the answer to the question of what Woolf really means by her feminist rhetoric, what her "I" really figures, is not simply indeterminate but irrelevant; for Woolf as much as her persona is a composite figure, somebody each of you has constructed. In Sandra Bernhard's words, without "you," "I" am nothing. In writing that "'I' is only a convenient term for somebody who has no real being," Woolf acknowledges that her own identity is immaterial. Therefore, while Woolf's composite "I" may well function to undercut the authority of the traditional male lecturer (an argument many feminists endorse), it also undercuts the authority of the historical female author (an argument many feminists resist). Or rather, it relocates authority, in the rhetorical performance not in the empirical author. So when we read at the end, "I will end now in my own person" (*Room* 109), we are uncertain just who that person is, whom to make responsible.

But, then, it's not a matter of any importance; for the writer is responsible not to an identity that lies behind her "I", but to the concept of identity her rhetoric advocates.

I will end now in *my* own person. If a presentation such as this requires a peroration, then mine might go something like this: The difference between postmodernism and feminism would seem to lie in the difference between a rhetorical and a non-rhetorical use of language. But—I do not believe a word that I am saying. After this performance, I no more than Woolf can be comfortable in the subject position of a conventional peroration. What's more, such categorical distinctions, "all this pitting of sex against sex" (*Room* 110), "ism" against "ism," would hail us right back to "the dominance of the letter "I," the "I" of Mr. A's novel, the "I" that led Woolf to cry, "But—I am bored!" (104), and to perform alternative subject positions that have enabled you and I to take the podium today.

---

[1] In *The Colonizer and the Colonized*, Albert Memmi uses the phrase "anonymous collectivity" to refer to the representation of the colonized in colonial discourse. Henry Louis Gates cites the relevant passage in "Critical Fanonism," page 459.

Works Cited

Bordo, Susan. "Feminism, Postmodernism, and Gender Scepticism." In *Feminism/Postmodernism*, ed. Linda Nicholson (New York and London: Routledge, 1990): 133-156.

Butler, Judith. *Gender Trouble*. New York and London: Routledge, 1990.

Foucault, Michel. "What Is an Author?" *The Foucault Reader*, ed. Paul Rabinow. New York: Pantheon, 1984.

Furman, Nelly. "Textual Feminism." In *Women and Language in Literature and Society*, ed. Sally McConnell-Ginet, Ruth Borker and Nelly Furman (New York: Praeger, 1980): 45-54.

Gates, Henry Louis, Jr. "Critical Fanonism." *Critical Inquiry* 17, 3 (Spring 1991): 457-70.

Hutcheon, Linda. *The Politics of Postmodernism*. London and New York: Routledge, 1989.

LaCapra, Dominick. *History and Criticism*. Ithaca: Cornell, 1985.

Marcus, Jane. *Virginia Woolf and the Languages of Patriarchy*. Bloomington: Indiana University Press, 1987.

Meese, Elizabeth. *Crossing the Double-Cross*. Chapel Hill: University of North Carolina Press, 1986.

Waugh, Patricia. *Feminine Fictions: Revisiting the Postmodern*. London and New York: Routledge, 1989.

Woolf, Virginia. *A Room of One's Own*. New York: Harcourt, Brace, Jovanovich, 1929; 1957.

The Rhetoric of Virginia Woolf's Feminism

Catherine Sandbach-Dahlström
Tradition, Resistance and Rewriting
in Virginia Woolf's Essays

I would argue here for a reading of Woolf's essays, both the familiar and the critical, on the model of Julia Kristeva's renowned essay, "Women's Time."[1] Kristeva sees the contemporary women's movement as existing in three spaces: identification with the symbolic order; resistance to that androcentric order through recognition of sexual difference, and finally the disintegration of the concept of the subject upon which difference is based. Woolf's text works in three similar spaces; one involves an attempt to integrate her project into mainstream masculine culture; another encloses textual resistance to that culture, and the last is the reproduction in her essays—as elsewhere—of a multiple, unstable concept of self.

For Woolf as a critic, integration consists of accepting the conventions of the essay genre and of reproducing the "great man" tradition of English letters by building on the notion of art "as an expression of character or personality" that she shares with male precursors, notably Pater.[2] One consequence of integration into the tradition is a tendency to disregard, or even denigrate, some of her female predecessors such as the Duchess of Newcastle or Elizabeth Heywood; another is the way the author is regularly conceived in terms of the masculine signature. Moreover, in her subject matter and critical standards Woolf owes an important debt to the past and to her father.

Nonetheless, it is in this relation that the resistance of the second space manifests itself. In rewriting Stephen's criticism Woolf resists the moralizing tendency of the Victorians through subjective identification with the objects of her critique and she comes to openly criticize his simplistic binary conception of life and literature. Resistance is also manifested through open recognition of sexual difference as textual configuration. Not only is the realist author's method of manipulating his subject matter made a trope for the repression of women by men in "Mr. Bennett and Mrs. Brown," but the act of writing itself is represented by metaphors of sexuality, of power and of control.[3]

In the third space the concept of a unified gendered subject

223

is displaced by the figure of the Common Reader—in "itself" both one of Woolf's genderless company of outsiders and a device for deflecting the usual gender correspondence between the author and the persona of the critic. For Woolf the unified subject is always associated with the sterile limitations of egocentricity from which a multiple self can escape. Thus the unified writing subject is undermined from within by such devices as generalized and impersonal pronouns. These in turn engender an explicit exposé of the disintegration of self in such essays as "Flying Over London" or "Evening Over Sussex."[4] Finally, Orlando is, I suggest, paradigmatic of this concept of self for his very being encompasses many selves and multiple time; he is both tradition and liberation from it.

Notes

[1] Julia Kristeva, "Women's Time", trans Alice Jardine & Harry Blake, *The Kristeva Reader*. ed Toril Moi, Oxford: Basil Blackwell, 1986.

[2] cf. Perry Meisel, *The Absent Father: Virginia Woolf and Walter Pater*. New Haven: Yale U.P., 1980.

[3] Virginia Woolf, "Character in Fiction," *The Essays of Virginia Woolf*, vol 3, ed. Andrew McNeillie. London: The Hogarth Press, 1988, cf. Rachel Bowlby, *Virginia Woolf: Feminist Destinations*, Oxford: Basil Blackwell, 1986.

[4] Virginia Woolf, "Flying over London" in *The Captain's Death Bed*. New York: Harcourt Brace Jovanovich, 1978 & "Evening over Sussex" in *The Death of the Moth and Other Essays*. New York: Harcourt Brace Jovanovich, 1970.

From *Melymbrosia* to *Between the Acts*

Laura Davis-Clapper
Why Did Rachel Vinrace Die? Tracing the Clues from
Melymbrosia to *The Voyage Out*

As we read toward the outcome of Virginia Woolf's *The Voyage Out*, the death of Rachel Vinrace, we pass directly stated allusions to 88 different historical figures and 40 figures from mythology and literature; the titles of 50 creative works; and 30 quotations from external works. About 100 different explicit allusions draw Rachel Vinrace's character. Critics agree that many of these allusions link love and marriage with death and that Woolf reshapes allusions as she composes the text. An allusion that can be added to the list of those that explain Rachel Vinrace's death shortly before she is to return to England to be married is a reference to one of Sir Walter Scott's Waverly novels, the historical romance *Kenilworth*.

The treatment of the *Kenilworth* allusion varies in three versions of the text: the earliest nearly complete draft of the novel, edited by Louise DeSalvo and published as *Melymbrosia by Virginia Woolf: An Early Version of The Voyage Out* (1982), contains two allusions to *Kenilworth*; the first English edition (Duckworth, 1915) contains one allusion to *Kenilworth*; and the first American edition (Doran, 1920) contains no direct mention of *Kenilworth*. Redrafting *Melymbrosia*, Woolf changed the book the character Susan Warrington was reading from the popular, but respectable *Kenilworth* to a fictitious, third-rate work, *Miss Appleby's Adventure*, to better express Susan's dullness, conformity, and insensitivity. Still, because Susan Warrington, like Rachel Vinrace, becomes engaged during *The Voyage Out*, we look for connections.

One of those connections comes in a scene after Susan's engagement party when Terence Hewet and Rachel Vinrace are discovering that they may be in love and go for a walk together to talk. The second allusion to *Kenilworth* in *Melymbrosia* and the single direct allusion in the first English edition is contained in the phrase 'Regent of the Skies' spoken by Terence as he tries to explain the stylistic difficulties of writing. "Regent of the Skies" alludes to line two of "Cumnor Hall," the ballad that inspired Scott to write *Kenilworth*, a novel that begins with the captivity of its protagonist, Amy Robsart, and ends with her death. This remarkably beautiful young woman loves passionately and is loved passionately by her courtier husband, the Earl of Leicester. But thinking that Queen Elizabeth, who does not know of Leicester's marriage, is making up her mind to marry him, and tricked without much difficulty into believing his wife has cuckolded him, Leicester allows Amy to be held prisoner and murdered. The plot sounds like the typical stuff of historical romance, but *Kenilworth* may be seen as a surprisingly unconventional novel. Queen Elizabeth's desire to avoid compromising her dignity and authority by marrying is well reasoned. Marriage is associated with chaos, confinement, and violence in *Kenilworth*. Men, rather than women, are indemnified as fickle in the novel, a reversal of the typical outlook in courtly love literature during the period when the novel is set, and it is the women in *Kenilworth* who insist upon honorable conduct. To preserve her honor, Amy Robsart defies the command of her husband and she convinces her husband to examine his own dishonorable behavior.

By alluding to *Kenilworth*, Woolf is not only signalling that her own novel will end with the death of Rachel Vinrace, but also suggesting that the views in *The Voyage Out* on the relations between women and men parallel those in Scott's novel. Against

From Melymbrosia to Between the Acts

the backdrop of *Kenilworth*, the response of the sexually inexperienced Rachel Vinrace to what amounts to an assault by Richard Dalloway when he kisses her does not seem overly sensitive, hysterical, or absurd. Rachel is repulsed by Richard's kiss; the kiss is, furthermore, an act of infidelity to Richard's wife. Rachel's nightmare that follows expresses her revulsion, the threats of violence she feels, and her entrapment, all as she lies "[s]till and cold as death." On a conscious level, too, Rachel condemns Richard's action: "'men are brutes,'" she concludes. Her death after her engagement will be a kind of moral choice against the violence marriage can bring.

Woolf's final word on her novel, as Elizabeth Heine points out in the Definitive Collected Edition of *The Voyage Out* (1990), was to choose the first English edition for the Hogarth Uniform Edition of 1929. The *Kenilworth* allusion and all that it represents remains a part of this densely allusive text. On the other hand, when Woolf deletes "Regent of the Skies" from the American text, relations among parts of the novel shift. One result is that we see more evidently in Terence Hewet the snobbery and insensitivity characterized by Susan Warrington. Looking at that place in the American edition where *Kenilworth* is no longer alluded to begins a process of discovery about other techniques Woolf uses in her first novel to express her answer to the question, Why does Rachel Vinrace die?

Elizabeth Heine
New Light on *Melymbrosia*

The "new light" that I brought to *Melymbrosia*, the version of the earlier form of *The Voyage Out* transcribed by Louise DeSalvo and published by The New York Public Library in 1982, was that cast by the intense gaze of the scholarly textual editor. In this case, I was returning to the surviving transcripts and manuscripts of Virginia Woolf's first novel after more than a decade, now bringing skills honed by editing the Abinger Edition, including E.M. Forster's unfinished fiction and unpublished Indian diaries. Of course, as readers and critics we all bring our own "light" to the texts we approach, seeing and shadowing as we choose or as we must. There is, happily, no foreseeable limit to the prismatic, diamond-shattered illuminations (even fireworks) that sparkle and flare from reader to reader and critic to critic. But at the same time, factual accuracy about the words of the writers themselves, the words actually on the page—the text itself—is to me essential.

I returned to *The Voyage Out* in order to edit the text for the Definitive Collected Edition of Virginia Woolf's novels published by The Hogarth Press in 1990; the full account of my findings appears in that volume. At the conference, I emphasized the importance of the dating of the version published as *Melymbrosia*. It is the version completed by Virginia Stephen in July 1912, just before her marriage to Leonard Woolf. Although it includes pages which may have been typed as early as October 1907, and although the content of the whole must have built up gradually in the lost versions written and typed, and rewritten and retyped, between 1907 and 1912, the two dated holograph notebooks and the surviving typescripts unquestionably corroborate both the 1912 dating for the *Melymbrosia* version and the later, post-marriage dating for the massive revisions of 1912-13.

This dating, however, is not new. I explained it in print in 1979, when The New York Public Library announced in its *Bulletin* the discovery of the *Melymbrosia* version. Both Louise DeSalvo and I, each working independently, had discovered the sequences of early pages, although, as our articles indicated, we differed in their dating. I was therefore the more delighted to see my earlier findings working out again before my much more experienced eyes as I checked the manuscripts, still safe in the Berg Collection, one more time. And this time, I also had the pleasure of using *Melymbrosia*, which makes the tracking of earlier pages a much easier task. The later pages, however, are incompletely transcribed, and one must (as one should in any case) make a pilgrimage to the originals to study Virginia Stephen's handwritten, blue-inked proofreadings and revisions of the later typescript pages transcribed in *Melymbrosia*. These revisions were omitted on a principle that works well enough for the

From Melymbrosia to Between the Acts

earlier pages, many of which Virginia Woolf used again as she revised the novel after her marriage, but it shortchanges the later pages, omitting their revisions even from the appendix.

Nonetheless, it is a salutary lesson for an editor (or a reader or a critic) to be reminded of the effects of conclusions reached too soon, or principles too rigidly applied. And for an editor, it is always a wonderfully lucky accident to have independent pairs of eyes shedding light on the same manuscripts. With the aid of *Melymbrosia*, I also realized that my own eyes, after a decade, seemed to be renewed. In the light of my later experience, the pages of the various pre-marriage and post-marriage revisions fell into place with much greater clarity, yielding results explained in the new Hogarth edition (399-463).

For *Melymbrosia*, perhaps as a reward for my return to the originals, a "new" page revealed itself. Formerly identified merely as an unplaced fragment, it too has now been published in the Hogarth edition (428). It is included here because, by the time I distributed copies for my talk, in the last hour of the conference, it had become obvious that this early page of fiction, long discarded, nonetheless illustrated major themes of our discussions. The still omniscient narrator, half-mocking her characters, comments on their silent sympathies and records their unspoken words. Ideas of abuse and violence, dominance and revenge, parental authority and imperialism, all move naturally to questions of Christianity and submission, vividly sexual in the apparently Freudian mistyping of "sin" for "sun" in the passage bracketed for deletion. The coming of night then ends the chapter—uncannily, characteristically foreshadowing "Time Passes" and *The Waves*.

> When one guest rises, as every hostess knows, it is as a stone knocked out of a wall, and the wall tumbles. Mrs. Paley commanded Susan to fetch her shawl, hire a carriage, and take her for a drive. She thereby destroyed a palace of happiness, but as Susan smiled, Mrs. Paley had some excuse, and would have been incredulous if Mr. Venning's words had come out aloud in the air. "Oh you old slave driver how I'd like to lash you with your own whip!" She was no more of

a slave driver than many parents, and as she would certainly have driven no slaves had there been none to drive it was partly Susan's fault, who was a Christian. [But the sin went down without having seen the great happiness expressed which was hovering as it were disembodied.] The gong was sounded punctually at seven thirty; by which hour the light in the air was replaced by an infinite number of lights on the earth. The dining room filled; the lounge filled; Miss Willett executed a piece on the violin, irresistibly reminding one of a terrier in a yard with a bone; billiard balls clicked; then the bedrooms were all lit up, and the sitting rooms deserted. The moon swung high and once more the sound of the sea was heard, as the waves broke regularly upon the beach. [F/5]

Works Cited

DeSalvo, Louise A. "Sorting, Sequencing, and Dating the Drafts of Virginia Woolf's *The Voyage Out.*" *Bulletin of Research in the Humanities* 82 (1979): 271-93.
Heine, Elizabeth. "The Earlier *Voyage Out*: Virginia Woolf's First Novel." *Bulletin of Research in the Humanities* 82 (1979): 294-316.
———. "Virginia Woolf's Revisions of *The Voyage Out.*" Woolf, *The Voyage Out* 399-463.
Woolf, Virginia. *Melymbrosia: An Early Version of The Voyage Out*. Edited with an Introduction by Louise A. DeSalvo. New York: New York Public Library, 1982.
———. *The Voyage Out*. Ed. Elizabeth Heine. With an Introduction by Angelica Garnett. London: Hogarth, 1990.

G. Patton Wright
Virginia Woolf's Uncommon Reader:
Allusions in *Between the Acts*

Virginia Woolf's final novel, *Between the Acts*, contains more allusions to and quotations from literature outside itself than perhaps any of her other fictional works. In part, this is the result

From Melymbrosia to Between the Acts

of Woolf's desire to combine fiction and criticism in a "new novel," originally entitled "Pointz Hall." In October, 1938, Woolf noted in her diary that she wanted to write "lots of little poems to go into P[ointz] H[all] and to "collect... my innumerable T.L.S. notes: to consider them as material for some kind of critical book: quotations? comments? ranging all through English lit: as I've read it & noted it during the past 20 years" (*Diary* 5:180). More so than any of her other novels, Woolf treated this new novel as a place for presenting, often in parodic form, a critique of literature from Chaucer to the present time. In composing this novel, she drew heavily on her own reading of works in English literature, both major and minor. Like Miss La Trobe who arranges and directs the pageant around which the action of this novel occurs, Virginia Woolf found herself in the rather awkward position of writing for two very different audiences.

One audience she herself had called "common readers," taking the phrase from Dr. Johnson, who had used the term without the same degree of irony with which it appears in Woolf's criticism, particularly in her final novel. The "common" reader is depicted as one who is rather careless, hard to please, idiosyncratic, and often unpredictable in determining what is truly important. Moreover, the common reader is forgetful and inaccurate, pulling together a scrap of this poem or a fragment of that play in an attempt to construct what Woolf called a "ramshackle fabric" of a worldview (*The Common Reader*, 1st Series, 1). This is the person whom Woolf considered her audience for her critical essays, collected in two series under that title, although one hastens to add that the actual content of many of these essays suggests a more literate audience than the one that she describes in the introductory essay.

The second audience is anything but "common." In fact, this audience is privy to the most obscure of allusions, the smallest portion of a phrase or quotation that triggers in the mind certain thematic connections and volumes of meaning. This is an ideal audience, whom I call Woolf's "uncommon reader," and it is best exemplified by Virginia Woolf herself. Although she too could be hasty and inaccurate in her recall of passages that she had read, and although many of her allusions undergo a seachange as they are incorporated into her new novel, the allusions provide us a special window through which to view Woolf in the composing process.

Selected passages in the Early Typescript of "Pointz Hall," edited by Mitchell Leaska, can be compared with corresponding ones in the so-called final text in order to identify Woolf's probable intentions for making alterations in her composition. Some of the quoted passages contain errors that can be attributed either to the character in the novel who attempts to quote the lines in question or to Virginia Woolf herself whose memory was indeed fallible. In the first case, we have miscitations *by design*, whereas in the second case, the error occurs *by accident*.

Yet a third case occurs when the incorporated allusions are presented in passages of internal monologue of a character whose recall of such passages seems implausible or unlikely. In other words, Woolf creates a character, the content of whose internal monologue is inconsistent with the kind of person whom she has described. The most interesting and revealing instance in the novel is that of Giles Oliver whose internal monologue contains allusions that reveal his deepest anxieties and anger, explaining to some extent his immediate dislike of William Dodge, his condescending attitude toward his wife's poetry, and his brief attraction to Mrs. Manresa. In short, the allusions that are presented narratologically as occurring to him are inconsistent with the presentation of him as a character; nevertheless, this allusive material reveals to the uncommon reader Giles's abiding fears of homosexuality and mortality.

Virginia Woolf was capable of weaving into the text of her novel the strands of many quotations that create an extremely complex picture of human life and emotions. Not always was she accurate in her quoting, but even when she misremembered a passage, she used the material to her advantage and worked the re-formed ideas into her own themes. Exasperated at times with her common readers, who like the audience for Miss La Trobe's pageant might see only the "scraps, orts and fragments" of themselves (*BTA* 188), Woolf wrote for an ideal reader, an "uncommon" reader, whose mind was as attuned to the music and rhythm of a phrase as her own mind was. This uncommon reader would not be distracted by the occasional misquotation (although might find it curious), but instead would be able to receive the communication between author and reader almost instantaneously. Above all, it was an uncritical audience, in the sense that it would not find fault with the writing or even the content, in much the same way that the implied audience for the *Diary* was Woolf's most understanding and sympathetic reader. Writing for this audience reduced her anxieties that had so often accompanied the composition of her previous novels, especially as she prepared them for final publication and release to what she sometimes saw as a hostile public. Beyond the purely personal level of this kind of writing, however, the allusive material in *Between the Acts* invites her best readers to become engaged in the creation of these characters' lives and to share with the author those judgments about them that would escape the attention of the more superficial reader.

Appendix: Program for Virginia Woolf Miscellanies, June 7 - 9, 1991

Friday, June 7

1:45 - 3:00 **Woolf, Reading, and Readers**
"Maternal Reading: Woolf and Feminist Reader-Response Theory" Elizabeth A. Flynn, *Moderator* (Michigan Technological U)
"Virginia Woolf, Conversation, and the Common Reader" Beth C. Rosenberg (New York U)
"The Coterie and the Common Reader" Alex Zwerdling (U of California, Berkeley)

3:15 - 4:30 **A Modernist Abberation: Reading Woolf in the Context of Postmodernism** Ruth Johnston, *Moderator* (Pace U)
"Preserving a Discourse of Difference and a Difference of Discourse" Roseanne Hoefel (Iowa State U)
"'What Does it Mean? How Do You Explain it All?' Virginia Woolf: A Postmodern Modernist" Ann Marie Hebert (Case Western Reserve U)
"Fascism and Madness: Woolf Writing Against Modernism" Teresa Heffernan (U of Toronto)

3:15 - 4:30 **Woolf, Class and Empire** Esther Labovitz, *Moderator* (Pace U)
"Woolf's Criticism of the British Empire in *The Years*" Kathy J. Phillips (U of Hawaii at Manoa)
"Taking a Leaf from Virginia Woolf's Book: Empowering the Student" Beth Rigel Daugherty (Otterbein C)
"Vast Nests of Chinese Boxes, or Getting from Q to R: Critiquing Empire in 'Kew Gardens' and *To the Lighthouse*" Jeanette McVicker (SUNY at Fredonia)

4:45 - 6:00 **Woolf and Contemporary Writers** Eileen Barrett, *Moderator*

Appendix

(California State U, Hayward)
"Virginia Woolf from a Latin American Perspective" Antonia Garcia-Rodriguez (Pace U)
"Tea with Virginia: Woolf as an Early Mentor to May Sarton" Deborah Straw
"Reading to Write: *The Waves* as Inspiration" Carol Ascher
"Placing the Salt Cellar: The Structures of Art and the Anarchy of Emotion" Jane Lazarre (Eugene Lang C)

4:45 - 6:00   **Elegies: Death and Mourning** George Warner *Moderator* (Pace U)
"Virginia Woolf's Grief Work" Susan Bennett Smith (Stanford U)
"Woolf's Elegiac Enterprise" Karen Smythe (U of Regina)
"Death and Woolf's Festive Vision" Christopher Ames (Agnes Scott)
"Eternal Renewal: Death and Grieving in *The Waves*" Louise Poresky (Marist C)

6:15 - 7:00
"Woolf as 'Landscape Artist' and Cultural Historian: Talland House, *To the Lighthouse* and *The Waves*" A video project. Leslie K. Hankins (U of N Carolina at Chapel Hill)

Saturday, June 8

10:00 - 11:15 **Virginia Woolf and Her Experimentalist Contemporaries: Mansfield, Richardson, and Stein** Judith Allen, *Moderator* (U of Delaware)
"After the Invention of the Gramophone: Hearing the Woman in Stein's *Autobiography* and Woolf's *Three Guineas*" Georgia Johnston (Rutgers, New Brunswick)
"Woolf, Richardson, and the Search for Elastic Form: Getting 'Everything' In" Julie Mody (U of Delaware)
"Virginia Woolf and Katherine Mansfield, or The Case of the Déclassé Wild Child" Evelyn Haller (Doane C)

10:00 - 11:15 **"A Rope to Throw the Reader": The Reading of Rhythm in Virginia Woolf** A Discussion *moderated* by Patricia Laurence (Vassar C/City College of CUNY) with John Briggs (W Connecticut State U); Marilyn Zucker (SUNY at Stony Brook); Elizabeth Cabot (Stonehill College); Beth C. Schwartz (U of Florida at Gainesville); Leslie K. Hankins (U of North Carolina at Chapel Hill).

11:30 - 12:45 **Woolf and War**
"Patriarchy and War" Andy Delohery (W Connecticut State U)
"A Woolfian Perspective on the Persian Gulf Crisis" Gail Fay (W Connecticut State U)

11:30 - 12:45 **Intertextualities: Woolf, Dostoevsky, Yourcenar, Weldon**
"Interiors: Woolf and Dostoevsky" Penny Colburn-McGuire (Pace U)
"'Necessary Bore' or Brilliant Novelist?: What Yourcenar Understood about Woolf's Text" Judith L. Johnston, *Moderator* (Rider C)

Appendix

"Dear Reader: Transforming Romance and Intercepting Acculturation in Woolf and Weldon" Denise Marshall (Heidelberg C)

11:30 - 12:45 **Reading at Random** Walter Raubicheck, *Moderator* (Pace U)
"Virginia Woolf and Murasaki Shikibu: A Question of Perception" Catherine Nelson-McDermott (U of Alberta)
"The Influence of John Waller `Jack' Hills on Virginia Woolf" Penny Painter (Sonoma State U)
"Two Figures Standing in Dense Violet Light" John Milton, Virginia Woolf, and the Epic Vision of Marriage" Lisa Low (Pace U)

12:45 - 2:00 **Lunch**

2:00 - 3:15 **Life/Studies: Psychobiography and Virginia Woolf** Vara Neverow-Turk, *Moderator* (Southern Connecticut State U)
"'In a house with no privacy': *To the Lighthouse*, Co-Dependence, and Feminist Theory" Jane Lilienfeld (AIS)
"Virginia Woolf: Incest Survivor" Louise A. DeSalvo (Hunter C) "Woolf and Freud" Judith Lutzer, C.S.W.
"A Phenomenological Reading of certain Photographs" Roger Poole (Nottingham U) read by Mark Hussey

3:30 - 4:45 **Virginia Woolf Seeking Other Worlds With New Language, Vision, and Ritual** Karla Jay, *Moderator* (Pace U)
"Notes from Underground: Lesbian Myth and Ritual in the Writings of Virginia Woolf" Patricia Cramer (Xavier U)
"Virginia Woolf's Mountain Top—That Persistent Vision" Penelope Cordish (Goucher C)
"*Between the Acts*: Feminist Theory, Feminine Language" Merry Pawlowski (California State U at Bakersfield)

3:30 - 4:45 **Time, Embodiment and the Problem of Separation in the Novels of Virginia Woolf** John Briggs, *Moderator* (W Connecticut S U)
"Life Without Boundaries" Amanda Grant (Pace U)
"Silence, Time, and Space" Kathy Brady (Western Connecticut S U)
"Embodiment and Language in Virginia Woolf" Jane Moore (Western Connecticut State U)

5:00 - 6:15 **A Writer's Workshop With Virginia Woolf** A performance piece by Robin Gunther (W Connecticut State U) with Virginia Hromulak, Timothy Francisco, Ed Hagen, Charles Gardner (WCSU)

5:00 - 6:15 **A Roundtable Discussion on Teaching *To The Lighthouse*** Beth Rigel Daugherty, *Co-moderator* (Otterbein C); Mary Beth Pringle, *Co-moderator* (Wright C); Marcia McClintock Folsom (Wheelock C); Nancy Topping Bazin (Old Dominion U); Sally Jacobsen (Northern Kentucky U); Katherine Hill-Miller (Long Island U, C. W. Post Campus); Susan Yunis (C of St. Scholastica).

6:30 - 7:30 "Mrs. Dalloway and the Airplane" music-theatre by Lisa Peterson

Appendix

with music by David Bucknam

Sunday, June 9

10:00 - 11:15 **Leonard and Virginia Woolf Working Together** Mark Hussey *Moderator* (Pace U)
"Leonard and Virginia Woolf Working Together" Wayne Chapman (Washington State U)
"Leonard Woolf, the League of Nations Society, and the Journal *War and Peace*, 1916-1918" Janet M. Manson (Kansas State U)
"Leonard Woolf: The Pivot or Outsider of Bloomsbury" Jean Moorcroft Wilson

10:00 -11:15 **The Rhetoric of Virginia Woolf's Feminism** Helane Levine-Keating, *Moderator* (Pace U)
"Was Virginia Woolf a Feminist Critic?" Elaine K. Ginsberg (W Virginia U)
"Virginia Woolf and Postmodern Feminism" Pamela Caughie (Loyola U)
"Tradition, Resistance and Rewriting in Virginia Woolf's Essays" Catherine Sandbach-Dahlström (Stockholm U)
"Writing the Feminine: Virginia Woolf and the Making of Feminist Histor(iograph)y" Sara Blair (U of Virginia)

11:30 - 12:45 **From *Melymbrosia* to *Between the Acts*** Muriel Shine *Moderator* (Pace U)
"Why Did Rachel Vinrace Die? Tracing the Clues from *Melymbrosia* to *The Voyage Out*" Laura Davis-Clapper (Kent State U)
"New Light on *Melymbrosia*" Elizabeth Heine (Bermuda C)
"Virginia Woolf's Uncommon Reader: Allusions in *Between the Acts*" G. Patton Wright (UCLA)

11:30 - 12:45 **The Oscillating Vision Of Virginia Woolf: Views of Women and Children** Patricia Laurence, *Moderator* (City C/Vassar)
"*To the Lighthouse*: Virginia Woolf and Victorian Childhood" Camille Guthrie (Vassar C)
"Women Creating: Mothers, Artists, and Social Reformers" Jennifer Smith (Vassar C)

Notes on Contributors

Christopher Ames has written about Woolf in a variety of contexts: in the *Miscellany*; in a forthcoming article in *Twentieth Century Literature* on the "canon narrative"; and in his book *The Life of the Party: Festive Vision in Modern Fiction*. He is currently an Assistant Professor of English at Agnes Scott College.

Carol Ascher is the author of *The Flood*, a novel, and *Simone de Beauvoir: A Life of Freedom*, a critical study. Her short fiction and essays have appeared most recently in *The Virginia Quarterly*, *Boulevard*, and *Ms*. She has received four PEN/NEA Syndicated short fiction awards. Carol Ascher supports her literary work by a part-time position as Senior Research Associate at the ERIC Clearinghouse on Urban Education at Teachers College, Columbia University. "Reading to Write: *The Waves* as Muse" also appeared in *The American Voice*, Summer 1992.

Nancy Topping Bazin is Professor of English at Old Dominion University in Norfolk, Virginia. Her *Virginia Woolf and the Androgynous Vision* (1973) was an important contribution to the reevaluation of Woolf as a major writer that began in the 1970s. She is co-editor of *Conversations with Nadine Gordimer* (1990).

Kathy Brady received her B.A. in English from Western Connecticut State University. Currently she is a Teaching Assistant in the English Department at W.C.S.U. and is pursuing an M.A. in English. She lives in New Milford, Connecticut with her husband and two daughters. Never willing to limit her options, like Clarissa Dalloway, she says "I could never say of myself, I am this or I am that."

John Briggs is an Associate Professor of English at Western Connecticut State University. He is author of *Fire in the Crucible* (St. Martin's, 1988) and *Fractals: The Patterns of Chaos* (Simon & Schuster, 1992); co-author of *Looking Glass Universe* (Simon & Schuster, 1984), *Turbulent Mirror* (Harper Collins, 1990) and *Metaphor: The Logic of Poetry* (Pace University Press, 1990).

Notes on Contributors

Pamela L. Caughie teaches twentieth-century literature and literary theory at Loyola University of Chicago. She is author of *Virginia Woolf and Postmodernism* (Illinois, 1991) and articles on Woolf, feminism and postmodernism. Anne Callahan presented this paper at the conference. She teaches French literature at Loyola and is currently writing a book on George Sand and the question of female impersonation in literature.

Wayne K. Chapman, Assistant Professor of English, Clemson University, is the author of *Yeats and English Renaissance Literature* (1991), numerous articles in *Yeats Annual*, *Yeats*, *Virginia Woolf and War* (with Janet Manson) and elsewhere; he is co-editing *The Countess Cathleen* manuscripts and an essay collection on the politics of Bloomsbury women.

Penny Colburn-McGuire is currently a senior at Pace University majoring in English Literature. She is particularly interested in the relationship between English authors of the 1900-1940 period and the literature of the nineteenth century.

Penelope Cordish is an Assistant Professor of English and a member of the Women's Studies faculty at Goucher College, where she also directs a new Division of Interdisciplinary Studies. She holds an M.A. from the University of California at Berkeley and a Ph.D. from Johns Hopkins University.

Pat Cramer teaches English and is the Coordinator of the Women's Studies Program at the University of Connecticut at Stamford. She has published articles on William Blake, Chaucer, Virginia Woolf, and Women's Studies teaching. She is currently working on a book on Virginia Woolf.

Beth Rigel Daugherty, Associate Professor of English at Otterbein College, is interested in Woolf's relationship with her reader and how that relationship affects her revisions. An essay on *To the Lighthouse* recently appeared in *Twentieth Century Literature*. She is currently expanding the Morley College paper, exploring Woolf's use of short stories as rough drafts, and examining the writer/reader relationship in *Between the Acts*.

Laura Davis-Clapper is an Associate Professor at the East Liverpool campus of Kent State University. Her dissertation (currently being expanded) was *An Index to Character, Place, and Allusion in the Literature of Virginia Woolf*. She has just joined the editorial staff of the Cambridge Edition of the Works of Joseph Conrad and is one of the editors for a new computer discussion group for Modern British & Irish Literature: 1895-1955 (ModBrits@KentVm).

Andy Delohery received a Bachelor of Arts degree in English at Western Connecticut State University and is now working on his Master of Arts degree while he is a Graduate Assistant at Western. He lives with his wife in Danbury.

Louise DeSalvo is author of *Virginia Woolf: The Impact of Childhood Sexual Abuse on Her Life and Work*, and *Nathaniel Hawthorne: A Feminist Reading*, editor of *Melymbrosia*, an early version of Woolf's first novel *The Voyage Out*, and co-editor with Mitchell Leaska of *Vita Sackville-West's Letters to Virginia Woolf*. She is Professor of English at Hunter College.

Gail Fay received a Bachelor of Science degree in Elementary Education with an English endorsement from Western Connecticut State University. She is currently enrolled at Western in the Graduate Assistantship program for a Master of Arts degree in English. She resides in Waterbury, Connecticut, with her husband and two sons, Kenny and Kevin

Marcia Folsom is Professor of English and Chair of Liberal Arts at

Notes on Contributors

Wheelock College in Boston. She has published essays on teaching *A Room of One's Own* and on Sarah Orne Jewett. She is editor of an MLA volume on teaching Jane Austen's *Pride and Prejudice*.

Antonia García-Rodríguez is an Assistant Professor of Spanish in the Department of Modern Languages at Pace University. She has a Ph.D. in Comparative Literature (Spanish and French) from The State University of New York at Binghamton. She has written a book on two Latin American women writers (Rosario Ferre and Elena Poniatowska) which she hopes to publish soon.

Amanda Grant graduated from Pace University in 1990 with a Bachelor's Degree in English Literature. She is currently pursuing a Master's Degree at Hunter College. She will proceed with a Ph.D. when her Master's has been completed. Her primary aspiration is to become a professor at the university level and a writer.

Evelyn Haller, who graduated from Barat, holds the Ph.D. from Emory, and teaches at Doane College near Lincoln, Nebraska, is completing books on Woolf's use of ancient cultures and the forms of Willa Cather's fiction as influenced by the other arts including architecture. She is also writing a biography of artist Hildreth Meière (1892-1961).

Leslie Hankins has an M. A. in Comparative Literature and a Ph.D. in English from University of North Carolina, Chapel Hill. Her dissertation was entitled "Virginia Woolf's Spatial Art and Critique: Trespassageways for the Twentieth Century and Beyond." She has written on Woolf and cinema, Woolf and Benjamin, and on the *Kunstlerroman*.

Ann Marie Hebert, pursuing her Ph.D. in English at Case Western Reserve University, is interested in feminist theory and contemporary literature. She is contemplating a dissertation that explores the problem of how representation becomes self-representation and how women might rewrite the feminine script which has, to a large extent, been written by and for men.

Teresa Heffernan is working on a doctoral thesis entitled "The Post-Apocalypse and the Reflexive Text" at the University of Toronto. Other work includes: "Tracing the Travesty: Constructing the Female Subject in Susan Swan's *The Biggest Modern Woman of the World*," *Canadian Literature* and "There is More to Reading than Signs: McDonald's and Postmodern Culture," The Toronto Semiotic Circle.

Elizabeth Heine is a visiting Professor in Humanities at the New Jersey Institute of Technology and was previously at Bermuda College. She is Editor of the Abinger Edition of E. M. Forster and edited *The Voyage Out* for the Hogarth Press Definitive Edition of Virginia Woolf's novels.

Roseanne Hoefel teaches Enlgish and coordinates the Women's Studies Program at Alma College in Michigan. She has published articles in *Studies in Short Fiction, The Emily Dickinson Journal, Transformations, Phoebe, Feminisms*, and *The Women's Studies Review*. She is currently working on a study which places Emily Dickinson and Virginia Woolf in a French feminist context.

Mark Hussey is Assistant Professor of English at Pace University in New York. He is author of *The Singing of the Real World: The Philosophy of Virginia Woolf's Fiction* and editor of *Virginia Woolf and War: Fiction, Reality, and Myth*. He is an editor of *Virginia Woolf Miscellany* and currently Secretary/Treasurer of the Virginia Woolf Society.

Notes on Contributors

Sally Jacobsen has a Ph.D. from Purdue University, teaches at Northern Kentucky University, and is co-editor of *Reading and Writing Poetry* (1991). Recently she taught *To the Lighthouse* to Kentuckians studying "Literature and the Other Arts" at Oxford University.

Judith L. Johnston is Associate Professor of English and past Director of Women's Studies at Rider College in Lawrenceville, NJ. An active member of the Virginia Woolf Society, she initiated and chaired an MLA session on Virginia Woolf and Class Consciousness. She has published articles on the sexual politics in Virginia Woolf's *Between the Acts* and on the sexual politics in Marguerite Yourcenar's *Coup de Grâce*; these will reappear within a book-length study of women novelists responding to fascism.

Jane Lazarre is Director of the Writing Program at the Eugene Lang College of the New School for Social Research in New York City. She is author of several critically acclaimed novels—including *The Mother Knot, On Loving Men, Some Kind of Innocence, The Powers of Charlotte,* and *Worlds Beyond My Control*— and has written for *The Village Voice, Ms., The Nation, Harper's,* and *Feminist Studies*.

Jane Lilienfeld has published essays on Virginia Woolf, James Joyce, Willa Cather, Margaret Atwood, Colette, mother/daughters in literature, and feminist theory. She has chaired or co-chaired five Virginia Woolf Society panels at the Modern Language Association. Currently she is an Assistant Professor of English at Lincoln University and is at work on an anthology of feminist theory to be co-edited with Vara Neverow-Turk and a book entitled *"To Want, To Want, and Not To Have": Alcoholism as Family Illness and Narrative Strategy in Selected Novels of Hardy, Joyce, and Woolf.*

Lisa Low is Assistant Professor of English at Pace University in New York City. She has published in *The Massachusetts Review, Massachusetts Studies in English, Crosscurrents,* and *Kritikon Literrarum*. Harold Bloom selected her essay "Ridding Ourselves of Macbeth" for his Chelsea House Series *Macbeth*. She is currently editing a volume of essays on Milton and the romantics for Cambridge University Press. Lisa Low delivered this essay—"Milton, Woolf, and the Epic Vision of Marriage"—both at the Woolf conference at Pace University in June and at Yale University in November, 1991.

Judith Lutzer is a psychoanalyst practicing in Smithtown, NY who writes on psychoanalytic and literary topics. She is on the faculty of the Long Island Institute of Psychoanalysis, and the Department of Psychiatry at SUNY Stony Brook. She is a member of the New York Freudian Society, the International Psychoanalytical Association, and the Virginia Woolf Society.

Janet M. Manson, Visiting Assistant Professor of History, Clemson University, is the author of *Diplomatic Ramifications of Unrestricted Submarine Warfare, 1939-1941* (1990); "Regulating Submarine Warfare, 1919-1945," *Encyclopedia of Arms Control and Disarmament,* (1992); and (with Wayne Chapman) "Carte and Tierce: Leonard, Virginia Woolf and War for Peace," *Virginia Woolf and War* (1991).

Denise Marshall is on the faculty at SUNY-Oswego. Her work includes study of Woolf's comic strategies as empowerment, Woolf's linguistic revolts, and Woolf's ethical philosophy. She is editing a volume of women's travel letters for Beacon, and is working on film adaptations of P.D. James' mysteries. Her work on female development and romance is continued in an article on *The*

Notes on Contributors

Terminator.
Jeanette McVicker, currently Assistant Professor of English at SUNY College at Fredonia, received her Ph.D. in Comparative Literature in 1988. She has published in *boundary 2* and *Translation Perspectives*, and is spending 1991-92 teaching in Romania on a Fulbright. She is at work on an essay on feminism in Eastern Europe, as well as a book on cultural critique in the writings of Virginia Woolf, Simone de Beauvoir, and Katherine Anne Porter.

Katherine Hill-Miller is a Professor of English at C.W. Post College, Long Island University. She is author of articles on Virginia Woolf, Jane Austen, Anne Thackeray Ritchie, Mary Shelley, James Joyce, and Thomas Hardy.

Catherine Nelson-McDermott is doing research into the relationship between Bloomsbury and Orientalism for her Ph.D. at the University of Alberta. This work is being funded by the Social Science and Humanities Research Council of Canada. Other research areas include gender and modernism and post-colonial theory.

Vara Neverow-Turk is Co-Coordinator of the Women's Studies program at Southern Connecticut State University where she is an Assistant Professor of English. She is currently editing two collections of contributed essays, *When Laughing Matters: The Politics of Humor in the Works of Virginia Woolf*, and, with Jane Lilienfeld, *Urgent Questions, Necessary Actions: Feminisms and the Real World*. She has published work in the *Virginia Woolf Miscellany, College English,* and *College Composition and Communication.*

Penny Painter is a graduate student in English at Sonoma State University. She is a California Pre-Doctoral Scholar and teaches ESL and Business English for the Sonoma City Office of Education. She hopes to pursue a Ph.D. in English coupled with linguistics.

Merry M. Pawlowski is an Assistant Professor in the English Department at California State University, Bakersfield. Her dissertation, an investigation into Woolf's uses of language in the 30s, is entitled "'. . . til the visionary becomes a part of the fictitious . . .': Feminine Discourse in Virginia Woolf's Final Decade." She received her Ph.D. from Tulane University in 1990. Her areas of specialization and teaching are modern British literature and feminist literary theory.

Kathy Phillips, Associate Professor of English at the University of Hawaii, has a Ph.D. in comparative literature from Brown University. She has published *Dying Gods in Twentieth-Century Fiction* (Bucknell UP, 1990) and articles in such journals as *Twentieth Century Literature, Mosaic,* and *Comparative Literature Studies.* She is completing a book on Virginia Woolf and the British Empire.

Roger Poole is Reader in Literary Theory at the University of Nottingham, England, and author of *Towards Deep Subjectivity* (1972), *The Unknown Virginia Woolf* (1978, 1982, 1990), and *The Laughter is On My Side* (1989, with Henrik Stangerup).

Louise Poresky is a Visiting Assistant Professor of English at Marist College in Poughkeepsie. Her book on Virginia Woolf's novels, entitled *The Elusive Self,* was published in 1981 by Associated University Presses. Since that time, she has presented papers on Virginia Woolf and George Eliot at colleges and conferences in the New York area. Her most recent article, in which she shows thematic correspondences between Woolf and Dorothy Richardson,

Notes on Contributors

appeared in the *Marist Working Papers* in January, and in *Virginia Woolf Miscellany*. Dr. Poresky, also a fiction writer, read her story "Old Blood," an account of a daughter's experience of her mother's death, at SUNY-New Paltz in 1990. She is currently researching modern mythologies for her next work of scholarship.

Mary Beth Pringle, Professor of English at Wright State University, has published on several women modernists, on feminist topics and on Samuel Beckett and James Joyce. She and Beth Daugherty are co-editing *Approaches to Teaching Woolf's To the Lighthouse*.

Beth Rosenberg received her Ph.D. from New York University. Her dissertation concerned Virginia Woolf and Samuel Johnson.

Catherine Sandbach-Dahlström was born in Great Britain in 1940 and took her first degree (in history) at Oxford. On marrying she moved to Sweden and taught school for several years. Her dissertation (1984) is on Charlotte Yonge and she teaches literature and writing. She is now working on a longer text, *Virginia Woolf: The Feminist as Essayist and Critic*, and an anthology of women's polemics from 1600 onwards.

Deborah Straw of Burlington, Vermont is a writing and literature Instructor and a Writing Assessment Mentor at Community College of Vermont. Her particular area of interest is women's journals and memoirs. She interviewed May Sarton for the winter 1991 issue of *Belles Lettres* and will present at the May Sarton conference in June 1992.

Jean Moorcroft Wilson teaches at London University. Her recent book, *Virginia Woolf, Life and London*, was published in America by Norton. She has also written a book on the First World War poets, Issac Rosenberg and Charles Sorley. She is currently working on a full-scale biography of another First World War poet, Siegfried Sassoon.

G. Patton Wright is editor at Cambridge Wordwright in Cambridge, Massachusetts. He is textual editor of the definitive edition of *Mrs. Dalloway* published by The Hogarth Press in 1990 and has written articles and papers on Woolf, T.S. Eliot, James Joyce, and Wallace Stevens.

Susan Yunis is Assistant Professor of languages and literature at the College of Saint Scholastic in Duluth, Minnesota, although she taught the course described during the roundtable discussion—an undergraduate seminar on the Bloomsbury Group—at the University of Minnesota in Duluth.

Alex Zwerdling is a Professor of English at the University of California, Berkeley. He is the author of *Yeats and the Heroic Ideal*, *Orwell and the Left*, and *Virginia Woolf and the Real World*. He is currently at work on a study of the American expatriates who settled in London.